Edmund's

UNITED STATES
COIN
PRICES

*CURRENT MARKET VALUES
FOR ALL UNITED STATES COINS AND GRADES*

**COMPLETE WITH
480 COIN ILLUSTRATIONS
AND VALUABLE
COLLECTING INFORMATION**

"THE ORIGINAL CONSUMER PRICE AUTHORITY"

Lincoln Cents (Good or Better)

09, 18-S, 31, 39D or 55S	$.50 ea.
12P, 16S, 21S, 24S or 33P	$.95 ea.
09VDB, 13D, 23S, 32 or 32D	$1.50 ea.
11D, 12D, 22D or 26S	$4.25 ea.
31D or 33D	$2.50 ea.
10S, 13S or 15S	$6.50 ea.
14S or 24D	$9.25 ea.
09S ... $42.00 14D ... $84.00 31-S $32.95	
1943 Steel Cent Set BU PD&S	$5.95
1955-S BU	$.75 ea.
1960 P&D Sm/Lg Date BU Set	$3.95
1982 7-piece Variety Set BU	$2.95

Starter Sets with Whitman Folder (Good or Better)

Jefferson Nickel 1938-61	$5.95
25 diff. Plus 3 Warnick	
Roosevelt Dimes 1946-64	$9.95
15 diff.	
Mercury Dimes 1916-45	$9.95
15 diff.	

Indian Head Cents Good/better	2/$1.95
Silver War Nickel Av. Circulation	5/$2.25
1950D Jefferson Nickel BU	$6.95
$1 Silver Certificate Uncirculated	$3.95
$1 Silver Certificate Circulated	3/$5.45
Foreign Banknotes	3/$1.00 or 9/$2.75
Mercury Dime 1945-S Micro "s" circulated	$1.95
BU Mercury Dimes	$5.95 or 3/$15.00
Proof: Kennedy Half	$6.95
Franklin Half	$6.95
Morgan Dollar Fine/btr	$9.95
5 diff $48.50 10 diff $94.95	
Peace Dollar Fine/btr	$9.45
3 diff $24.95 7 diff $59.95	
Bulk Foreign Coins	8/$1.00

SATISFACTION GUARANTEED
FREE PRICE LIST

14 DAY RETURN PRIVILEGE
** PLEASE ADD $2.50 P&H **
Member ANA NHNA

Jon L. Chickering and Co.
Box 1011-E296 • Manchester, NH 03105-1011

Free Price List

Thousands of coins, graded filler to proof, issued bi-monthly.

Send self-addressed stamped envelope for free copy.

Phone **1-800-366-6320**.

BETTER COINS
POR 266664 E
Houstin, TX 77207

Free 56-Page Catalog

Packed with U.S. and Canadian coins, U.S. currency, books, supplies and more!

30 Day Money-Back Guarantee.

Allen's
Dept LF
399 South State Street
Westerville, Ohio 43081

PREFACE

This book is intended to be a useful guide for novice and experienced collectors of United States coins as well as for investors who wish to include rare U.S. coins in their investment portfolio. To serious coin collectors or "numismatists", the investment potential of coins is secondary to their historical and educational value. However, collectors cannot ignore the increasing value of their collection over the years. This is one hobby in which one can gain both financially and educationally.

The prices listed in this book have been carefully compiled through the study of the current trends in the coin market, including auction results, dealer prices, and several references as to the relative values of various coins within a series.

In certain instances, due to the increased bullion values of coins in some modern series, a minimum numismatic value has been set. In these series, it would be unwise numismatic practice to purchase coins in lesser grades than the lowest priced grade because their price would be the same due to the bullion content of the coin.

On the Cover

The 1804 DOLLAR - "THE KING OF AMERICAN COINS" pictured here is one of the most sought after American rarities. It is a prime example of scarcity and demand. There are only fifteen known specimens of the 1804 Dollar, most of which are permanently impounded in the collections of museums, leaving very few specimens available to the private collector. Because of the extreme rarity and considerable demand for the coin, its price increases considerably each time one is put on the market. There are, however, several other coins in the United States series that are even rarer. Some of these coins can be purchased for considerably less than the 1804 Dollar because they are not as popular for one reason or another. An example is the 1829 Large Planchet Half Eagle. There are only six known specimens of this coin, making it more than twice as rare as the 1804 Dollar. However, the 1804 Dollar, renowned as the "King of American Coins," brings considerably more money because of its greater demand.

EDITOR'S NOTE: Neither the Editor nor the Publisher of this book are dealers in United States Coins. The prices contained herein are therefore not an offer to buy or sell coins. They are intended to serve the reader as a guide to the current market value of United States coins as of the time of publication. Because of the volatile nature of the coin market, this book is revised and updated on a semi-annual basis so that we can give the reader the most accurate prices possible. All information and prices published herein are gathered from sources which, in the editor's opinion, are considered reliable, but under no circumstances is the reader to assume that this information is official or final. The advertisements included herein are not operated by nor are they the responsibility of the publisher.

Publisher: Peter Steinlauf

Published by:
Edmund Publications Corp.
300 N. Sepulveda Bl., #2050
El Segundo, CA 90245

ISBN: 0-87759-607-7
ISSN: 0270-8949

President:
Michael G. Samet, Ph. D.

Coin Editor:
Daniel J. Goevert

Copy Editor:
Zachary Shrier

Creative Director:
Debra Katzir

Photos & Cover Design:
Ray Kerns
Brian Kerns

Database Specialist:
Victor Friedman

Photography Courtesy of The United States Mint and the Museum of the American Numismatic Association

© 1996 by Edmund Publications Corporation.
All rights Reserved.
No reproduction in whole or in part may be made without explicit written permission from the publisher.

Printed in Canada

Edmund's
UNITED STATES COIN PRICES

FALL/WINTER 1996   **VOL 18 NO. 2**

TABLE OF CONTENTS

Introduction 6
   A Brief History of The American
      Coinage System 8
   Why Coins are Desirable Investments 14
   Speculators, Investors, and Collectors 16
   More Advice About Coin Investing 18
   Buying and Selling Coins 22
   An Introduction to Grading 25
   Basic Grading Information for U.S. Coins .. 26
   Handling & Storing Numismatic
      Treasures 37
   Collecting Coins for Fun 40
   The American Numismatic
      Association (ANA) 42

Investor's Tips 43

U.S. Regular Issue Coins
   Half Cents 47
   Large Cents 52
   Small Cents 58
   Two Cent Pieces 70
   Three Cent Pieces 72
   Half Dimes 76
   Nickels 83
   Dimes 94
   Twenty Cent Pieces 112
   Quarter Dollars 113
   Half Dollars 133
   Silver Dollars 156

Bicentennial Coins 174

On the cover:
The 1804 Silver Dollar
"The King of American Coins"

U.S. Gold Coins 176
  Gold Dollars 178
  Quarter Eagles ($2.50 Gold) 183
  Three Dollar Gold Pieces 193
  Four Dollar Gold Pieces 195
  Half Eagles ($5.00 Gold) 196
  Eagles ($10.00 Gold) 208
  Double Eagles ($20.00 Gold) 216
Mint Sets 224
Proof Sets 226
U.S. Commemorative Coins 228
  Quarter Dollar 230
  Silver Dollar 230
  Half Dollar 231
  Gold Coins 248
  1982 G. Washington 250th Anniversary 250
  1984 Olympic Games 251
  1986 Statue of Liberty 252
  1987 Constitution Bicentennial 253
  1988 Olympiad 254
  1989 Bicentennial of Congress 255
  1990 Eisenhower Centennial 256
  1991 Mount Rushmore 257
  1991 Korean War 258
  1991 U.S.O. 50th Anniversary 258
  1992 Olympic Games 259
  1992 Columbus Quincentenary 260
  1992 White House 200th Anniversary 261
  1993 James Madison/Bill of Rights 262
  1991-1995 WWII 50th Anniversary 263
  1993 Thomas Jefferson 264
  1994 Prisoner of War. 264
  1994 Vietnam Veterans Memorial 265
  1994 Women in Military Service 265
  1994 World Cup Soccer 266
  1994 U.S. Capitol Bicentennial 267
  1995 Civil War Battlefields 268
  1995 Special Olympics World Games 269
  1995-1996 XXVI Olympiad 270
U.S. Bullion Coins
  American Eagles 276
  Silver Eagles 280
  Bullion Values of U.S. Coins 281
U.S. Mints and Mintmark Locations 282
Recommended Reading 284

Edmund's

COIN PRICES

OMUND'S 1996 U.S. COIN PRICES

INTRODUCTION

It is a well demonstrated fact that investing in United States coins can be a very profitable venture. A few years ago, the Salomon Brothers of New York, a well known investment firm, conducted a survey on various investment vehicles and discovered that United States coins have enjoyed a compounded annual return of 21.4 percent over the previous ten years. In the early 1990's, the same company reported a 14.6 percent return on a selected group of coins over a twelve month period. This is not to imply that a person can simply walk into the nearest coin shop, purchase the first coin they see, and expect that coin to appreciate at such a high rate. Having some basic knowledge of the mechanics propelling the coin industry forward is a very important factor in wisely purchasing American coins as investment mediums. The following is intended to provide the reader with some essential background information.

The coin industry has witnessed significant changes over the last decade. Inconsistent grading practices had become a highly vocalized issue by the mid 1980's. While one dealer might assign a coin a certain grade, another dealer might give the same coin a slightly higher or lower grade. In the numismatic profession, subtle grade differences can mean literally thousands of dollars in trading value. In 1986, several companies began offering third party grading services. Coins submitted to these organizations were evaluated through consensus by a panel of experts. Each coin was then encapsulated in a tamper-proof container, certified, and returned to the owner. The coins submitted were mostly high grade uncirculated and proof specimens, or otherwise "expensive" material. By the late 1980's, the large grading services captured the trust of the coin industry, at last providing the much desired consistency in coin grading.

The impact of the grading services has been enormous. Encapsulated coins (known as "slabs" by insiders) have become highly liquid commodities, being traded readily by confident buyers and sellers, often sight unseen. Computer networks connected bidders to further facilitate coin transactions more quickly. Suddenly, coins were being merchandised much in the same way as stocks, resulting in extremely volatile price movements, generally upward. The activity won the attention of millions of first-time coin investors and several large Wall Street brokerage firms, pushing the slabbed market to dizzying heights by the spring of 1989.

Eventually, many slabbed coin prices plunged back towards reality as grading services began releasing the population reports. These reports indicated the volumes, types, and grades of coins that passed through their systems, thus revealing a more likely approximation of each coin's true scarcity. Especially hard hit were the "generic" coins (i.e. common date coins), which

INTRODUCTION

even in mint condition were much more abundant than realized just a few years earlier. In the early 1990's, the great run-up of the 1980's crash landed to become nothing more than a memory. In fact, many top quality generic coins across the board fell almost 80% off their 1989 record highs. Notably, truly rare material displayed strong resistance to price dips, and in some instances even continued to post gains throughout the entire ordeal. This wasn't enough to sustain the overall robust trading (of the 80's), however, and by 1992, the once furious coin onslaught was reduced to a slow trickle.

In the aftermath of the slabbed market's collapse, tremendous bargains exist at present. Given the market's cyclical nature, coupled with seriously undervalued numismatic merchandise, we are on the verge of an upwardly mobile market. For those able to react in an informed manner, great purchases can be made. Because of the many intricacies involved with numismatics, a prudent investor should establish a relationship with a professional engrossed daily in the coin business.

While the higher-end investment side of the coin industry has vacillated radically, collectors are still actively purchasing their favorite interest. Public awareness of the coin hobby has grown, as evidenced by the record turnouts at coin shows across the nation. In truth, collector purchases have increased over the last several years, a fact overshadowed by the monumental transformations mentioned above. The demand for key and semi-key dates in lesser grades than top quality is increasing. Although not nearly as volatile as most slabbed items, some of these coins have been known to experience downward price corrections as well, and to go up again as interest expanded. On the other hand, certain key and semi-key dates have risen consistently over time, with virtually no record of abrupt reversals. The collector pressure presents investment opportunities as well. By studying retail price trends, informed investors may have a clue about future performance. They can learn how to recognize which coins have temporarily reached the maximum value levels and which ones are due for several more years of healthy appreciation. In addition, they can spot those "blue chips," which have solid, long term investment potential, and identify "dogs"—those coins with poor investment potential. Armed with the knowledge, these investors maximize the chances to realize profit in the numismatic marketplace.

Much of today's numismatic investment literature deals only with the slabbed material, practically ignoring the less expensive market currently occupied by collectors and relatively few investors. The scope of this book explores not only the terrific potential of purchasing certain slabbed coins, but also those

INTRODUCTION

"collector" coins as investment possibilities. Hopefully, along the way, the reader will be encouraged to study and learn about coins as a hobbyist might. Not only will the guide be a help in reaching financial objectives; it will open avenues of adventure not found in other income producing opportunities.

A Brief History of the American Coinage System

Understanding the historical aspect of coins is an important factor in adopting a successful investment program. From the earliest colonial times to the birth of our nation, through the great gold and silver debates dominating American politics for much of the 19th century, and during generations of war and peace, American coins have always been indicative of the times. Coins are visible links to the past, placing us face-to-face with history itself. If only that 1839 half dollar in your collection could speak, what stories it could tell!

The story of American money goes back more than three centuries ago. The early settlers of New England relied heavily upon foreign coins for conducting the day to day business affairs. At any given time, coins from England, France, Germany, Holland, Spain, and many other countries could be found in circulation. Also in use, and of special importance, were the coins that migrated to the colonies from Spanish possessions in the New World. Included in these were the Spanish milled dollar and the doubloons (worth then about $16). The Spanish milled dollar, also called the "piece of eight" or the "Pillar dollar" was the equivalent of eight Spanish reales. One real equaled 12½ cents and was known as a "bit." Thus a quarter came to be known as "two bits," an expression still used today. The Spanish milled dollar and its fractional parts were the principal coins of the American colonists, and served as the model for our silver dollar and its sub-divisions in later years. For the most part, however, much larger quantities of coins were needed. Because of the scarcity of coins, especially in the more remote areas, the colonists sometimes used other mediums of exchange, such as bullets, mussel shells (called *wampum*), and animal skins.

Unfortunately, for the early American settlers, our mother country, England, failed to seriously consider the coinage problems mounting in her colonies across the Atlantic. Since the English Parliament evidently was not going to provide more coins for the hard-pressed colonists, some of the more industrious Americans opted to take the matter into their own hands. Whether or not it

INTRODUCTION

had the authority to do so, the General Court of the Massachusetts Bay Colony granted John Hull permission to begin minting coins. Hull set up a mint in Boston and began producing the well-known "N.E. pine tree" coins in 1652, the denominations being threepence, sixpence, and one shilling. These were the first coins ever minted in the New World, outside of Mexico. As time went on, other coins and tokens of various types were introduced and used by the colonists regularly.

After the Revolutionary War broke out, there was little change in the pattern of coins circulating in America. To be sure, there were new pieces always entering from abroad, as usual, which were quickly accepted in the coin-starved colonies. It was during the time that the first unified currency system was established, which consisted of notes issued by the Continental Congress to finance the Revolution.

Although these notes were originally declared to be redeemable after the war in gold and silver coins, it was found impossible because of the excess of printed notes over metal reserves. Consequently, the notes depreciated rapidly and became worthless. Following the Revolution, the governing document of the infant nation, the Articles of Confederation, adopted March 1, 1781, maintained that Congress had the authority to regulate coinage, but specifically reserved the right of coinage to each individual state. And so, during the 1780's we find a healthy variety of these state issues, minted mostly in copper, circulating throughout the country. These post-Revolution, pre-Constitution coins represent a truly unique era of American history, and are admired by all true numismatists today.

By the mid 1780's, many Americans saw the advantages of having a national mint and a standardized coinage system. The money situation at the time was still woefully inadequate and confusing. To further promote the cause, Thomas Jefferson, in 1784, recommended the use of the decimal system with the dollar as the basic unit of trade; and on July 6, 1785, the United States Congress voted in favor of Jefferson's plan. However, it was not until after the Constitution was implemented and George Washington sworn in as our first president, that Congress turned its attention to solving the "money mess"— by beginning to create the United States coinage system, as it is known today.

On April 2, 1792, Congress approved a law allowing coins to be minted bearing the words "United States of America." The was the first major step in establishing our national coinage system. President Washington appointed a famous scientist and philosopher named David Rittenhouse to be the first Director of the Mint. Construction of the new minting facility, located in

INTRODUCTION

Philadelphia, began in the summer of 1792. The coin denominations specified in the 1792 law were as follows:

	VALUE OF
Gold Eagle	$10.00
Gold Half-Eagle	5.00
Gold Quarter-Eagle	2.50
Silver Dollar	1.00
Silver Half-Dollar	.50
Silver Quarter-Dollar	.25
Silver Dime (originally spelled disme)	.10
Silver Half-Dime (same as above)	.05
Copper Cent	.01
Copper Half-Cent	.005

The first coin struck by the United States was the half-dime in July 1792, several months before the mint facility was fully completed. Fifteen hundred of these pieces were minted, but only as pattern coins, not intended for circulation. The first coins to actually reach the general population were the copper half cent and one cent coins of 1793. The following year, the first silver issues were released: the five cent silver piece (the half-dime), the half-dollar, and the silver dollar. Dimes and quarters were first issued in 1796. Gold coins arrived on the scene in 1795, in the form of the ten dollar gold eagle and the five dollar gold half eagle. Quarter eagles, valued at two and one-half dollars, were introduced in 1796. Because the minting process was primitive by today's standards, some of the early United States coins bear file marks, a result of weight adjustments made by the mint's original employees.

For many years after the Philadelphia Mint began operating, coins failed to appear in sufficient numbers throughout the United States. The problem did not arise because of the mint's inability to produce money in adequate volumes. The expected movement of new coinage into the channels of trade was greatly impaired by metals speculators, who exported overseas as many gold and silver coins as they could obtain. The reason for the one-way flow was the weight ratios between the American money and foreign currency: the bullion value of the American coins caused them to find their way to foreign markets for sale and melting.

INTRODUCTION

It wasn't until 1834 that Congress reduced the weight standard of gold, a move which helped to alleviate the exportation of American coins. The passage of another act in 1837 to further revise and standardize the mint and coinage laws proved beneficial to the American nation. More Congressional legislation in 1853 reduced the weight of silver coins by about 7%, to make the metal value less than face value, causing more smaller coins to be retained in circulation.

As the number of United States coins in circulation increased, the necessity for the use of foreign and private coins decreased. In fact, Congress enacted a law in 1857 to prohibit the continued use of foreign and private coins. When the Philadelphia Mint began regular production in 1793, it was thought that the facility would fulfill the coinage demands of our new nation. Within forty years, however, pioneers had extended the American frontier so far from Philadelphia the mint could no longer serve the entire nation. To meet the needs of the growing country, several branch mints were opened, the first ones in 1838. To distinguish the place of origin, small letters, or "mint marks," were added to the coins' surface, differentiating one mint from another. A rundown of all United States mints that saw active duty follows:

Charlotte, North Carolina—Mint Mark "C"—in operation from 1838-1861. One of America's earliest productive gold mining districts, situated in the southern Appalachian region, was concentrated sixty miles west of Charlotte. The mint here created a boom for the mining industry nearby. The Charlotte mint struck only gold dollars, quarter eagles and half-eagles.

The Confederate States of America seized the Charlotte mint in 1861, and operations stopped after the remaining gold bullion had been coined into half-eagles of the federal design. Although reopened as an assay office in 1868, the facility never produced coins again. The original building was relocated and reconstructed, and today it is known as the Mint Museum of Art.

Dahlonega, Georgia—Mint Mark "D"—in operation 1838-1861. The story of the Dahlonega Mint is similar to that of the Charlotte Mint. In addition to gold dollars, quarter-eagles and half-eagles, the mint produced a few three dollar gold pieces.

Soon after the Civil War began, this mint also closed its doors. In 1871, the state of Georgia became the rightful owner of the property, and converted the building into an agricultural college; and that same year, a fire destroyed the building. Today the administration building of North Georgia College sits atop the foundation of the original building.

INTRODUCTION

New Orleans, Louisiana—Mint Mark "O"— in operation 1838-1909. The New Orleans Mint was the third mint opened in 1838. The facility was much larger than its sister branches, and eventually it produced all gold and silver coins with the exception of the twenty cent piece.

In 1861 operations ceased when the government of Louisiana took control of the mint, and later passed control to the Confederacy. It was here that coins began bearing the identity of the Confederate States of America. Also struck by the Confederates were some 1861 half dollars of federal design, which are impossible to distinguish from the halves issued by the United States government in early 1861.

Following the Civil War, the New Orleans Mint was closed, but it was reactivated in 1879 with the production of silver dollars, gold eagles and double eagles. After the mint permanently shut down as a coinage facility in 1909, it continued to serve as an assay office until 1942. Parts of the old mint building have been restored within the last few years, and are now open to the public as a tourist site.

San Francisco, California—Mint Mark "S"—in operation 1854 to present. The discovery of gold at Sutter's Mill in 1848 started a westward stampede, bringing both statehood and a mint to California. During the early days of the gold rush, coins were badly required to fill the needs of the growing population. Several private mints popped up in the San Francisco area prior to the establishment of the government mint. The San Francisco Mint has been housed in three separate buildings, the last move taking place in 1937.

The Old Mint Museum, housed in San Francisco's second mint building at Fifth and Mission streets, is open to the public free of charge. This museum was expanded in 1993.

Carson City, Nevada—Mint Mark "CC"—in operation 1870-1893. The discovery of silver at Nevada's famous Comstock Lode brought another westward migration of fortune seekers. Although established, perhaps because of political pressure from the powerful mining industry, the Carson City Mint produced some of the coins most highly prized by today's collectors, due to scarcity and the allure of owning an artifact from the "Wild West." The Carson City Mint passed into oblivion for several reasons: the glitter of silver eventually dimmed, the overabundance of coins available to the local economy, and because the Mint was unable to cleanse its reputation following a government scandal resulting in the suspension of the mint from 1886 to 1888.

From 1893 to 1933, the Carson City facility operated as an assay office. In time, the old mint became occupied as the Nevada State Museum, where visitors will find an exhibit dedicated to the building's original purpose.

INTRODUCTION

Denver, Colorado—Mint Mark "D"—in operation 1906 to present. The establishment of the mint was provided for in a law passed in 1862, but operations did not begin until 1906. The mint mark ("D") cannot be confused with that of the Dahlonega Mint (also "D") because the Dahlonega Mint last issued coins in 1861. The Denver Mint is still housed in its original building, completed in 1904, upgraded and modernized several times since then.

In recent years, the Denver Mint has been one of the world's most prolific producers of coins, with billions of coins turned out annually.

West Point, New York—Mint Mark "W"—the newest facility, granted mint status in 1988. Actually, coinage has taken place at the location since 1974, when it was used to help the Philadelphia Mint meet the demand for one cent coins. The 1984 Olympic commemorative coins were struck at West Point, and carry the mint mark "W," the first coins to bear a distinguishing mark from West Point. Today it is used primarily to produce coins for collector programs and bullion coins, although it has also struck coins for circulation in recent years. The coins released into general circulation are identical to those struck in Philadelphia.

Philadelphia, Pennsylvania—No Mint Mark, except "P" on 1942-1945 nickels, 1979 Susan B. Anthony dollars, and all coins 1980 or newer, except cents - in operation 1792 to present. Today the largest and most modern mint in the world, the facility creates all dies for United States coins and sends them to the branch mints (dies are pieces of metal, with designs imposed upon them and are used in pairs to strike a blank disc to make a coin). The present mint was dedicated in 1969, just a short walk from the original 1792 building.

Since the inception of the United States coinage system in 1792, mint officials have attempted to monitor the number of coins struck each year. Collectors should be advised that these mint reports were probably not always accurate, and should not be the sole factor in estimating rarity of coins. To confuse the matter even more, large quantities of gold and silver coins were never released for actual circulation, but were stored in United States Treasury vaults as backing for paper money. Many of these coins were eventually melted and re-minted into new coins. The reports from the Mint Directors do have some merit, however, as they provide a starting point for a numismatist to estimate scarcity of certain coins. Many other factors also need to be considered before arriving at an accurate estimation.

INTRODUCTION

Why Coins Are Desirable Investments

In recent decades, the price appreciation of many United States coins has been spectacular, capturing the imagination of countless investors. Many collectors have joyfully discovered that one of the world's most productive investment vehicles also happens to be their favorite hobby! For example, the collections of R.H. Gore, Jr. and Dennis I. Long were auctioned off together in 1990 for a combined total of nearly $5 million; the collections were assembled for only a small fraction of that total!

What makes a coin valuable? Ultimately, values are based on essentially the same set of rules as any other investment medium. If everyone wants to buy, prices go up, but if everyone wants to sell, prices drop. For coins, however, the supply/demand factor is closely associated with a number of other factors specific to the coin industry. Each of these must be carefully considered to arrive at a general evaluation of a coin, and in particular analyzed which factor has the greatest influence on the price movements of that coin. All collectors and investors should learn to recognize how these diverse factors determine the market value of a coin.

First of all, let's take a look at the supply/demand theory and how it relates to coin values. What exactly is the supply? Simply stated, the supply can be defined as the number of coins available for sale at a specific point in time. Mintage is the first indicator to be studied when guessing the available supply of a given coin. The mintage figure for a given date and mint mark tells you that the existing total today can be no larger than the number. Survivorship is the key modifier to the original mintage figure. As mentioned earlier, many coins were never released by the Mint, or were melted down. For instance, the Pittman Act authorized the melting down of over 270 million silver dollars in 1918! In 1979 and 1980, bullion prices set record highs, causing more coins to be withdrawn and converted to the metal form and resold at a profit. Moreover, millions of coins have been lost or destroyed by methods other than melting, further reducing the supply. More concisely, the volume of coins issued in the past is finite, can never increase, and in all likelihood will shrink even more over time due to attrition. This provides the basic upward momentum behind the coin market.

Collectors and investors comprise the demand position of the equation. If there is no demand, there is no market. Over the past thirty years, a higher and higher percentage of our population have become coin buyers. The number of collectors and investors has increased from about half a million in the 1950's to perhaps as many as 20 million today, depending upon one's definition of a collector. In all likelihood, that number will continue to increase,

INTRODUCTION

and more buyers competing for, at best, a fixed supply of collectible coins points to only one thing: higher prices in the future.

Besides the supply and demand factor, there are several other considerations determining the value of a coin. The most critical of these is condition, or state of preservation. Coins are very durable, but seldom can collectible coins be found in the pristine condition they enjoyed when first minted. From the moment a coin is removed from the dies, it is scratched, scraped, mishandled, and worn from everyday use. The degree of deterioration is measured by the "grade" or "condition" assigned to a coin. There are several typical grades widely recognized by numismatists, and just as with diamonds or antiques, these grades can significantly affect a coin's value. For instance, take a look at the 1892-S Morgan silver dollar. In Almost Uncirculated (AU-50) grade, the coin retails for around $2,500. In the next grade up, MS-60 Uncirculated, it sells for around $10,000! Such an incredible jump in price from one grade to the next is not uncommon, so you see how critical the coin's condition is in determining its value. Grading is discussed more throughout in subsequent sections of this book.

A common misconception held by the general public is that age is an important factor in setting coin values. Actually, it is one of the least important considerations. Many of the coins of the 20th century are far more expensive than some of the coins of the ancient Greeks or Romans, which can be purchased for as little as $10. To be sure, age does have some impact on the rarity of a coin, in that the older the coin, the longer the time for more of the original number of these coins to perish.

The design of a coin can have a bearing on its value. Many collectors enjoy acquiring every date and mint mark of an individual series of United States coins. Such a collector who focuses on, let's say Buffalo nickels, would want a specimen from each mint for every year the Buffalo nickel was issued. After the Buffalo nickel collection is completed, the collector may move on to some other series. While some collectors practice the hobby the way, others like to acquire a specimen of each design change in the entire United States series. They are called "type set collectors," and the method of collecting puts pressure on certain designs minted for only a short period of time. The 2½ dollar quarter-eagle design of 1808 lasted for that year only. Although not much rarer than other quarter-eagles of its time, demand from type set collectors has pushed the value of the 1808 quarter eagle to at least three times that of its contemporaries!

INTRODUCTION

Coin collecting is a profitable hobby. That's why millions of investors put their financial reserves into coins. While the appreciation rate in many instances is nothing short of spectacular, a word of warning to those hoping to use coins to turn a fast buck: forget it! Coins usually are a long term blue chip investment, not a short term 'get rich quick' scheme. The people who have earned the most outstanding profits on their coin investments held them for the long term. In other words, be prepared to hold your coins for at least two to five years before selling.

In summary, few investments opportunities offer as many advantages coupled with impressive performance and outstanding potential as numismatic investments do. The governing precept is this: In order to maximize your chances of value appreciation, obtain quality, scarce coins at competitive prices, and hold them for a reasonable length of time. Several negative risk aspects exist too, but they can be minimized through studying the subject and using good old-fashioned common sense. It's no wonder why coins receive so much attention from so many investors, large and small.

Speculators, Investors, and Collectors

There are basically three categories of coin buyers: s*peculators*, *investors*, and *collectors*. A combination of these groups comprises the demand side of the numismatic industry. The distribution of the types of buyers may vary from one small segment of the market to the next. Should you have the ability to identify what group exerts the greatest pressure on any one segment of the market at any particular time, you have a valuable clue as to what direction prices will take in the very near future. Each group possesses distinct personality traits, and you need to learn how to recognize them.

A speculator is someone who follows promotional advertising and hops aboard bandwagons when they appear. Speculation is based or the concept that another buyer will pay a higher price than what the seller has paid for it. Speculators operate with mass psychology. When word gets around about a certain "good" investment, everyone wants to get in on the act and make money. It doesn't take much arm twisting to convince a speculator to jump into a bull market.

In the coin world, an influx of speculators is evident when a coin series (or even a single coin) experiences sudden sharp price increases. Pandemonium continues until interest shifts to some new areas, which could be in a few days, a few months, or a few years, depending on how much promotion has

INTRODUCTION

been involved. Because of their nature, speculators don't stay with anything for a long period of time. When they lose interest in a specific item and move on to greener pastures, prices fall on that item.

Typically, few speculators familiarize themselves with the particulars of any investment vehicle, and this is especially true of numismatics. They simply migrate to wherever they believe most of the money is going.

A perfect example of the speculator phenomenon has already been touched on. For several years, it became popular to invest in high grade generic certified coins (i.e. common-dated slabbed Morgan silver dollars, Walking Liberty half dollars, etc., with a grading MS-65 or better). Interest in these issues heightened to unbelievable levels, causing prices to escalate accordingly, even though supplies were plentiful. In March 1990, interest waned, triggering a sharp fall in prices.

A coin investor is a person who strategically spends money on coins regularly, with the hope that someday they will be able to resell at a substantial profit. A notable difference between an investor and a speculator is that an investor doesn't jump in and out of the market when they see someone else doing it. Investors are consistently active in the marketplace year after year. The true investor understands the basic reasons underlying the value of a coin, the cyclical nature of the coin market, and other related facts. They observe, compare, and rationalize before each purchase, and leave hysteria to the masses of speculators. Most investors initiate their numismatic careers as speculators or collectors, and cross over into the investor class later on. For instance, during the 1979-1980 and 1988-1989 bull markets, countless thousands of speculators became collectors and investors upon discovering the rewards of owning historic United States coins. At the same time, some collectors realized how they could benefit financially from their numismatic skills, and they too became more like investors.

Collectors of coins have been around for many centuries. One definition of a coin collector is a person who assembles coins principally for the enjoyment received during the search. For them, coins are a hobby. Collectors come in all sizes and shapes, young and old, rich and poor. These days, a collector can't find too many worthy coins out of general circulation, and so is willing to pay a price to a dealer to acquire a desired specimen. The chief determinant for a collector is whether or not a coin is needed to fill an empty slot in a coin album, and of course, it must be affordable. When certain coins rise quickly in value, collectors typically redirect their enthusiasm to another segment of the market and return when prices have fallen.

INTRODUCTION

Even though the slabbed market has been declining for several years, collectors still remain consistent buyers of specific coins needed for their collections. Unquestionably, collectors serve as the price foundation of the coin market. Any coin of numismatic interest will have some value as far as collectors are concerned. Collectors are the reason why prices almost never fall beyond a certain point.

If you're an investor, watch closely the activities of the collectors and speculators. When the collector gets pushed out of a market because of escalating prices, and the buyers are made up almost entirely of speculators, that segment of the market is probably headed for a fall. Conversely, when collectors have shaped the basis for demand and prices have been stable for some time, the market is likely to be at basement levels and can only go up.

More Advice About Coin Investing

Simply stated, as an investor, your objective with numismatic coins is to assemble a collection of coins (or portfolio if you wish to call it that) that will appreciate handsomely over the years. There are numerous options available for achieving this goal, but you should adopt a strategy beforehand, structured by your desires and circumstances. You must determine, for instance, whether you want long term growth or short term growth coins (or both), and how much investment capital you can safely afford to tie up in each. Also, since there are many good investment prospects on the market at any given time (and especially now), you have to decide which coins, and in what condition, will be the most profitable to add to your numismatic portfolio. You should take all angles into consideration before you spend your hard earned money. It's alright to be skeptical. Remember, it's better to be safe than sorry, and for every "good" opportunity that slips through your fingers, there is always another to take its place.

Even though the basic motive for an investor in buying a coin is to resell someday at a profit, strategies change depending on your future goals. You may want to accumulate wealth for a down payment on a new home in five years or so, or perhaps you're starting a nest egg for retirement thirty years down the road. Persons wanting to register quicker profits should get into what industry analysts call "short term" coins. Begin by looking at the track record for different coins in various grades. There are literally hundreds to choose from with no particular preferred beginning point; the main thing is to

INTRODUCTION

start investing. Short term coins are those that rise fast in a relatively short time and drop quickly later on. Not coincidentally, short term coins historically have been linked with speculative involvement, as, for example, slabbed coins. When short-term investment coins are clearly undervalued in the market, and are therefore due for a price increase, that is the time to buy. You should expect to hold these coins an absolute minimum of two years, possibly as long as five years, and maybe even longer. After the short-term coins have recorded their anticipated increases, be disciplined enough to sell them. Many investors have the misconception that the coins will continue to perform fantastically every year, but they probably won't. Sell them and funnel your profits into other coins which are underpriced. Broadly speaking, coins grading MS-63 to MS-65 (or better) and Proof coins now fall into the underpriced category.

"Long term" coins are coins which cannot be expected to increase substantially within the next few years. The prices of these coins, when graphed, display a steady upward movement, with a few minor dips and plateaus here and there. Typically, a long term coin is one which has wide appeal among collectors, which explains its relatively smooth performance over the years. An investor should be prepared to hold these coins for at least ten years. Visualize long term coins as the "blue chip stocks" of the numismatic world because you can count on good, steady growth. If you're a fairly young person especially, you ought to seriously consider obtaining a few long term investment coins for your future.

What percentage of income should an investor spend on coins? Obviously the answer varies from person to person. Since you know your financial situation more intimately than anyone, including your income, obligations, plans, spending habits and lifestyles, you alone are the one who can best make that decision. Be careful: buying coins is enjoyable for many investors, and some find they cannot resist the temptation to convert much of their cash into numismatic holdings. Always leave yourself an emergency cash cushion, or you may be forced to liquidate some of your investment coins before they have reached their full potential.

The price of a coin gives little indication of whether or not it is a good investment. What is needed to determine the investment potential of a coin is an analysis of the demand for it, and its directional trend, not simply today's price. A coin currently selling for $3000 sounds impressive, but in reality, a coin selling for less than $100 may be a far better investment. When ready to buy, always keep in mind that good investment coins do not necessarily have big price tags.

INTRODUCTION

After studying this book, investors should develop a pattern for adding good potential coins to their portfolio. As with so many other financial areas, it is best to diversify. By diversifying, when some of your coins don't perform quite as you had anticipated, others will do well in the meantime. Should you ever be faced with having to sell some of your coins, a diversified portfolio will enable you to liquidate coins which have more closely reached their maximum potential. Prominent coin expert David Hall, along with a number of other numismatic advisors, recommends the following diversification program:

| 25% Type Coins | 20% Modern Singles | 10% Commemoratives |
| 25% Gold | 20% Silver Dollars | |

In each investment area, there are short and long term prospects available. Plan your purchases according to your objectives, concentrating on maintaining desired percentages for maximum satisfaction.

Type coins are coins in all denominations minted in the country between 1793-1916. "Type coin" got it's name from collectors trying to obtain an example of each type of coin minted during the period, because complete sets were too costly to assemble. Gold coins are generally the most expensive coins a collector can buy. In fact, the price of choice gold coins has put them out of reach for smaller investors. For marginal investors, you're best advised to buy the less expensive dates without compromising on quality or condition.

Modern singles are the coins of the 20th century. They include:

Lincoln Cents	1909-Present
Buffalo Nickels	1913-1938
Jefferson Nickels	1938-Present
Mercury Dimes	1916-1945
Roosevelt Dimes	1946-Present
Standing Liberty Quarter	1916-1930
Washington Quarters	1932-Present
Walking Liberty Half Dollars	1916-1947
Franklin Half Dollars	1948-1963
Kennedy Half Dollars	1964-Present
Eisenhower Dollars	1970-1978

INTRODUCTION

This list of coins, in particular, offers an array of tremendous long term investment opportunities. The prices of many of these coins can fit nearly anyone's budget, while even MS-65 coins can be had for only a few dollars more than MS-60 coins. Great potential exists in the modern singles. The top grade coins from the area will probably become extremely valuable in twenty or thirty years, in comparison to what they cost presently.

Silver dollars are the most commonly bought investment coin today. Dollars minted from 1794 to 1873 are not as widely traded as the more common Morgan and Peace dollars of 1878-1935. Probably in no other series has there been more price manipulation and speculation. Extreme caution is advised because of the volatility, but therein lies fantastic possibilities. See the section on silver dollars for more information.

Commemoratives are coins specially minted to commemorate an event or honor some person from the past. Commemoratives are sanctioned by Congress. Speculation influence has been heavy here also.

Don't be uneasy if you can't adjust your coin portfolio immediately to reflect the guidelines listed above. Naturally, if you purchase only one coin at a time, it will take a while to diversify your collection accordingly.

One very important decision an investor must make is what condition of coins to buy. Dealers usually tell customers to buy coins in the very best conditions — namely, MS-65+ and PR-65+ coins. From an investment viewpoint this year, this is generally good advice, and as such, gem material will be prominently mentioned in most of the upcoming sections on individual coin series. However, all grades can do well from time to time and from coin to coin. For instance, scarce coins and many early American coins have done extremely well in Good and Very Good condition at various intervals in the past. To no one's surprise, countless issues in Uncirculated and Proof have performed spectacularly. There is no absolute rule of thumb when it comes to grade selection. Each coin in every condition must be judged on its history, potential, and current price.

Always avoid coins that have been bent, holed, gouged, or damaged in any way. They almost never possess good investment potential.

If you're seriously contemplating spending your investment dollars on coins, it is highly recommended to first spend a little money on building a small numismatic library. It's a purchase that can literally pay for itself many times over. "Buy the book before the coin" was a quote attributed to Aaron Feldman, a well-known dealer. See the "Recommended Reading" list at the back of this book.

INTRODUCTION

Buying and Selling Coins

More often than not, when you buy or sell a coin, you will be doing business with a coin dealer. It is worth the effort to check out the background of any dealer you're considering working with, because there is a small minority of unscrupulous dealers waiting to sell overgraded and overpriced coins. By carefully choosing a dealer with expertise and an unchallenged reputation, you will take another large step toward becoming a successful numismatic investor.

If you are considering doing business with a dealer, first ask a lot of questions. A legitimate dealer expects to receive many questions, and they'll be happy to answer them for you. Questions to bring up are: What return privilege, if any, does the dealer offer? Do they guarantee their coins to be genuine? Do they belong to any of the trade organizations, such as the American Numismatic Association (ANA) or the Professional Numismatists Guild (PNG)? Professional affiliations are clues the dealer is willing to obey certain industry guidelines and accept responsibility, at least superficially. Also, the memberships are indicators that the dealer has an established network of contacts within the industry.

Be sure to inquire outright if the dealer uses ANA grading standards, and if not, find out how they determine the grade of a coin. Will they allow their coins to be submitted to an unbiased grading service? What price guides, if any, do they base coin values on? Do they both buy and sell coins based on that guide? Will they buy back coins that they originally sold to you? Examine their policies in depth. If an individual or company can't answer all of your questions to your complete satisfaction, or if the firm simply won't take the time to field your inquiries, take your business elsewhere. There are numerous other honest companies in the coin business which will work hard to serve your needs, whether you are a small collector or a wealthy investor.

The best place to start in your search for a good dealer is the community where you live. Most cities of 10,000 or more usually have at least one coin dealer. Get answers to questions similar to those above. In addition, contact a coin club in your area, if any, and listen to what they have to say about the dealer. Try to obtain references from the banks, the chamber of commerce, credit bureaus, or anywhere the dealer has done business in the past. Bad reputations are hard to shake, and chances are good that if the dealer has been incompetent or dishonest, you'll discover it, but only if you investigate. On the other hand, a good reputation is difficult to build, and is usually well deserved.

INTRODUCTION

There are hundreds of very fine coin dealers scattered across the nation who do a large volume of business through the mail. Unfortunately, there are a few con artists using the postal system to their advantage also. Before you send off any money in the mail, you should adopt the same investigative tactics for out of town dealers as for any other dealer. One good aspect of mail order firms is that they usually maintain a much larger inventory to choose from than your local dealer. Furthermore, if they offer certified coins by the better known grading services, there is only a very slim chance of getting shortchanged. A quick check with the publisher who prints their advertising can also yield useful information.

A great place to acquire coins is at coin shows. Unless you live in a remote area, there will likely be a show coming to your general vicinity soon. Shows range in size from just a few tables to full scale events featuring hundreds of world renowned dealers. Shows also provide an excellent venue to expand your numismatic knowledge.

One area that has given the numismatic industry a black-eye is telemarketing fraud. Not every company using the approach is dishonest, but a good rule to abide by is this: if you receive an unsolicited phone call from someone in an attempt to sell you coins, be on guard. What occasionally happens is that a slick-talking salesperson disguising themselves as a knowledgeable numismatist tries to impress you with their fantastic stock of coins, part of which they are willing to "sacrifice" for you, their prized customer. In reality, what they have is a group of overpriced coins, worth only a fraction of their cost to you. If you feel a necessity to do business with a telemarketer, follow the guidelines mentioned above. Also, ask them if you could stop by their place of business the next time you're in their area. Most con artists don't want you to see their operation in person. Even if a telemarketer has "good" answers to your questions, never abandon caution. Some of these professionals are so clever at handling objections that even a well-versed customer can be fooled. At the risk of offending sincere telemarketers, the safest and best advice is to avoid numismatic telemarketers altogether.

If you believe that you have been cheated by a coin dealer, you have several options. If the dealer's stated policy includes a money back guarantee, use it. Be sure to retain copies of all receipts and written correspondence between both parties. If you're still not satisfied, complain to the ANA or PNG if the offending dealer is a member. These organizations carefully monitor their members under a strict code of ethics. If you purchased your problem coin through an ad in one of the hobby publications, file a grievance with the publisher against the dealer. Publishers don't want unhappy readers spreading bad

INTRODUCTION

news about their magazines, so they may exert pressure upon the dealers, threatening to refuse them advertising space, unless the problem is rectified promptly. Another recourse is to notify federal and state authorities who enforce mail fraud laws. They can assist you if you've been the victim of blatantly deceitful advertising.

Assuming that you have chosen to buy coins of sound investment quality, and you have maintained them in as good a condition as when they were bought, you should have little difficulty in finding a buyer. However, there are a few facts you should be mindful of before you approach dealers to ask them for an offer on your coin.

Coin dealers are in business to make a profit; as numismatics is their chosen profession, they are certainly entitled to one. Like other businessmen, coin dealers have numerous overhead expenses, including salaries to employees, rent, taxes, advertising, insurance, travel, and many other miscellaneous items. About 70% to 90% of the retail value of a coin is the best dealers can offer to buy it for, sometimes less.

When dealers are solicited to buy a coin that they think will sell quickly, they'll probably be willing to pay closer to the 90% figure. If there is a chance of a slower sale, dealers will discount their offer accordingly. Slow selling coins are the dread of coin dealers. It means having capital tied up while the coin lies idle; they cannot buy other coins or pay expenses with the money already spent for the idle coin.

Other factors make it worth your while to shop around when selling coins. Not all dealers are in identical economic positions, and while one dealer may want your coin to replenish their inventory, another may be well stocked with the same coin. These factors can have a bearing on how much a dealer will offer for your merchandise.

An alternate method of liquidating your investment coins is to sell them to other investors. Should you opt for this method, be prepared to allot more time and out-of-pocket expenses than if you sold directly to a dealer. A classified ad in the local newspaper or hobby circular usually brings respondents willing to buy your coins at or near their fair retail price. Try to avoid letting strangers know much about yourself and your investment. Take precautions not to publish your phone number and home address, and if at all possible, meet with interested buyers on neutral ground. A good option would be the bank where you keep the coins.

You may choose to try putting your coins on the auction block.. Many of the larger, better known coin auction companies are always seeking collectible coins from the general public as a way to round out their sales, and would

INTRODUCTION

welcome your contributions. The average commission ranges from 12% to 20%, usually paid by the seller, but increasingly today the commission charge is split evenly between the buyer and seller. Frequently, an auction sale for an especially "hot" coin is likely to draw a higher price than if you sold it otherwise, because auctions are emotional platforms where bidders often react beyond reason to acquire a popular item. Be certain to make all the usual inquiries about the auction company before you go the route.

No matter what your preferred method for selling your coins, be aware that in nearly all circumstances, certified coins are more liquid than uncertified.

Most dealers are honest, forthright professionals committed to helping their customers find the right coin in the right grade at the right price. Because there are a few bad apples in every barrel, a coin investor should never abandon caution when dealing with an unknown company. You may never be as familiar with grading and numismatics, in general, as professional coin people are, but if you arm yourself with some knowledge about the hobby and always be inquisitive, the rip-off artists will have to look beyond you to carry out their scams.

An Introduction to Grading

Grade (the condition or state of wear of a coin) is one of the main determining factors of a coin's value. Until relatively recently, grading was by "instinct." Based on their own knowledge and personal observations, one seller would have their own system, and another seller, with another set of observations, experiences, and opinions, a different one. There was little standardization.

In recent times coin values have increased sharply. In many instances coins that were worth $10 twenty years ago are worth $200 or more now. A very small difference in grade can mean a very large difference in price. The exact grade of a coin is more important now than ever before.

Recently, the continued escalation of coin values has brought about finer grading distinctions than ever before. For example, the Mint State or Uncirculated grade is often divided into three classifications: Uncirculated (typical) or, in the numerical scale MS-60; Choice Uncirculated or MS-65, and Perfect Uncirculated or MS-70. The official ANA Grading System defines these and many other distinctions. It also gives important information concerning surface characteristics, methods of striking, different gradations of wear, and much other information which enables the user to accurately grade any United States coin from 1793 to the present.

INTRODUCTION

In the pages immediately following, you will find basic information from the official ANA Grading System. The information is far from complete because of the size limitations of the book. The complete official ANA Grading System is a sizable reference book of 352 pages and is highly recommended by the editor as a very useful adjunct to the book.

Basic Grading Information for United States Coins

OFFICIAL ANA GRADING SYSTEM

The grading information on the following pages is intended to inform the reader about the basics of grading United States Coins. The information is being reproduced from The Official American Numismatic Association Grading Standards For United States Coins with the courtesy of the American Numismatic Association.

PROOF COINS

The term "Proof" refers to a manufacturing process which results in a special surface or finish on coins made for collectors. Most familiar are modern brilliant proofs. These coins are struck at the mint by a special process. Carefully prepared dies, sharp in all features, are made. Then the flat surfaces of the dies are given a high mirror-like polish. Specially prepared planchets (pieces of metal ready to receive an impression) are fed into low-speed coining presses. Each Proof coin is slowly and carefully struck more than once to accentuate details. When striking is completed, the coin is carefully taken from the dies. The result is a coin with mirror-like surface. The piece is then grouped together with other denominations in a set and offered for sale to collectors.

From 1817 through 1857 inclusive, Proof coins were made only on special occasions and not for general sale to collectors. They were made available to visiting foreign dignitaries, government officials, and those with connections at the mint. Earlier (pre-1817) United States coins may have proof-like surfaces and many proof characteristics (1796 Silver Coins are a good example), but they were not specifically or intentionally struck as proofs; these coins are sometimes designated as "specimen strikings."

INTRODUCTION

Beginning in 1858, Proofs were sold to collectors openly. In that year, 80 Silver Proof sets (containing silver coins from the three-cent piece through the Silver Dollar), plus additional pieces of the Silver Dollar denomination, were produced as well as perhaps 200 (the exact number is not known) Copper-Nickel cents and a limited number of Proof Gold coins.

The traditional or "brilliant" type of proof finish was used on all American proof coins of the nineteenth century. During the twentieth century, cents through the 1909 Indian, nickels through the 1912 Liberty, regular issued silver coins through 1915, and gold coins through 1907 were of the brilliant type. When modern proof coinage was resumed in 1936 and continued through 1942, then 1950 to 1964, and 1968 to date, the brilliant finish was used. While these types of proofs are referred to as "brilliant proofs," actual specimens may have toned over the years. The mirror-like surface is still evident, however.

From 1908 through 1915, matte proofs and sandblast proofs (the latter made by directing fine sand particles at high pressure toward the coin's surface) were made of certain gold coins (exceptions are 1909-1910 proofs with Roman finish). While characteristics vary from issue to issue, generally all of these pieces have extreme sharpness of design detail and sharp, squared-off rims. The surfaces are without luster and have a dullish matte surface. Sandblast proofs were made of certain commemoratives also, such as the 1928 Hawaiian issue.

Roman finish proof gold coins were made in 1909 and 1910. These pieces are sharply struck, have squared-off edges, and have a satin-like surface finish, similar to an Uncirculated coin (which causes confusion among collectors today, and which at the time of issue was quite unpopular as collectors resented having to pay a premium for a coin without a distinctly different appearance).

Matte proofs were made of Lincoln cents 1909-1917 and Buffalo Nickels 1913-1917. Such coins have extremely sharp design detail, squared-off rims, "brilliant" (mirror-like) edges, but a matte or satin-like (or even satin surface, not with flashy mint luster) surface. In some instances matte proof dies may have been used to make regular circulation strikes once the requisite number of matte proofs were made for collectors. So, it is important that a matte proof, to be considered authentic, have squared-off rims and mirror-like perfect edges in addition to the proper surface characteristics.

INTRODUCTION

Additional Points Concerning Proofs: Certain regular issues or business strike coins have nearly full prooflike surfaces, which were produced in several ways. Usually regular issue dies (intended to make coins for circulation) were polished to remove surface marks or defects to extend use. Coins struck from these dies were produced at high speed, and the full proof surface is not always evident. Also, the pieces are struck on ordinary planchets. Usually such pieces, sometimes called "First Strikes" or "Prooflike Uncirculated" have patches of Uncirculated mint frost. One characteristic is the shield on the reverse (on coins with the design feature). The stripes within the shield on proofs are fully brilliant, but on proof-like no-proofs the stripes usually are not mirror-like. Also, the striking may be weak in areas and the rims might not be sharp.

The mirror-like surface of a brilliant proof coin is much more susceptible to damage than surfaces of an Uncirculated coin. For the reason, proof coins which have been cleaned often show a series of fine hairlines or minute striations. Also, careless handling has resulted in certain proofs acquiring marks, nicks, and scratches.

Some proofs, particularly nineteenth century issues, have "lint marks." When a proof die was wiped with an oily rag, sometimes threads, bits of hair, lint, and the like would remain. When a coin was struck from such a die, an incuse or recessed impression of the debris would appear on the piece. Lint marks visible to the unaided eye should be specifically mentioned in a description.

Proof-70 (Perfect Proof). A Proof-70 or Perfect Proof is a coin with no hairlines, handling marks, or other defects; in other words, a flawless coin. Such a coin may be brilliant or may have natural toning.

Proof-65 (Choice Proof). Proof 65 or Choice Proof refers to a proof which may show some very fine hairlines, usually from friction type cleaning or friction type drying or rubbing after dipping. To the unaided eye, a Proof-65 or Choice Proof will appear to be virtually perfect. However, 5-power magnification will reveal some minute lines. Such hairlines are best seen under strong incandescent light.

Proof-60 (Proof). Proof-60 refers to a proof with some scattered handling marks and hairlines which may be visible to the unaided eye.

INTRODUCTION

Impaired Proofs. If a proof coin has been excessively cleaned, has many marks, scratches, dents or other defects, it is described as an impaired proof. If the coin has seen extensive wear then it will be graded one of the lesser grades—Proof-55, Proof-45, or whatever. It is not logical to describe a slightly worn proof as "AU" (Almost Uncirculated) for it never was "Uncirculated" to begin with—in the sense that Uncirculated describes a top grade of normal production strike. So, the term "Impaired Proof" is appropriate. It is best to describe fully such a coin, examples being: "Proof with extensive hairlines and scuffing," or "Proof with numerous nicks and scratches in the field," or "Proof-55, with light wear on the higher surfaces."

UNCIRCULATED COINS

The term "Uncirculated," interchangeable with "Mint State," refers to a coin which has never seen circulation. Supposedly, such a piece has no wear of any kind. A coin as bright as the time it was minted or with very light natural toning can be described as "Brilliant Uncirculated." Except in the instance of copper coins, the presence or absence of light toning does not affect an Uncirculated coin's grade. Indeed, among silver coins, attractive natural toning often results in the coin bringing a premium price.

The quality of luster or "mint bloom" on an Uncirculated coin is an essential element in correctly grading the piece, and has a bearing on its value. Luster may in time become dull, frosty, spotted or discolored. Unattractive luster will normally lower the grade.

With the exception of certain Special Mint Sets for collectors, Uncirculated or normal production strike coins have been produced on high speed presses, stored in bags together with other coins, run through counting machines, and in other ways handled without regard for numismatic prosterity. As a result, it is the rule and not the exception for an Uncirculated coin to have bag marks and evidence of coin-to-coin contact, although the piece might not have seen actual commercial circulation. Differences in criteria in the regard are given in the detailed individual grading sections of the Official ANA Grading Guide.

INTRODUCTION

Uncirculated coins can be divided into three major categories:

MS-70 (Perfect Uncirculated). MS-70 or Perfect Uncirculated is the finest quality available. Such a coin under 4-power magnification will show no bag marks, lines, or other evidence of handling or contact with other coins.

A brilliant coin may be described as "MS-70 Brilliant" or "Perfect Brilliant Uncirculated." A lightly toned silver or nickel coin may be described as "MS-70 Toned" or "Perfect Toned Uncirculated." Or in the case of particularly attractive or unusual toning, additional adjectives may be in order such as "Perfect Uncirculated with attractive iridescent toning around the borders."

Copper and Bronze coins: To qualify as MS-70 or Perfect Uncirculated, a copper or bronze coin must have its full luster and natural surface color, and may not be toned brown, olive, or any other color (coins with toned surfaces which are otherwise perfect should be described as MS-65 as the following text indicates).

MS-65 (Choice Uncirculated). The refers to an above average Uncirculated coin which may be Brilliant or Toned (and described accordingly) and which has fewer bag marks than usual; scattered occasional bag marks on the surface or perhaps one or two very light rim marks.

MS-60 (Uncirculated). MS-60 or Uncirculated (typical Uncirculated without any other adjectives) refers to a coin which has a moderate number of bag marks on its surface. Also present may be a few minor edge nicks and marks although not of serious nature. Usually, deep bag marks, nicks, and the like must be described separately. A coin may be either brilliant or toned.

Striking and Minting Peculiarities on Uncirculated Coins

Certain early United States gold and silver coins have mint-caused planchet or adjustment marks, a series of parallel striations. If these are visible to the naked eye, they should be described adjectivally in addition to the numerical or regular descriptive grade. For example: "MS-60 with adjustment marks," or "MS-65 with adjustment marks," or "Perfect Uncirculated with very light adjustment marks," or by some similar qualification.

If an Uncirculated coin exhibits weakness due to striking or die wear, or unusual (for the variety) die wear, they must be adjectively mentioned in addition to the grade. Examples are: "MS-60, lightly struck", or "Choice Uncirculated, lightly struck," and "MS-70, lightly struck."

INTRODUCTION

CIRCULATED COINS

Once a coin enters circulation it begins to show signs of wear. As time goes on, the coin becomes more and more worn until, after decades, only a few original features are left.

Dr. William H. Sheldon devised a numerical scale to indicate degrees of wear. According to the scale, a coin touched by even the slightest trace of wear (below MS-60) cannot be called Uncirculated.

Although intended to be a finely continuous scale, it has been found practical to designate specific intermediate numbers to define grades. Hence, the text uses the following descriptions and their numerical equivalents:

Choice About Uncirculated-55. Abbreviation: AU-55. Only a small trace of wear is visible on the highest points of the coin. As in the case with the other grades here, specific information is listed in the Official ANA Grading Guide under the various types, for wear often occurs in different spots on different designs.

About Uncirculated-50. Abbreviation: AU-50. With traces of wear on nearly all of the highest areas. At least half of the original mint luster is present.

Choice Extremely Fine-45. Abbreviation: EF-45. With light overall wear on the coins highest points. All design details very sharp. Mint luster is usually seen only in protected areas of the coin's surface such as between the star points and in the letter spaces.

Extremely Fine-40. Abbreviation: EF-40. With only slight wear but more extensive than the preceding, still with excellent overall sharpness. Traces of mint luster may show.

Choice Very Fine-30. Abbreviation: VF-30. With light even wear on the surfaces; design details on the highest points lightly worn, but with all lettering and major features sharp.

Very Fine-20. Abbreviation: VF-12. As preceding but with moderate wear on highest parts.

Fine-12. Abbreviation: F-12 Moderate to considerable even wear. Entire design is bold. All lettering, including the word LIBERTY (on 28 coins with the feature on the shield or headband), visible, with some weaknesses.

Very Good-8. Abbreviation: VG-8. Well worn. Most fine details such as hair strands, leaf details, and so on are worn nearly smooth. The word LIBERTY if on a shield or headband is only partially visible.

INTRODUCTION

Good-4. Abbreviation: G-4. Heavily worn. Major designs visible, but with faintness in areas. Head of liberty, wreath, and other major features visible in outline form without center detail.

About Good-3. Abbreviation AG-3. Very heavily worn with portions of the lettering, date, and legends being worn smooth, the date barely readable.

Editor's Note: The exact descriptions of circulated grades vary widely from issue to issue, so the preceding commentary is only of a very general nature. Once again, we highly recommend the Official ANA Grading Guide be referred to for specific information about grading the various types.

SPLIT AND INTERMEDIATE GRADES

Often, because of peculiarities striking, or a coin's design, one side of the coin will grade differently from the other. When the is the case, a diagonal mark is used to separate the two. For example, a coin with an AU-50 obverse side and a Choice Extremely Fine-45 reverse side can be described as: AU/EF or, alternately, 50/45.

The ANA standard numerical scale is divided into the following steps: 3, 4, 8, 12, 20, 30, 40, 50, 55, 60, 65, and 70. Most advanced collectors and dealers find that the gradations from AG-3 through choice AU-55 are sufficient to describe nearly every coin showing wear. The use of intermediate grade labels such as EF-42, EF-43, etc., is not encouraged. Grading is not that precise, and using such finely split intermediate grades implies a degree of accuracy not verified by other numismatists. A split or an intermediate grade, such as that between VF-30 and EF-40 should be called choice VF-35 rather than VF-EF or about EF.

An exception to intermediate grades can be found among Mint State coins—coins grading from MS-60 through MS-70. Among Mint State Coins there are fewer variables. Wear is not a factor; the considerations are usually the amount of bag marks and surface blemishes. While it is good numismatic practice to adhere to the numerical classifications of 60, 65, and 70, it is permissible to use intermediate grades.

INTRODUCTION

In all instances, the adjectival description must be of the next lower grade. For example, a standard grade for a coin is MS-60 or Uncirculated Typical. The next major category is MS-65 or Uncirculated Choice. A coin which is felt to grade, for example MS-64, must be described as "MS-64, Uncirculated Typical." It may not be described a Choice Uncirculated for the minimum definition of Choice Uncirculated is MS-65. Likewise, an MS-69 coin must be described as: MS-69, Uncirculated Choice. It is not permissible to use Uncirculated Perfect for any coin which is any degree less than MS-70.

The ANA Grading System considers it to be good numismatic practice to adhere to the standard 60, 65 and 70 numerical designations. Experienced numismatics can generally agree on whether a given coin is MS-60 or MS-65. However, not even the most advanced numismatists can necessarily agree on whether a coin is MS-62 or MS-63; the distinction is simply too minute to permit accuracy. In all instances, it is recommended that intermediate grades be avoided, and if there is any doubt, the lowest standard grade would be used. The use of plus or minus signs is also not accepted practice.

GRADING ABBREVIATIONS

Corresponding numbers may be used with any of these descriptions.

MS-70	Perfect Uncirculated	Perf. Unc.	UNC.-70
MS-65	Choice Uncirculated	Ch. Unc.	UNC.-65
MS-60	Uncirculated	Unc.	UNC.-60
AU-55	Ch. Abt. Unc.	Ch. Abt. Unc.	CH. AU.
AU-50	About Uncirculated	Abt. Unc.	AU
EF-45	Choice Extremely Fine	Ch. Ex. Fine	CH. EF
EF-40	Extremely Fine	Ex. Fine	EF
VF-30	Choice Very Fine	Ch. V. Fine	CH. VF
VF-20	Very Fine	V. Fine	VF
F-12	Fine	Fine	F
VG-8	Very Good	V. Good	VG
G-4	Good	Good	G
AG-3	About Good	Abt. Good	AG

INTRODUCTION

CLEANING COINS

Experienced numismatists will usually say that a coin is best left alone and not cleaned. However, most beginning collectors have the idea that "Brilliant is best" and somehow feel that cleaning a coin will "improve" it. As the penchant for cleaning seems to be universal, and also because there are some instances in which cleaning can actually be beneficial, some important aspects are presented here.

All types of cleaning, "good" and "bad," result in the coin's surface being changed, even if only slightly. Even the most careful "dipping" of a coin will, if repeated, result in the coin acquiring a dullish and microscopically etched surface. It is probably true to state that no matter what one's intentions are, for every single coin actually improved in some way by cleaning, a dozen or more have been decreased in value. Generally, experienced numismatists agree that a coin should not be cleaned unless there are spots of oxidation, pitting which might worsen in time, or unsightly streaking or discoloration.

PROCESSING, POLISHING, AND OTHER MISTREATMENT OF COINS

There have been many attempts to give a coin the appearance of being in a higher grade than it actually is. Numismatists refer to such treatment as "processing." Being different from cleaning (which can be "good" or "bad"), processing is never beneficial. Often one or more methods of treating a coin are combined. Sometimes a coin will be cleaned or polished and then by means of heat, fumes, or other treatment, artificial toning will be applied; there are many variations.

Types of processing include polishing and abrasion which removes metal from a coin's surface, etching and acid treatment, and "whizzing". The latter usually refers to abrading the surface of a coin with a stiff wire brush, often in a circular motion, to produce a series of minute tiny parallel scratches which to the unaided eye or under low magnification often appear to be like mint luster. Under high magnification (in the instance a very strong magnifying glass should be used) the surface of a whizzed coin will show countless tiny scratches. Also, the artificial "mint luster" will usually be in a uniform pattern throughout the coin's surfaces, whereas on an Uncirculated coin with true mint luster, the sheen of the luster will be different on the higher parts than on the field. Some whizzed coins can be extremely deceptive. Comparing a whizzed coin to an untreated coin is the best way to gain experience.

INTRODUCTION

The American Numismatic Association's bylaws make members subject to disciplinary action if they advertise or offer for sale or trade any coin that has been whizzed and is represented to be of a better condition than it was previously. When a coin has been polished, whizzed, artificially retoned, or in any other way changed from its original natural appearance and surface, it must be so stated in description.

For example, a coin which is Extremely Fine but whizzed to give it the artificial appearance of Uncirculated should be described as "Extremely Fine, Whizzed." An AU coin which has been recolored should be described as "AU, Recolored." The simple "dipping" (without abrasion) of an already Uncirculated or Proof coin to brighten the surface does not have to be mentioned unless such dipping alters the appearance from when the coin was first struck (for example, in the instance of a copper or bronze coin in which dipping always produces an unnatural color completely unlike the coin when it was first struck).

NATURAL COLORATION OF COINS

Knowledge of the natural color which coinage metals acquire over a period of years is useful to the collector. To an extent, a coin's value is determined by its coloration. Also, certain types of unnatural color might indicate that a coin has been cleaned or otherwise treated.

The basic coinage metals used in the United States are alloys of copper, nickel, silver, and gold. Copper tends to tone the most rapidly. Gold is the least chemically active and will tone only slightly and then over a long period of years.

Copper. Copper is among the most chemically active of all coinage metals. Half cents and large cents of 1793-1857 were made of nearly pure copper. Later "copper" coins are actually bronze.

When a copper coin is first struck it emerges from the dies with a brilliant pale-orange surface, the color of a newly minted Lincoln set. There were some exceptions in the early years among half cents and large cents. Copper was obtained from many different sources, traces of impurities varied from shipment to shipment, and some newly minted coins had a subdued brilliance, sometimes with a brownish or grayish cast.

Once a freshly minted coin enters the atmosphere it immediately begins to oxidize. Over a period of years, especially if exposed to actively circulating air or if placed in contact with sulphites, the coin will acquire a glossy brown surface. In between the brilliant and glossy brown stages, it will be part red and part brown.

INTRODUCTION

An Uncirculated coin with full original mint brilliance, usually slightly subdued in coloration, is typically described as Brilliant Uncirculated (our example here is for a typical Uncirculated or MS-60 coin); a choice piece would be called Choice Brilliant Uncirculated, and so on. One which is part way between brilliant and brown surface hues would be called Red and Brown Uncirculated. Specimens with brownish surfaces can be called Brown Uncirculated. Particularly valuable coins can have the coloration described in more detail. Generally, in any category of grading, the more explanation given, the more accurate is the description.

Brilliant Proof (with mirrorlike fields) copper and bronze coins are pale orange when first struck. Over a period of time they, like Uncirculated pieces of the same metal, tend to tone brown. Often attractive iridescent hues will develop in the intermediate stages. A Proof copper coin can be described as Brilliant Proof (if the surfaces are still "bright"), Red and Brown Proof, or Brown Proof.

Matte Proofs were made at the Philadelphia Mint in the Lincoln cent series from 1909 to 1916. When first introduced, these were stored in yellow tissue paper which tended to tone them quickly to shades varying from deep reddish-brown to dark brown with iridescent tones. The surface coloration is normal today for a Matte Proof bronze coin and should be expected. Most "bright" Matte Proofs have been cleaned or dipped.

Early copper and bronze coins with full original mint brilliance are more valuable than Red and Brown Uncirculated pieces. The more original mint brilliance present, the more valuable a coin will be. The same is true of Proofs.

Circulated copper coins are never fully Brilliant, but are toned varying shades of brown. Certain early large cents and half cents often tone black because of the presence of impurities in the original metal.

Nickel. Uncirculated nickel (actually an alloy of copper and nickel) coins when first minted are silver-gray in appearance, not as bright as silver but still with much brilliance. Over a period of time nickel coins tend to tone a hazy gray, gray, or golden coloration, sometimes with bluish overtones. Proof nickel coins will tone in the same manner.

The presence or absence of attractive toning does not affect an Uncirculated or Proof nickel coin's value. Many collectors, particularly those with great experience, will actually prefer and will sometimes pay a premium for very attractive light toning. Very dull, heavily toned, or spotted coins are considered less valuable. Circulated nickel coins have a gray appearance.

INTRODUCTION

Silver. When first minted, silver coins have a bright silvery-white surface. Over a period of time, silver, a chemically active metal, tends to tone deep brown or black. Uncirculated and Proof silver pieces often exhibit very beautiful multi-colored iridescent hues after a few years. The presence or absence of attractive toning does not affect a silver coin's value one way or the other. Old timers and museums will often prefer attractively toned coins. Beginners sometimes think that "brilliant is best." Circulated silver coins often have a dull gray appearance, sometimes with deep gray or black areas.

Gold. When first struck, gold coins are a bright yellow-orange color. As gold coins are not pure gold but are alloyed with copper and traces of other substances, they do not tend to tone over a period of time. Over several decades, a gold coin will normally acquire a deep orange coloration, sometimes with light brown or orange-brown toning "stains" or streaks in areas (resulting from improperly mixed copper traces in the alloy). Light toning does not affect the value of a gold coin.

Very old gold coins, particularly those in circulated grades, will sometimes show a red oxidation. Gold coins which have been recovered from treasure wrecks after centuries at the sea bottom will sometimes have a minutely porous surface because of the corrosive action of sea water. Such pieces sell for less then specimens which have not been so affected. Care must be taken to distinguish these from cast copies which may have a similar surface.

Handling and Storing Numismatic Treasures

Some handling and storage methods are known to contribute to the deterioration of coins, lowering values considerably along the way. If you don't want the shock of someday discovering that the condition of a half dollar bought at MS-65 must be seriously downgraded because of treatment received from you, read the chapter carefully. It could save you much mental anguish later on.

Never handle an unprotected coin any other way except by its edges. If your fingers come in contact with either one of its sides, small amounts of oil and acid in the skin could be left behind. Always place a soft surface below the coin in case it should accidentally slip from your grasp. There will be a lesser risk of damage by doing so. Do not allow any collectible coin to come in contact with other coins or hard objects. Any bump or scrape could leave scratches. By no means should a person scoot a valuable coin along any surface, no matter how soft or slick the surface is.

INTRODUCTION

The best way to protect and store your coins is to keep them in special holders or albums available through coin dealers and bookstores. Not all containers are of equal quality, so it's best to get advice before you place your most valuable coins in any of them.

Never use paper envelopes for storing coins. Most paper products contain sulfur, which can cause an ugly black or yellow tone to appear on your coins. If a coin is shipped to you in a paper envelope, be certain to remove it right away. As an additional precaution, maintain separate storage facilities for your important papers and your numismatic investments.

Some types of coin holders, one kind in particular called a "flip," contains a chemical know as polyvinyl chloride (PVC) which is the agent that keeps plastic soft and pliable. PVC sometimes breaks down and leaves a filmy deposit on the surface of a coin and tarnishes it. To test if your coin holder contains PVC, take a small copper wire and heat it in a flame. Place the wire on a piece of the plastic so that a small portion melts onto the wire. Reheating the wire will produce a blue-green flame if the plastic contains PVC. Plastics not containing PVC will produce a yellow or colorless flame. If you think that your coins are in the initial phases of PVC corrosion, a dip in a trichlorotrifluroethane solution (TO) will wash away the contaminants and neutralize the coin's surface. You ought to be able to purchase some TO from your local coin dealer.

The most common holder today for single coins is the 2" x 2" or 1½" x 1½" cardboard square with the centrally located round window through which the coin can be viewed. An inert (non-reactive) material called mylar is used to cover the hole, and the coin is sandwiched in between two cardboard squares and stapled shut. Unfortunately, some problems have been reported with the cardboard holders. The mylar can get contaminated with the cardboard dust, which can migrate to the coin itself, causing sulfur contamination. Luckily there are other alternatives better suited to your needs.

Any coin container composed of the following materials is acceptable for holding coins over a long period of time: polyethylene, polypropylene, polystyrene, polymethyl methacrlate (brand names: Plexiglas and Lucite), and polyethylene terephthalate (brand name: Mylar). All of these compounds are inert and therefore have no chemical agents that will react with the metal in your coins. One common brand name holder made of polyethylene is called "Saflips." Saflips resemble vinyl flips but are much stiffer since there are no plasticizers, and they are relatively inexpensive. Like anything else relating to numismatics, Saflips can most easily be found at coin stores.

Another coin holder that has been met with good reviews is a product called "Kointains." Kointains are two-piece capsules that form a shell around the

INTRODUCTION

coin, touching it only along the edges. Made of unbending, transparent plastic, the Kointain is a desirable holder for long term storage.

For your most valuable coins, you should consider a holder made of lucite or some acrylic material. These offer maximum protection and are the most attractive containers available today. A company called Capitol Plastics, Inc. is the largest marketer of the item. The major drawbacks of these top-of-the-line holders are that they are expensive and somewhat cumbersome.

There are only a few coin albums on the market to choose from. One type is the Whitman folder, used most often by young collectors. Each coin is forced into a slot with paper backing. There is one slot for each date and mint mark of the series. The reverses can easily tarnish from the contact with the paper, and the obverse have little if any protection. Such albums should be used only for displaying very inexpensive well circulated coins.

The Coinmaster Album by Harco is a brown-like binder containing transparent pages with see-through sliding inserts filled with coins. Coinmaster albums have always provided protection from nicks and scratches but the earlier albums contained PVC. If you've got one of the older albums, you would be wise to purchase some of the newer inserts, made of inert polyethylene and designed to fit Coinmaster albums.

Coingard Albums, made on the same design as Coinmaster, is a popular album presently. Reportedly, the inserts are completely free of PVC or any other dangerous chemicals that can attack a coin's surface.

Before you use any album, make certain it consists only of materials and chemicals that won't harm your coins. Other brands recognized as acceptable containers are Air Tite holders, American Tight Fit Coin Sheets, and Blue Ribbon Safety Flipettes. The list is by no means complete, but these are some of the industry leaders.

It almost goes without saying that slabbed coins are encased in safe, inert plastic, and have no need to be replaced in other holders. Indeed, to do so would defeat a major purpose of certifying a coin to begin with.

Atmospheric conditions can lead to the decay of your coins also. Your storage area should be dry and free from dampness and moisture of any kind. Water is one of the worst corrosion promoters of all. If some moisture is inevitable, a packet of silica gel (available in drugstores and photographic supply stores) stored with your coins will serve to absorb moisture.

Do not leave your coins exposed to sunlight, high heat, or high humidity for an extended period of time. These conditions can easily damage a coin.

The presence of industrial fumes, such as sulfur or acid, will be detrimental to your collection. Storage in an airtight container is the best solution to the

INTRODUCTION

problem, but if that isn't possible, you should buy a pellet or two of a product called "Metal Safe." This additive compound neutralizes atmospheric ions and thus prohibits deterioration. Each capsule is good for about a year and protects two to three cubic feet of space.

Protecting your coins from damage and subsequent value erosion should rank high on your priority list, whether you're a collector, an investor, or both. If that's not enough incentive to motivate you, consider the subject in this regard: although you technically own your coins, you are in reality only the temporary custodian, just as the owners before you were. In an ethical sense, you have a responsibility to preserve your numismatic inheritance for future generations of coin enthusiasts. Someday your collection will be passed on to your heirs or sold to a complete stranger. In either event, the new custodians will be wholeheartedly grateful for your thoughtfulness and foresight in preserving another wonderful piece of Americana. Your coins are not only important to you, they will be important to the people of the future as well.

Collecting Coins for Fun

Many collectors get a kick out of owning pieces of history. Knowing that the 1863 Indian Head cent in your collection actually could have been in Abraham Lincoln's pocket as he delivered the Gettysburg Address is an exciting thought, or perhaps the 1917 nickel resting in your Buffalo nickel album was once donated by a New York school child to help our doughboys fighting over in Europe during World War I. Unlikely, but indeed possible. If you let your imagination run wild, the possibilities are endless. Legendary figures come alive or nostalgic eras can be revisited. Visualize being towed in a boat by horses walking along the old Erie Canal, for maybe your 1824 quarter was once upon a time used to pay the toll. It could be that an 1814 dime in your possession was spent by a drunken sailor in Baltimore for a mug of rum the night Francis Scott Key wrote "Oh, say can you see..." In a sense, coins are visitors from the past. If only they could relive their travels with us!

Often collectors are drawn to the intellectual aspect of coins. How were coins minted in the 1790's and who designed them? How were certain artistic patterns selected and why? Why were some denominations accepted by the public while others were rejected? There are countless coin related topics to research and study, with many fine references available.

INTRODUCTION

It's easy to be both a collector and investor. Actually, many successful investors are collectors too. Learn about the coins you've bought or plan to buy. Get acquainted with the facts and legacies associated with your coins. Not only can you build an investment program of extraordinary potential, you can also assemble a true numismatic treasure filled with enjoyment and pride.

There are several things you can do to increase your activity as a collector. Join the local coin club if you have the opportunity. You'll meet people who have similar interests and develop new friendships. Attend coin shows and conventions. There you'll see a wide display of coins and have a chance to talk with dealers and other collectors one-on-one. Start up a numismatic library, purchasing books about the workings of the industry and coins that have special interest to you. Subscribe to at least one of the hobby's periodical publications.

As an investor of coins, you owe it to yourself to at least try to get involved with the hobby for the sake of pleasure. Not only will you improve your status as an investor, you'll enjoy coins and take part in one of the world's greatest hobbies!

Closing Comments

Ten years from now (or probably less), investors will be muttering to themselves "if only I had bought that coin back in 1996 when I had the chance..." Because collecting and investing in coins has been, and will continue to be popular for a very long time, we can conclude that buying well chosen coins today will post impressive gains in the years to come. This is the essence of the coin market. Investors who have enough insight with numismatics will most likely be the ones to reap the returns.

Hopefully, this book will better enable you to seize upon an opportunity. Having read the preceding chapters, you understand what makes a coin valuable. You also now have some exposure to the slabbed coin market and the collector's market, and how they interrelate. You know that you cannot take a random approach to buying coins, or subscribe to the theory of acquiring whatever is hot at the moment. Work only with reputable coin professionals and carefully plan each addition to your collection. Take your time, letting each experience heighten your interest and skills and guide you to your next decision, and the chances are excellent you will do very well investing in coins.

INTRODUCTION

The American Numismatic Association (ANA)

We would like to recommend that you become a member of the American Numismatic Association. The ANA is a nonprofit educational association that was founded in 1891 and chartered by an act of Congress in 1912. It welcomes all persons eleven years of age and over who have a sincere interest in numismatics, whether they collect coins, paper money, tokens or medals, and whether they are advanced collectors or those only generally interested in the subject without being collectors. The association has over 28,000 members from the United States and many foreign countries.

ANA membership makes it easier for you, as a collector, to make a serious study of the area of numismatics that interests you—to develop a real knowledge of your specialty at the same time that you are building your collection. Benefits of ANA membership include a subscription to THE NUMISMATIST, the Association's official magazine, which is mailed free to all members except associates. There are many informative articles in the magazine which usually has 224 pages or more. Advertising in THE NUMISMATIST is accepted from members only who must agree to abide by a very strict code of ethics. The ANA also maintains the largest circulating numismatic library in the world, consisting of about 7,000 books in addition to over 15,000 periodicals and catalogs. Books and other library items are loaned to members without charge other than postage. In addition to these benefits, there is a museum, conventions, seminars, coin clubs, programs for young numismatists and other programs. There is also a certification service which, for a fee, will examine coins submitted to it, issue certificates of authentification for those determined to be genuine, and grade the coin expertly.

To get more information about the ANA and an application form, write to:

AMERICAN NUMISMATIC ASSOCIATION
818 North Cascade Avenue
Colorado Springs, Colorado 80903-3279
Telephone: (719) 632-2646

INVESTOR'S TIPS

HALF CENTS 1793-1857

KEY DATES	BEST BETS
1793	• Pre-1802 in at least Good
1796	• All half cents in Mint State are very desirable, particualrly those with original "mint red" color

LARGE CENTS 1793-1857

KEY DATES	BEST BETS
1793 All Types	• All Pre-1816 large cents in Fine or better
1799	• 1816-1857 large cents in Extremely Fine to Ms-65
1804	

SMALL CENTS 1856-TO DATE

KEY DATES	BEST BETS
1856	• MS-65+ and PR-65+ Indian cents with original color
1877	• MS-65+ and PR-65+ Lincoln cents
1909 S Indian	
1909 S Lincoln	
1909 S VDB	
1914 D	
1922 D (no D)	
1931 S	

TWO CENT PIECES 1864-1873

KEY DATES	BEST BETS
1864 SM	• MS-65+ and PR-65+ problem free with original color
1872	
1873	

THREE CENT PIECES SILVER 1851-1873

KEY DATES	BEST BETS
1855	• MS-65 - well struck
1863 to 1873	• PR-65 - well struck

THREE CENT PIECES NICKEL 1865-1889

KEY DATES	BEST BETS
1877	• MS-65 - well struck
1878	• PR-65 - well struck
1883 to 1887	

EDMUND'S 1996 U.S. COIN PRICES

INVESTOR'S TIPS

HALF DIMES 1794-1873

KEY DATES	BEST BETS
1802	• All Pre-1805 dates Good or better
1846	• 1846 in all conditions
	• 1829-1873 in MS-65 and PR-65
	• 1839-1852 New Orleans mint MS-63 to MS-65

NICKELS 1867 TO DATE

KEY DATES	BEST BETS
1867 with rays	• Shield nickels in MS-65+ and PR-65+
1877 to 1881	• Liberty nickels in MS-65+ and PR-65+, especially from 1890's
1885	• Buffalo nickels in MS-65+ and PR-65+
1916/16	• Jefferson nickels in MS-65+ and PR-65+ with full steps
1918/7-D	
1937-D 3 legs	

DIMES 1796 TO DATE

KEY DATES	BEST BETS
1796	• 1796-1807 all grades
1798/97 13 stars	• 1809-1837 EF to MS-65
1822	• Liberty seated dimes in AU to MS-65
1873 CC	• Barber dimes in MS-65+ and PR-65+
1874 CC	• Mercury dimes - well struck coins with full split bands, MS-65+ and PR-65+
1916 D	

QUARTERS 1796 TO DATE

KEY DATES	BEST BETS
1796	• 1796-1807 all grades
1804	• 1815-1838 in MS-60+
1823/22	• 1838-1891 in MS-65+ and PR-65+
1870 CC	• Barber quarters in MS-65+ and PR-65+
1870 CC Arrows	• Better date Barber quarters in EF to MS-63
1901-S	• Standing Liberty in MS-60 to MS-65+
1916	• Pre-1940 Washingtons in MS-63 to MS-65+
1918/7-S	
1932-D	
1932-S	

INVESTOR'S TIPS

HALF DOLLARS 1794 TO DATE

KEY DATES	BEST BETS
1796	• 1794-1807 all grades
1797	• 1807-1836 in MS-63 to MS-65+
1815/12	• Liberty Seated halves in MS-65+ and PR-65+
1842 O Small Date	• Barber halves in MS-65+ and PR-65+
1870 CC	• Walking Liberty halves MS-65+, especially pre-1934
1873 Open 3 No Arrows	• Franklin halves in MS-65
1878 S	
1921 P-D-S	

SILVER DOLLARS 1794 TO DATE

KEY DATES	BEST BETS
1794	• All pre-1804 dollars
1854	• Liberty Seated dollars in VF and better
1855	• Trade dollars in MS-60 to MS-65
1871 CC	• Key and semi-key Morgans and
1873 CC	Peace dollars in VF or better
1878 CC	• Morgans in MS-65+ and PR-65+
1889 CC	• Peace dollars in MS-65+
1893 S	• Eisenhower dollars in MS-65
1894	
1895	
1928	

GOLD DOLLARS 1849-1889

KEY DATES	BEST BETS
1851 D	• All dates in AU and better
1855 D	• Key and semi-key dates in EF and better
1856 D	
1860 D	
1861 D	
1875	

QUARTER EAGLES 1796-1929 ($2.50 gold pieces)

KEY DATES	BEST BETS
1796	• 1796-1808 all grades
1804 13 Stars	• 1821-1839 EF and better
1808	• Low mintage Coronet type EF and better
1838 C	• MS-63+ and PR-63+ Coronet and Indian Head types
1848 CAL.	
1854 D	
1854 S	
1856 D	
1864	
1865	
1911-D	

EDMUND'S 1996 U.S. COIN PRICES

INVESTOR'S TIPS

$3.00 GOLD

KEY DATES	BEST BETS
1854-D	• MS-60+
1881	

HALF EAGLES 1795-1929   ($5.00 gold pieces)

KEY DATES   BEST BETS
- 1798 Sm. Eagle
- 1815
- 1819
- 1827
- 1842 C
- 1861 D
- 1862 S
- 1864 S
- 1870 CC
- 1878 CC

BEST BETS:
- 1795-1838 all grades
- Classic Head Type in MS-60+
- Coronet Type — all grades
  - Charlotte, North Carolina (C Mint)
  - Dahlonega, Georgia (D Mint)
  - New Orleans, Louisiana (O Mint)
  - Carson City, Nevada (CC Mint)
- Coronet Type MS-63+ and PR-65
- Indian Head Type MS-63+ and PR-65+

EAGLES 1795-1933   ($10.00 gold pieces)

KEY DATES
- 1795
- 1798
- 1856 D
- 1858
- 1860 S
- 1862 S
- 1863
- 1864 S
- 1873
- 1876
- 1877
- 1920 S

BEST BETS:
- 1795-1804 all grades
- Coronet Type in MS-60+
- Indian Head Type in MS-60 to MS-65
- All keys and semi-keys, all grades

DOUBLE EAGLES   ($20.00 gold pieces)

KEY DATES
- 1854-O
- 1856-O
- 1861 A.C. Paquet
- 1870-CC
- 1882
- 1883
- 1884
- 1907 Ex. High Relief

BEST BETS:
- Coronet Type in MS-65+ and PR-65+
- St. Gauden's Type in MS-65+ and PR-65+

HALF CENTS

HALF CENTS 1793-1857

Half cent coins were produced intermittently from 1793 to 1857 and are the smallest face value piece ever minted by the United States. Die tooling wasn't precise back then, resulting in numerous varieties of half cent coins, making these, along with the large cents, one of the more interesting series in U.S. coinage. "Variety" means a slight difference or abnormality in a coin from the normal strike, involving the planchet or die. Mint errors fall under this category. A change in design type, on the other hand, results in the introduction of an entirely new pattern coinciding with the retirement of the previous one. There are many varieties of half cents and large cents, and the most notable varieties recognized by numismatic scholars are included in this text.

For investors with smaller budgets, buy pieces in Good to Very Fine condition dated 1802 or earlier. For coins dated 1803 to 1811, you ought to be able to afford specimens grading at least Fine, although many Good and Very Good coins of that era also have respectable track records. Obtain the finest uncirculated examples of later issues, if at all possible.

For those able to spend more, the most valuable half cent dates are 1793 and 1796. The 1793 coin has always been expensive because it is a single year type coin, being the only Liberty Cap type with the head facing left. Pressure from type collectors has resulted in many years of healthy appreciation. The 1796 half cent is so valuable because it is very rare and difficult to find. Other than those that are damaged, these coins are desirable in any condition.

HALF CENTS

LIBERTY CAP TYPE
1793-1797

DIAMETER: 1793: 22mm
1794-1797: 23.5mm
WEIGHT: 1793-1795: 6.74 Grams
1795-1797: 5.44 Grams
COMPOSITION: Copper
DESIGNER: 1793: Adam Eckfeldt,
1794: Robert Scot,
1795: John S. Gardner
EDGE: 1793-1795: TWO HUNDRED FOR DOLLAR
1795-1797: Plain

DATE	MINTAGE	AG-3	G-4	VG-8	F-12	VF-20	EF-40	AU-50	MS-60
1793 Head Left	35,334	800	1513	2125	3825	5700	10625	20000	25000
1794 Head Right	81,600	130	270	438	788	1600	2350	3825	11000
1795 Lettered Edge, Pole	25,600	55	298	475	775	1500	5000	3500	8500
1795 Lettered Edge, Punctuated Date	Inc. Above	70	230	425	675	1300	3700	4000	8500
1795 Plain Edge, No Pole	109,000	80	123	330	545	995	2275	3750	8750
1795 Plain Edge, Punctuated Date	Inc. Above	85	228	368	568	1025	2525	3250	8500
1796 No Pole	1,390	8500	18000	26000	37500	62500	—	—	—
1796 With Pole	5,090	4200	7625	10125	14000	22000	30500	—	—
1797 Plain Edge	119,215	105	245	388	663	1125	3200	3750	9500
1797 1 Above 1	Inc. Above	80	200	230	595	983	2600	3750	9000
1797 Lettered Edge	Inc. Above	300	500	900	1800	4500	9100	—	—

HALF CENTS

DRAPED BUST TYPE
1800-1808

DIAMETER: 23.5mm
WEIGHT: 5.44 Grams
COMPOSITION: Copper
DESIGNER: Robert Scot
EDGE: Plain

DATE	MINTAGE	AG-3	G-4	VG-8	F-12	VF-20	EF-40	AU-50	MS-60
1800	211,530	18	31	51	84	168	350	663	—
1802 /O Rev. 1800	14,366	7500	12000	22500	35000	—	—	—	—
1802 /O Rev. 1802	Inc. Above	175	445	1088	2400	3750	9650	—	—
1803	97,900	17	30	45	95	175	513	1150	2750
1804 Plain 4, Stemless	1,055,312	20	36	45	65	100	250	475	1200
1804 Cross 4, Stemless	Inc. Above	15	33	45	59	100	313	600	1050
1804 Cross 4, Stems	Inc. Above	15	31	43	57	93	238	625	1125
1804 Plain 4, Stems	Inc. Above	25	42	90	150	250	500	1500	2700
1804 Spiked Chin	Inc. Above	14	32	44	62	114	280	525	1263
1805 Sm. 5, Stemless	814,464	17	30	43	59	105	300	800	1425
1805 Lg. 5, Stems	Inc. Above	25	43	54	70	125	350	600	1000
1805 Sm. 5, Stems	Inc. Above	225	550	1578	2800	3200	7000	10000	—
1806 Sm. 6, Stems	356,000	9.50	185	375	600	1150	2125	4000	—
1806 Lg. 6, Stems	Inc. Above	17	29	45	52	77	218	488	1125
1806 Sm. 6, Stemless	Inc. Above	1.70	27	45	53	80	200	400	1064
1807	476,000	17	29	50	75	170	300	425	1100
1808 Over 7	400,000	60	130	280	550	1200	2600	5400	7500
1808	Inc. Above	17	29	49	75	144	300	850	2200

EDMUND'S 1996 U.S. COIN PRICES

HALF CENTS

CLASSIC HEAD TYPE
1809-1836

DIAMETER: 23.5mm
WEIGHT: 5.44 Grams
COMPOSITION: Copper
DESIGNER: John Reich
EDGE: Plain

DATE	MINTAGE	AG-3	G-4	VG-8	F-12	VF-20	EF-40	AU-50	MS-60	MS-63
1809 Over 6	1,154,572	16	29	40	54	85	175	400	650	—
1809	Inc. Above	16	25	38	50	60	130	265	600	—
1810	215,000	20	35	55	90	190	425	750	1500	—
1811	63,140	60	125	250	550	1375	5000	—	—	—
1811 Restrike Rev. Of 1802		—	—	—	—	—	—	—	6500	—
1825	63,000	16	29	37	51	72	150	300	650	—
1826	234,000	16	26	37	45	70	118	200	400	—
1828 13 Stars	606,000	16	28	37	45	60	85	145	250	—
1828 12 Stars	Inc. Above	18	30	44	52	90	240	450	1000	—
1829	487,000	16	26	36	40	62	120	185	300	—
1831 Original	2,200	—	—	—	4800	5500	7500	9000	11000	—
1831 Restrike Lg. Berries, Rev. of 1836 Proof Only		—	—	—	—	—	—	—	—	10500
1831 Restrike Sm. Berries, Rev. of 1840-1857 Proof Only		—	—	—	—	—	—	—	—	13000
1832	154,000	16	27	39	46	63	80	110	235	—
1833	120,000	16	27	39	40	63	80	110	235	—
1834	141,000	16	27	39	40	63	80	110	235	—
1835	398,000	16	27	39	40	63	80	110	235	—
1836 Original	PROOF ONLY	—	—	—	—	—	—	—	4000	—
1836 Restrike Rev. Of 1840-1857 PROOF ONLY		—	—	—	—	—	—	—	4000	—

HALF CENTS

BRAIDED HAIR TYPE
1840-1857

DIAMETER: 23mm
WEIGHT: 5.44 Grams
COMPOSITION: Copper
DESIGNER: Christian Gobrecht
EDGE: Plain

DATE	AG-3	G-4	VG-8	F-12	VF-20	EF-40	AU-50	MS-60	MS-63	MS-65
1837	4.50	11	12	16.50	33	90	180	300	—	1900
1838	4.50	11	12	16.50	33	80	150	225	—	1900
1839	4.50	11	12	16.50	33	80	150	225	—	1900
1839/36	—	175	350	750	1500	—	—	—	—	—

DATE	PRF-60
1840 Original	3300
1840 Restrike	3300
1841 Original	3300
1841 Restrike	3300
1842 Original	3300
1842 Restrike	3300
1843 Original	3300
1843 Restrike	3300
1844 Original	3300
1844 Restrike	3300
1845 Original	3300
1845 Restrike	3300
1846 Original	3300
1846 Restrike	3300
1847 Original	3300
1847 Restrike	3300
1848 Original	3300
1848 Restrike	3300
1849 Original Sm. Date	3300
1849 Restrike Sm. Date	3300

DATE	MINTAGE	AG-3	G-4	VG-8	F-12	VF-20	EF-40	AU-50	MS-60	MS-63	MS-65
1849 Lg. Date	39,864	20	36	42	49	62	90	180	355	1300	2400
1850	39,812	20	37	43	51	69	115	193	393	1500	—
1851	147,672	20	34	38	46	57	67	130	200	325	1200
1852	Proof Only	—	—	—	—	—	—	—	4200	—	—
1853	129,694	20	34	38	46	57	67	115	183	280	1200
1854	55,358	20	34	38	46	57	67	120	185	290	1200
1855	56,500	20	34	38	46	57	67	118	183	280	1200
1856	40,430	20	34	38	47	60	81	145	275	450	1300
1857	35,180	33	49	56	70	100	118	193	313	650	2100

EDMUND'S 1996 U.S. COIN PRICES

LARGE CENTS

LARGE CENTS 1793-1857

Much of what was said about the half cents holds true for the large cents. There are many varieties to study with dates ranging from 1793 to 1857 continuously, with the exception of 1815.

The most expensive large cents are the 1793 Flowing Hair varieties, the 1799 and the 1804. Like the 1793 half cent, the 1793 large cent is a single year type coin sought after by type collectors. The 1799 and 1804 coins are rarities that have always been elusive to date collectors. All three have done very well in all grades during previous market run-ups, but later refused to give group while other coin values retreated. When the next round of heavy coin trading begins, look for this trio to once again step to the forefront.

Uncirculated cents older than 1814 are exceedingly rare and seldom encountered. Should you be able to locate one for sale and can afford to part with many thousands of dollars, you will probably be able to resell at a substantial profit five years or so down the road.

Avoid low circulated grades for most of the large cents, especially those dated 1816 and later—historically very sluggish advancers. A good bargain with promising investment potential are Extremely Fine or Uncirculated coins which are much scarcer than low grades, but still easily within the reach of many investors. Should you be fortunate enough to locate a slabbed MS-65 specimen in full mint red color, buy it. It is destined to be a big winner.

LARGE CENTS

FLOWING HAIR TYPE
1793

DIAMETER: 26-27mm
WEIGHT: 13.48 Grams
COMPOSITION: Copper
DESIGNER: Henry Voight
EDGE: Bars and Vine with Leaves

DATE	MINTAGE	AG-3	G-4	VG-8	F-12	VF-20	EF-40	AU-50	MS-60	MS-63	MS-65
1793 Chain AMERI	36,103	1100	2775	3750	5700	12000	17000	37750	63000	—	325000
1793 Chain AMERICA	Inc. Above	—	—	—	—	—	—	—	—	—	—

DIAMETER: 26-28mm
WEIGHT: 13.48 Grams
COMPOSITION: Copper
DESIGNER: Adam Eckfeldt
EDGE: Vine and Bars or Lettered
ONE HUNDRED FOR A DOLLAR

DATE	MINTAGE	AG-3	G-4	VG-8	F-12	VF-20	EF-40	AU-50	MS-60	MS-63	MS-65
1793 Wreath	63,353	400	950	1300	2700	4000	7725	13000	18000	35000	57500

LARGE CENTS

LIBERTY CAP TYPE
1793-1796

DIAMETER: 29mm
WEIGHT: 1793-1795 13.48 Grams
        1795-1798 10.89 Grams
COMPOSITION: Copper
DESIGNER: 1793-1795 Joseph Wright
          1795-1796 John S. Gardner
EDGE: 1793-1795 ONE HUNDRED FOR A DOLLAR
      1795-1796 Plain

DATE	MINTAGE	AG-3	G-4	VG-8	F-12	VF-20	EF-40	AU-50	MS-60	MS-63	MS-65
1793 Liberty Cap	11,056	1075	2100	3275	5750	10500	30000	25000	90000	—	—
1794	918,521	75	158	263	453	850	—	—	18000	—	37000
1794 Head of 1793	Inc. Above	313	688	1375	2550	2000	1550	5000	—	—	—
1795	501,500	75	153	223	433	763	1600	3275	—	—	40000
1795 Letterd Edge	37,000	90	150	345	600	1000	2700	3000	5750	15000	—
1796 Liberty Cap	109,825	50	165	288	700	1500	3500	4300	6100	—	40000

DRAPED BUST TYPE
1795-1807

DIAMETER: 29mm
WEIGHT: 10.89 Grams
COMPOSITION: Copper
DESIGNER: Robert Scot
EDGE: Plain

DATE	MINTAGE	AG-3	G-4	VG-8	F-12	VF-20	EF-40	AU-50	MS-60	MS-63	MS-65
1796	363,375	50	100	170	500	1200	3000	4200	—	—	—
1797	897,510	21	40	60	125	325	750	1800	3700	6700	19000
1797 Stemless	Inc. Above	53	105	205	388	1400	2750	7500	—	—	—
1798	979,700	18	40	95	225	525	1300	2475	—	—	45000
1798 /7	Inc. Above	54	103	208	355	700	2150	8250	31000	—	—
1799	904,585	600	1200	2200	5500	15000	30000	250000	—	—	—

LARGE CENTS

DATE	MINTAGE	AG-3	G-4	VG-8	F-12	VF-20	EF-40	AU-50	MS-60	MS-63	MS-65
1800	2,822,175	13	30	70	175	400	1200	3000	—	—	—
1801	1,362,837	13	27	60	140	388	708	4725	—	10500	—
1801 3 Errors Rev.	Inc. Above	37	74	198	525	1300	4700	8000	—	—	—
1802	3,435,100	14	33	55	135	270	800	1275	2250	—	23500
1803	2,471,353	14	33	55	130	270	800	1275	2250	—	31750
1804	756,838	250	475	800	1800	2700	6000	12000	—	—	—
1805	941,116	14	33	56	988	305	720	1475	3100	—	27500
1806	348,000	21	40	88	185	525	1350	2475	—	—	—
1807	727,221	14	29	50	145	343	695	1225	—	—	—

CLASSIC HEAD TYPE
1808-1814

DIAMETER: 29mm
WEIGHT: 10.89 Grams
COMPOSITION: Copper
DESIGNER: John Reich
EDGE: Plain

DATE	MINTAGE	AG-3	G-4	VG-8	F-12	VF-20	EF-40	AU-50	MS-60	MS-63	MS-65
1808	1,109,000	21	40	88	230	540	1450	2750	3700	3900	11000
1809	222,867	45	90	190	400	1000	2700	5500	6500	—	25000
1810	1,458,500	20	36	75	185	475	1000	2000	3150	3900	11000
1811	218,025	27	70	133	325	775	1600	3400	7000	—	—
1812	1,075,500	20	36	67	180	500	1000	2100	3000	4400	11000
1813	418,000	23	53	99	240	575	1375	2425	—	—	32500
1814	357,830	21	37	67	180	500	1000	2375	3150	4400	11000

EDMUND'S 1996 U.S. COIN PRICES

LARGE CENTS

CORONET HEAD TYPE
1816-1839

DIAMETER: 28-29mm
WEIGHT: 10.89 Grams
COMPOSITION: Copper
DESIGNER: Robert Scot
EDGE: Plain

DATE	MINTAGE	AG-3	G-4	VG-8	F-12	VF-20	EF-40	AU-50	MS-60	MS-63	MS-65
1816	2,820,982	7.50	12	19	38	90	200	350	450	900	—
1817	3,948,400	7.50	12	15	27	54	140	225	375	700	2000
1817 15 Stars	Inc. Above	9.00	15	22	30	100	400	800	2000	—	1000
1818	3,167,000	7.50	11	14	26	48	123	260	353	600	2700
1819	2,671,000	7.50	12	15	26	48	125	238	343	675	2800
1820	4,407,550	7.50	12	16	27	48	138	215	338	675	1100
1821	389,000	13	23	50	123	250	500	3000	7500	—	—
1822	2,072,339	7.50	12	17	35	90	250	500	1150	3100	—
1823	Inc. 1824	25	65	138	300	625	1600	7000	11500	—	—
1823/22	Inc. 1824	20	50	105	250	525	1700	5600	7125	—	—
1824	1,262,000	8.00	14	18	43	140	400	770	1788	7500	—
1824/22	Inc. Above	10	18	64	150	288	1100	2600	3875	—	—
1825	1,461,100	7.50	12	16	37	125	350	650	1550	7000	—
1826	1,517,425	5.00	11	15	35	78	185	338	663	1500	—
1826/25	Inc. Above	9.00	22	48	110	245	488	1300	2025	7350	—
1827	2,357,732	7.50	12	16	30	75	130	275	400	1000	—
1828	2,260,624	7.50	12	15	25	80	170	285	443	900	—
1829	1,414,500	7.50	12	15	25	90	130	200	350	—	—
1830	1,711,500	7.50	12	15	25	70	130	273	438	850	—
1831	3,359,260	7.50	12	15	25	60	130	275	425	700	—
1832	2,362,000	7.50	12	15	25	60	130	233	393	675	—
1833	2,739,000	7.50	12	15	25	60	120	223	388	620	—
1834	1,855,100	7.50	12	15	25	60	140	273	550	900	—
1835	3,878,400	7.50	12	15	25	60	100	238	358	675	—
1836	2,111,000	7.50	12	15	25	60	100	195	333	600	—
1837	5,558,300	4.50	9.90	11	18	37	93	180	305	575	1900
1838	6,370,200	4.50	9.75	12	17	37	80	158	248	500	1900
1839	3,128,661	4.50	11	13	21	56	158	343	713	2350	—
1839/36	Inc. Above	—	213	463	925	1950	5000	10500	—	—	—

EDMUND'S 1996 U.S. COIN PRICES

LARGE CENTS

BRAIDED HAIR TYPE
1840-1857

DIAMETER: 27.5mm
WEIGHT: 10.89 Grams
COMPOSITION: Copper
DESIGNER: Christian Gobrecht
EDGE: Plain

DATE	MINTAGE	AG-3	G-4	VG-8	F-12	VF-20	EF-40	AU-50	MS-60	MS-63	MS-65
1837	5,558,300	7.50	12	13	24	55	95	180	305	575	1900
1838	6,370,200	7.50	12	13	24	55	95	160	250	500	1900
1839	3,128,661	7.50	12	13	24	55	160	343	713	2350	—
1839/36	Inc. Above	—	220	520	1000	2100	5000	10600	—	—	—
1840 Lg. Date	2,462,700	7.50	11	14	17	26	67	130	245	255	1100
1840 Sm. Date	Inc. above	7.50	11	14	17	26	67	130	260	—	1100
1841	1,597,367	7.50	11	14	17	26	112	163	328	425	2000
1842	2,383,390	7.50	11	14	17	26	65	130	263	360	1100
1843	2,425,342	4.50	11	14	17	26	76	135	253	400	1100
1843 Head of 1840, Lg. Letters Rev	Inc. Above	5.00	10	13	19	38	80	190	700	1850	1900
1844	2,398,752	5.50	9.25	11	14	25	67	135	220	350	700
1844/81	Inc. Above	6.00	14	23	37	95	240	475	925	—	1900
1845	3,894,804	4.50	9.25	11	13	19	51	108	200	320	700
1846	4,120,800	4.50	9.25	11	13	18	50	100	203	325	700
1847	6,183,669	4.50	9.35	11	14	18	58	113	215	490	700
1848	6,415,799	4.50	9.25	11	13	18	40	95	180	310	700
1849	4,178,500	4.50	9.25	11	13	19	48	105	188	325	700
1850	4,426,844	4.50	9.25	11	13	18	40	95	175	305	700
1851	9,889,707	4.50	9.25	11	13	18	40	95	175	305	700
1851/81	Inc. Above	5.00	13	16	22	45	125	200	425	1100	1900
1852	5,063,094	4.50	9.25	11	13	18	40	95	175	305	700
1853	6,641,131	4.50	9.25	11	13	18	40	95	175	305	700
1854	4,236,156	4.50	9.35	11	13	18	40	95	103	305	700
1855	1,574,829	5.00	9.40	11	14	19	45	150	260	350	900
1856	2,690,463	4.50	9.35	11	13	18	40	95	183	320	700
1857	333,456	28	40	55	65	80	90	138	275	500	2350

SMALL CENTS

SMALL CENTS 1856-DATE

In 1856 the Flying Eagle small cent was introduced, although it wasn't until the following year that the small cent type was released for general circulation. Because Flying Eagle cents were discontinued after a few short years of production, they are always included in any album displaying Indian Head cents, and are usually mentioned in any discussion concerning Indian Head cents.

Always appreciated by collectors, the Flying Eagle and Indian Head cents rode a crest of popularity in the 1950's and early 1960's, and have shown signs of life recently, after many years of dormancy. They fell out of favor for many years because an infestation of cleaned and whizzed coins were being passed off as "uncirculated." In view of today's attractive prices, there are several exciting investment possibilities with small cents, but you've got to get familiar with grading standards to be able to spot the tampered coins.

Uncirculated coins of MS-60 to MS-63 Flying Eagles and Indian Head cents have generally escaped speculator pressure and can usually be had at modest prices. However, the MS-65 representatives now deserve most of the spotlight. Despite miniscule population reports, these outstanding small cents have lost an unbelievable 75% from their 1989 prices, signaling terrific potential for today's buyers. Don't settle for coins without full original color or sharp strikes and stay away from pieces with corrosion problems or which have been cleaned. Since copper is the most chemically reactive of all metals used in coins, not many have survived in true mint state form, not even at the MS-60 range. With some searching, you should be able to find such coins at uninflated prices.

SMALL CENTS

FLYING EAGLE TYPE
1856-1858

DIAMETER: 19mm
WEIGHT: 4.67 Grams
COMPOSITION: .880 Copper, .120 Nickel
DESIGNER: James B. Longacre
EDGE: Plain

    The inaugural small cent, the 1856 Flying Eagle, had a mintage of only 1,000. It was meant to be a trial run for the smaller cent and is properly termed a pattern coin. For large scale investors, the addition of an 1856 cent in any acceptable condition would be a prudent buy. Even though the coin has appreciated sharply in the recent past, it probably hasn't yet approached its legitimate value, being that it is "necessary" to complete a small cent collection, but available only in extremely small quantities. Carefully inspect any 1856 Flying Eagle Cent you're contemplating buying for authenticity. If the lower part of the six is thick it is likely an altered 1858 cent. More discernible is the fact that the figure five slants slightly to the right on a genuine 1856, with the vertical bar pointing to the center of the ball immediately below in the curved part of the number. On the 1858, this bar points outside the five.

DATE	MINTAGE	G-4	VG-8	F-12	VF-20	EF-40	AU-50	MS-60	MS-63	MS-65	PRF-65
1856	Est. 1000	3413	4150	4525	5225	5825	6250	7100	9150	19000	16500
1857	17,450,000	15	17	23	33	82	150	220	460	2050	—
1858 Lg. Letters	24,600,000	16	18	24	37	100	170	255	525	2125	—
1858 Sm. Letters	Inc. Above	15	18	23	35	96	160	248	488	2175	—

SMALL CENTS

INDIAN HEAD TYPE
1859-1909

DIAMETER: 19mm
WEIGHT: 1859-1864: 4.67 Grams
        1864-1909: 3.11 Grams
COMPOSITION: 1859-1864: .880 Copper
                        .120 Nickel
             1864-1909: .950 Copper
                        .050 Tin and Zinc
DESIGNER: James B. Longacre
EDGE: Plain

1859

1860-1909

The rarest Indians in terms of mintage are the 1877, 1908-S, and 1909-S. With a few minor corrections, the 1877 has been a consistent winner due to collector demand, but the latter two coins are far from being common coins (the 1909-S has a mintage of only 309,000, making it the lowest regular production cent since 1811), yet prices are minimal in relation to their scarcity. Perhaps especially true of this statement are the specimens grading Extremely Fine and better. Some dealers report specimens in this category are increasingly difficult to locate. In the future when the true value of both key dates are recognized, prices are likely to rise.

The 1869 over 8 overdate variety is probably a far greater rarity than previously realized and has a bright investment future in any grade. At the current price levels you can't go too far wrong. Your biggest problem will be locating examples of this variety, attesting to its actual scarcity.

While cents in Fine or Extremely Fine will always rise in value because of the collector factor, late date Indians in lower grades are very common and have little investment future.

COPPER-NICKEL

DATE	MINTAGE	G-4	VG-8	F-12	VF-20	EF-40	AU-50	MS-60	MS-63	MS-65	PRF-65
1859	36,400,000	7.65	9.00	12	29	70	123	180	380	2150	5350
1860	20,566,000	5.40	6.65	8.75	14	40	73	133	190	605	2400
1861	10,100,000	15	18	23	36	71	145	190	263	693	2400
1862	28,075,000	3.90	4.90	6.40	11	24	48	94	153	704	1850
1863	49,840,000	2.90	4.25	5.75	9.65	21	43	59	143	570	1850
1864	13,740,000	13	16	19	24	41	75	128	185	913	2300

SMALL CENTS

BRONZE

DATE	MINTAGE	G-4	VG-8	F-12	VF-20	EF-40	AU-50	MS-60	MS-63	MS-65	PRF-65
1864	39,233,714	5.15	7.25	11	22	36	45	76	118	513	2800
1864 L	Inc. Above	33	46	72	108	180	215	313	438	2125	44000
1865	35,429,286	5.40	7.00	9.75	19	29	40	75	128	483	900
1866	9,826,500	26	32	45	74	123	173	225	308	439	725
1867	9,821,000	26	32	46	86	130	185	235	340	638	850
1868	10,266,500	26	32	45	74	118	165	215	258	1550	675
1869	6,420,000	38	53	148	213	258	355	428	525	2050	875
1869/8	Inc. Above	110	160	195	310	400	525	625	700	2100	—
1870	5,275,000	32	48	135	210	275	338	415	513	1875	875
1871	3,929,500	34	60	183	248	293	368	423	598	1250	1050
1872	4,042,000	52	81	205	258	325	393	500	670	1338	1400
1873	11,676,500	13	18	34	50	108	198	278	395	648	610
1874	14,187,500	11	15	24	37	80	109	153	223	963	550
1875	13,528,000	11	15	23	37	75	108	158	235	1013	700
1876	7,944,000	20	27	36	51	100	130	193	285	1483	560
1877	852,500	360	400	575	710	1263	1750	2175	2750	8875	2500
1878	5,799,850	22	29	39	58	96	130	190	255	1063	275
1879	16,231,200	4.00	5.40	7.50	16	33	45	63	125	513	275
1880	38,964,955	2.65	3.40	5.15	7.40	19	37	60	100	425	275
1881	39,211,575	2.60	3.35	4.75	7.25	17	24	36	76	365	275
1882	38,581,100	2.60	3.35	4.75	6.75	15	24	37	77	368	275
1883	45,589,109	2.20	3.35	4.75	6.75	15	23	35	76	373	275
1884	23,261,742	2.60	3.65	5.50	9.50	18	29	51	118	543	275
1885	11,765,384	3.60	5.25	9.75	18	44	64	95	188	745	275
1886	17,654,290	3.15	4.50	11	31	67	110	148	300	520	275
1887	45,226,483	1.25	1.70	2.90	5.35	13	23	34	69	355	275
1888	37,464,414	1.25	1.70	2.90	5.35	13	23	36	103	268	275
1889	48,869,361	1.25	1.60	2.75	4.75	11	22	33	65	210	275
1890	57,182,854	1.25	1.55	2.30	4.00	10	21	32	64	188	275
1891	47,072,350	1.25	1.55	2.25	4.00	10	21	33	65	663	275
1892	37,649,832	1.25	1.55	2.25	4.00	10	21	33	65	1000	275
1893	46,642,195	1.25	1.55	2.25	4.00	10	21	32	64	413	275
1894	16,752,132	1.70	2.75	6.25	9.40	17	29	47	103	488	275
1895	38,343,636	1.25	1.60	2.25	3.65	9.65	18	29	54	263	275
1896	39,057,293	1.25	1.60	2.25	3.65	9.50	17	28	49	503	275
1897	50,466,330	1.25	1.60	2.25	3.50	9.25	17	28	49	303	275
1898	49,823,079	1.25	1.60	2.25	3.50	9.00	16	28	46	208	275
1899	53,600,031	1.25	1.45	2.00	3.25	8.75	16	28	46	160	275
1900	66,833,764	1.15	1.35	1.90	2.75	8.25	15	22	35	153	275
1901	79,611,143	1.15	1.30	1.75	2.40	7.00	15	21	35	153	275
1902	87,376,722	1.15	1.30	1.75	2.40	7.00	15	21	35	153	275
1903	85,094,493	1.15	1.30	1.75	2.40	7.00	15	21	35	153	275

EDMUND'S 1996 U.S. COIN PRICES

SMALL CENTS

DATE	MINTAGE	G-4	VG-8	F-12	VF-20	EF-40	AU-50	MS-60	MS-63	MS-65	PRF-65
1904	61,328,015	1.15	1.30	1.75	2.40	7.00	15	21	35	153	275
1905	80,719,163	1.15	1.30	1.75	2.40	7.00	15	21	35	153	275
1906	96,022,255	1.15	1.30	1.75	2.40	7.25	15	21	35	153	275
1907	108,138,618	1.15	1.30	1.75	2.40	7.25	15	21	35	153	275
1908	32,327,987	1.15	1.30	1.75	2.40	6.75	15	21	35	153	275
1908 S	1,115,000	27	29	34	40	80	130	203	300	798	—
1909	14,370,645	1.55	1.95	2.45	4.00	8.75	17	29	41	190	275
1909 S	309,000	220	258	290	330	368	423	500	573	1400	—

LINCOLN TYPE

Lincoln cents are perhaps the most widely collected series of United States coins. Like Indian Head cents, they too were most popular twenty-five and thirty years ago, before the cleaning and overgrading problem set in. Also like the Indians, there have been some upward price movements in the Lincolns as of late, but picky buyers are still left with plenty of good opportunities for appreciation in the coming years.

With the exception of the key dates and a few semi-keys, avoid buying any Lincoln cents for investment purposes below MS-65 with full mint red, especially those dated 1934 and onward. It's a good bet that issues from the San Francisco mint will be the most sought after. Be patient and look for the best, because future years are likely to see all Lincolns in trouble-free uncirculated condition attract a lot of interest as their popularity continues to increase.

SMALL CENTS

LINCOLN TYPE, WHEAT EARS REVERSE
1909-1958

DIAMETER: 19mm
WEIGHT: 3.11 Grams
          1943: 2.70 Grams
COMPOSITION: 1909-1942, 1947-1958:
              .950 Copper, .050 Tin and Zinc
              1943: Zinc Coated Steel
              1944-1946: .950 Copper, .050 Zinc
DESIGNER: Victor D. Brenner
EDGE: Plain

The key dates for the Lincoln series are the 1909-S, the 1909-S VDB, the 1914-D, and the 1931-S. Even in lower grades, these coins have experienced regular and steady value increases and are likely to retain their positions as the most valuable in the series.

Some dealers and collectors nowadays prefer to include the 1922-D (no D) cent on their lists of important Lincolns. Currently, collector demand is beginning to outstrip dealer supply. Be especially wary of who you do business with. Some 1922-D examples have had their mintmarks removed by hucksters in order to resemble authentic missing D specimens.

Some experts contend that Lincoln cent matte proofs of 1909 to 1916 are genuine sleepers (matte proof is a different manufacturing process than that used for later Lincoln proofs). By studying population reports, the survivorship of these pieces is relatively low, but current prices do not reflect this. These gems can be had for under $650, a price that could easily double in the next five years.

DATE	MINTAGE	G-4	VG-8	F-12	VF-20	EF-40	AU-50	MS-60	MS-63	MS-65	PRF-65
1909	72,702,618	0.50	0.55	0.90	1.55	2.50	6.15	14	20	70	450
1909 S	1,825,000	39	44	50	60	87	106	133	165	325	—
1909 S VDB	484,000	355	395	438	475	570	620	695	858	1875	—
1909 VDB	27,995,000	1.85	2.05	2.20	2.50	3.00	5.20	9.50	14	50	2800
1910	146,801,218	0.15	0.20	0.25	0.80	2.25	5.60	14	24	79	450
1910 S	6,045,000	6.40	7.15	8.00	11	21	49	65	74	235	—
1911	101,177,787	0.25	0.30	0.50	1.75	4.65	7.65	18	33	140	450
1911 D	12,672,000	4.15	5.15	6.40	12	31	50	76	105	625	—
1911 S	4,026,000	15	18	20	22	38	65	133	173	743	—
1912	68,153,060	0.65	0.90	1.70	3.70	8.40	13	24	69	165	450

EDMUND'S 1996 U.S. COIN PRICES

SMALL CENTS

DATE	MINTAGE	G-4	VG-8	F-12	VF-20	EF-40	AU-50	MS-60	MS-63	MS-65	PRF-65
1912 D	10,411,000	4.15	5.20	7.25	15	37	57	115	158	945	—
1912 S	4,431,000	11	12	14	17	34	55	96	130	913	—
1913	76,532,352	0.50	0.60	1.20	3.25	8.75	12	23	37	198	—
1913 D	15,804,000	1.80	2.40	3.50	7.00	22	40	80	130	710	—
1913 S	6,101,000	5.15	5.90	7.40	11	27	53	98	145	1288	—
1914	75,238,432	0.45	0.60	1.50	3.40	9.25	19	37	45	160	450
1914 D	1,193,000	78	87	118	183	415	585	870	1263	4400	—
1914 S	4,137,000	8.50	9.50	12	19	37	64	178	368	3825	—
1915	29,092,120	1.00	1.45	4.20	9.90	37	56	80	118	333	450
1915 D	22,050,000	0.85	1.10	2.00	3.65	11	22	50	81	353	—
1915 S	4,833,000	6.15	7.25	8.25	11	28	51	99	198	1600	—
1916	131,833,677	0.15	0.20	0.40	1.30	3.50	5.75	12	22	88	665
1916 D	35,956,000	0.25	0.40	1.25	2.75	8.65	17	51	90	1015	—
1916 S	22,510,000	0.80	1.10	1.55	2.65	8.50	19	60	118	3600	—
1917	196,429,785	0.10	0.15	0.35	0.90	2.50	5.15	11	25	143	—
1917 D	55,120,000	0.30	0.40	1.40	3.10	8.25	16	56	103	568	—
1917 S	32,620,000	0.45	0.50	0.90	2.10	6.40	18	58	118	1825	—
1918	288,104,624	0.10	0.15	0.35	0.75	2.25	5.15	11	26	130	—
1918 D	47,830,000	0.25	0.35	1.25	2.50	7.50	17	52	105	820	—
1918 S	34,680,000	0.45	0.50	1.00	2.00	6.25	18	58	128	3300	—
1919	392,021,000	0.10	0.15	0.30	0.65	2.00	5.00	8.75	22	67	—
1919 D	57,154,000	0.20	0.30	0.55	1.85	6.00	14	45	82	545	—
1919 S	139,760,000	0.15	0.30	0.50	1.00	2.00	9.50	31	74	1830	—
1920	310,165,000	0.10	0.15	0.30	0.60	2.25	4.50	10	18	74	—
1920 D	49,280,000	0.25	0.30	0.60	2.00	7.00	15	53	91	560	—
1920 S	46,220,000	0.20	0.30	0.45	1.20	3.90	16	80	178	2850	—
1921	39,157,000	0.20	0.30	0.50	1.80	5.15	12	36	60	140	—
1921 S	15,274,000	0.75	0.85	1.40	3.50	12	50	98	180	2550	—
1922 D	7,160,000	5.75	6.75	7.75	9.75	17	41	68	105	470	—
1922	Inc. Above	228	270	385	563	1775	3050	4975	9425	23500	—
1923	74,723,000	0.20	0.25	0.30	1.35	3.40	5.90	11	29	153	—
1923 S	8,700,000	1.60	1.90	2.90	5.00	18	65	183	355	2850	—
1924	75,178,000	0.20	0.25	0.30	1.15	4.40	7.75	22	44	153	—
1924 D	2,520,000	8.25	9.65	11	19	47	115	225	315	2775	—
1924 S	11,696,000	0.80	1.10	1.40	3.00	13	31	110	178	3475	—
1925	139,949,000	0.10	0.15	0.20	0.75	2.15	4.65	8.90	19	62	—
1925 D	22,580,000	0.35	0.45	0.65	2.45	7.25	15	45	71	900	—
1925 S	26,380,000	0.30	0.35	0.45	1.15	5.65	17	59	128	3500	—
1926	157,088,000	0.10	0.15	0.20	0.75	1.90	3.65	7.00	13	38	—
1926 D	28,020,000	0.30	0.35	0.65	1.65	4.75	12	43	79	975	—
1926 S	4,550,000	2.50	2.90	3.40	4.40	11	49	55	188	5100	—
1927	144,440,000	0.10	0.15	0.25	0.80	1.90	3.80	7.15	16	68	—
1927 D	27,170,000	0.25	0.30	0.50	1.00	3.40	10	31	61	788	—
1927 S	14,276,000	0.60	0.70	1.35	2.40	8.25	18	61	118	1800	—
1928	134,116,000	0.10	0.15	0.20	0.65	1.75	3.40	7.50	17	63	—
1928 D	31,170,000	0.25	0.30	0.35	0.90	2.40	7.75	22	48	435	—

SMALL CENTS

DATE	MINTAGE	G-4	VG-8	F-12	VF-20	EF-40	AU-50	MS-60	MS-63	MS-65	PRF-65
1928 S	17,266,000	0.45	0.50	0.65	1.65	3.50	12	46	85	553	—
1929	185,262,000	0.15	0.20	0.25	0.65	1.40	3.30	5.25	15	66	—
1929 D	41,730,000	0.20	0.25	0.30	0.80	1.90	5.25	17	26	120	—
1929 S	50,148,000	0.15	0.20	0.30	0.75	1.85	3.35	8.40	15	128	—
1930	157,415,000	0.10	0.15	0.25	0.40	1.25	2.40	4.00	5.25	27	—
1930 D	40,100,000	0.15	0.25	0.35	0.65	1.75	5.40	12	23	60	—
1930 S	24,266,000	0.20	0.30	0.35	0.70	1.40	2.95	6.25	11	48	—
1931	19,396,000	0.50	0.55	0.70	1.10	2.20	6.40	16	27	86	—
1931 D	4,480,000	2.15	2.65	3.15	3.95	6.90	27	45	76	373	—
1931 S	866,000	31	32	34	36	39	46	55	63	243	—
1932	9,062,000	1.35	1.65	1.90	2.15	3.50	9.00	18	23	55	—
1932 D	10,500,000	0.90	1.05	1.20	1.45	2.90	8.00	14	29	57	—
1933	14,360,000	1.10	1.20	1.45	1.80	3.15	8.25	16	24	52	—
1933 D	6,200,000	1.90	2.05	2.40	2.65	4.15	11	17	21	41	—
1934	219,080,000	—	0.10	0.20	0.30	0.75	1.50	3.00	4.65	14	—
1934 D	28,446,000	0.10	0.15	0.30	0.40	3.50	7.65	15	21	35	—
1935	245,338,000	—	0.10	0.30	0.30	0.70	0.95	1.40	3.40	6.90	—
1935 D	47,000,000	—	0.10	0.30	0.35	0.80	2.35	3.90	5.30	15	—
1935 S	38,702,000	—	0.20	0.45	0.90	2.40	4.65	9.00	13	50	—
1936	309,637,569	—	0.10	0.20	0.35	0.75	0.95	1.40	2.65	6.15	600
1936 D	40,620,000	—	0.10	0.25	0.35	0.80	1.25	1.80	3.75	9.50	—
1936 S	29,130,000	0.10	0.15	0.30	0.40	0.90	1.70	2.45	4.15	10	—
1937	309,179,320	—	0.10	0.20	0.25	0.60	0.75	0.90	1.75	5.65	135
1937 D	50,430,000	—	0.10	0.20	0.35	0.70	1.00	1.85	3.00	6.85	—
1937 S	34,500,000	—	0.10	0.20	0.35	0.65	1.25	1.65	2.65	9.50	—
1938	156,696,734	—	0.10	0.20	0.25	0.55	1.00	1.45	1.75	6.50	90
1938 D	20,010,000	0.15	0.15	0.35	0.55	0.80	1.25	1.95	3.40	7.75	—
1938 S	15,180,000	0.30	0.35	0.40	0.60	0.80	1.15	1.75	2.50	10	—
1939	316,479,520	—	0.10	0.15	0.25	0.30	0.40	0.60	1.15	5.40	85
1939 D	15,160,000	0.35	0.40	0.45	0.70	1.05	1.80	2.50	3.65	13	—
1939 S	52,070,000	—	0.15	0.25	0.35	0.60	0.95	1.25	2.00	14	—
1940	586,825,872	—	—	0.20	0.25	0.35	0.45	0.75	1.15	3.65	90
1940 D	81,390,000	—	0.10	0.25	0.35	0.45	0.85	1.10	1.40	5.40	—
1940 S	112,940,000	—	0.10	0.25	0.35	0.45	0.85	1.15	1.55	6.65	—
1941	887,039,100	—	—	0.23	0.30	0.35	0.45	0.90	1.35	4.15	93
1941 D	128,700,000	—	—	0.40	0.35	0.55	1.25	1.85	4.90	8.50	—
1941 S	92,360,000	—	—	0.50	0.40	0.50	1.15	1.90	2.90	8.65	—
1942	657,828,600	—	—	0.20	0.30	0.30	0.35	0.65	0.90	2.75	95
1942 D	206,698,000	—	—	0.25	0.25	0.30	0.45	0.70	0.90	4.00	—
1942 S	85,590,000	—	—	0.55	0.45	0.65	1.50	3.25	5.15	23	—
1943 D Steel	217,660,000	—	—	0.15	0.40	0.55	0.70	1.00	1.45	5.75	—
1943 S Steel	191,550,000	—	—	0.25	0.50	0.60	0.85	1.50	2.40	9.00	—
1943 Steel	684,628,670	—	—	0.10	0.25	0.40	0.65	0.80	1.10	3.40	—
1944	1,435,400,000	—	—	0.10	0.15	0.15	0.25	0.45	0.80	1.60	—
1944 D	430,578,000	—	—	0.20	0.25	0.20	0.25	0.45	0.85	2.00	—

SMALL CENTS

DATE	MINTAGE	G-4	VG-8	F-12	VF-20	EF-40	AU-50	MS-60	MS-63	MS-65	PRF-65
1944 D D/S	Inc. Above	—	—	37.50	72.50	123	180	280	413	1025	—
1944 S	282,760,000	—	—	0.15	0.20	0.20	0.30	0.45	0.65	2.65	—
1945	1,040,515,000	—	—	0.10	0.15	0.15	0.35	0.70	0.90	1.55	—
1945 D	226,268,000	—	—	0.15	0.20	0.20	0.30	0.60	0.70	1.50	—
1945 S	181,770,000	—	—	0.15	0.20	0.20	0.30	0.50	0.75	2.40	—
1946	991,655,000	—	—	0.10	0.15	0.15	0.20	0.30	0.55	1.35	—
1946 D	315,690,000	—	—	0.15	0.18	0.15	0.20	0.40	0.60	1.80	—
1946 S	198,100,000	—	—	0.20	0.25	0.25	0.30	0.50	0.80	2.05	—
1947	190,555,000	—	—	0.20	0.30	0.30	0.50	1.10	1.40	2.20	—
1947 D	194,750,000	—	—	0.15	0.18	0.15	0.20	0.35	0.55	1.60	—
1947 S	99,000,000	—	—	0.16	0.22	0.20	0.25	0.50	0.75	2.40	—
1948	318,570,000	—	—	0.20	0.30	0.25	0.40	0.65	0.85	1.90	—
1948 D	172,637,000	—	—	0.25	0.30	0.25	0.30	0.45	0.65	2.05	—
1948 S	81,735,000	—	—	0.30	0.40	0.35	0.55	0.70	1.20	2.90	—
1949	217,775,000	—	—	0.20	0.30	0.25	0.45	0.65	0.85	2.30	—
1949 D	153,132,000	—	—	0.30	0.40	0.30	0.45	0.60	0.85	2.80	—
1949 S	64,290,000	—	—	0.30	0.45	0.40	0.63	0.80	1.62	4.63	—
1950	272,686,386	—	—	0.07	0.15	0.17	0.37	0.63	0.98	1.63	35
1950 D	334,950,000	—	—	0.05	0.14	0.15	0.20	0.43	0.63	1.25	—
1950 S	118,505,000	—	—	0.07	0.15	0.20	0.55	0.80	0.95	1.90	—
1951	295,633,500	—	—	0.07	0.15	0.17	0.40	0.75	1.00	1.75	35
1951 D	625,355,000	—	—	0.05	0.10	0.15	0.30	0.45	0.55	1.15	—
1951 S	136,010,000	—	—	0.20	0.25	0.25	0.60	0.75	1.00	2.40	—
1952	186,856,980	—	—	7.00	0.12	0.20	0.45	0.55	0.70	1.75	30
1952 D	746,130,000	—	—	0.04	0.08	0.15	0.20	0.35	0.40	1.10	—
1952 S	137,800,004	—	—	0.07	0.12	0.20	0.50	0.75	1.30	2.50	—
1953	256,883,800	—	—	0.05	0.09	5.10	0.16	0.35	0.45	0.95	22.50
1953 D	700,515,000	—	—	0.04	0.08	0.15	0.16	0.35	0.40	0.95	—
1953 S	181,835,000	—	—	0.07	0.12	0.15	0.26	0.45	0.70	1.40	—
1954	71,873,350	—	—	0.12	0.16	0.20	0.30	0.55	0.75	1.40	12
1954 D	251,552,500	—	—	0.04	0.07	0.10	0.20	0.25	0.35	0.45	—
1954 S	95,190,000	—	—	0.05	0.08	0.15	0.18	0.30	0.40	0.80	—
1955	330,958,000	—	—	0.04	0.07	0.10	0.10	0.15	0.20	0.55	11.50
1955 Double Die	Inc. Above	—	—	315	390	460	555	713	1025	4675	—
1955 D	563,257,500	—	—	0.04	0.07	0.10	0.10	0.15	0.20	0.55	—
1955 S	44,610,000	—	—	0.15	0.18	0.25	0.25	0.45	0.70	1.15	—
1956	421,414,384	—	—	0.03	0.04	0.05	0.10	0.15	0.20	0.45	3.50
1956 D	1,098,201,000	—	—	0.03	0.04	0.05	0.10	0.15	0.20	0.45	—
1957	283,787,952	—	—	0.03	0.04	0.05	0.10	0.15	0.20	0.45	2.50
1957 D	1,051,342,000	—	—	0.03	0.04	0.05	0.10	0.15	0.20	0.45	—
1958	253,400,652	—	—	0.03	0.04	0.05	0.10	0.15	0.20	0.40	2.00
1958 D	800,953,300	—	—	0.03	0.04	0.05	0.10	0.15	0.20	0.40	—

SMALL CENTS

LINCOLN TYPE, MEMORIAL REVERSE
1959 TO DATE

DIAMETER: 19mm
WEIGHT: 1959-1982: 3.11 Grams
　　　　1983-Date: 2.50 Grams
COMPOSITION: 1959-1962, 1947-1958: .950 Copper
　　　　　　　.050 Tin and Zinc
　　　　　　　1962-1982: .950 Copper, .050 Zinc
　　　　　　　1982-Date: .976 Zinc, .024 Copper
DESIGNER: Obverse: Victor D. Brenner
　　　　　Reverse: Frank Gasparro
EDGE: Plain

If you like to gamble, take a look at the 1970-S small date variety and the 1972 double die version of the Lincoln cent. No one knows how many of these actually exist, but we can be certain that they always will be heartily welcomed by every collector of Lincoln cents now and in the future.

Lincoln cent popularity has gotten a boost lately, thanks to a goof by the Philadelphia mint. A small quantity of 1995 cents have a doubled-die appearance. Many dealers are paying $200 for the error coin, causing even non-collectors to scurry through pocket change. Such attention in the past (for example: the 1955 double-die phenomenon) has drawn in lots of new excitement to the hobby.

DATE	MINTAGE	MS-60	MS-65	PRF-65
1959	610,864,291	0.10	0.35	1.25
1959 D	1,279,760,000	0.10	0.35	—
1960 D Lg. Date	1,580,884,000	0.10	0.35	—
1960 D Sm. Date	Inc. Above	0.25	1.10	—
1960 Lg. Date	588,096,602	0.10	0.35	1.00
1960 Sm. Date	Inc. Above	1.75	5.25	19
1961	756,373,244	0.10	0.35	0.70
1961 D	1,753,266,700	0.10	0.35	—
1962	609,263,019	0.10	0.35	0.70
1962 D	1,793,148,400	0.10	0.35	—
1963	757,185,645	0.10	0.35	0.70
1963 D	1,774,020,400	0.10	0.35	—
1964	2,652,525,762	0.10	0.35	0.60
1964 D	3,799,071,500	0.10	0.35	—
1965	1,497,224,900	—	1.00	—
1966	2,188,147,783	—	0.60	—
1967	3,048,667,100	—	0.60	—
1968	1,707,880,970	—	0.15	—
1968 D	2,886,269,600	—	0.15	—
1968 S	261,311,510	—	0.50	0.90

EDMUND'S 1996 U.S. COIN PRICES

SMALL CENTS

DATE	MINTAGE	MS-60	MS-65	PRF-65
1969	1,136,910,000	—	0.80	—
1969 D	4,002,832,200	—	0.35	—
1969 S	547,309,631	—	0.35	0.90
1970	1,898,315,000	—	0.60	—
1970 D	2,981,438,900	—	0.35	—
1970 S	693,192,814	—	0.35	0.90
1970 S Sm. Date	Inc. Above	29	54	76
1971	1,919,490,000	—	0.80	—
1971 D	2,911,045,600	—	0.65	—
1971 S	528,354,192	—	0.60	0.90
1972	2,933,255,000	—	0.35	—
1972 D	2,665,071,400	—	0.35	—
1972 Double Die	Inc. Above	170	288	—
1972 S	380,200,104	—	0.15	0.90
1973	3,728,245,000	—	0.30	—
1973 D	3,549,576,588	—	0.30	—
1973 S	319,937,634	—	0.35	0.85
1974	4,232,140,523	—	0.30	—
1974 D	4,235,098,000	—	0.30	—
1974 S	412,039,228	—	0.50	0.85
1975	5,451,476,142	—	0.30	—
1975 D	4,505,245,300	—	0.30	—
1975 S	PROOF ONLY	—	—	3.75
1976	4,674,292,426	—	0.30	—
1976 D	4,221,592,455	—	0.30	—
1976 S	PROOF ONLY	—	—	3.00
1977	4,469,930,000	—	0.30	—
1977 D	4,149,062,300	—	0.30	—
1977 S	PROOF ONLY	—	—	2.35
1978	5,558,605,000	—	0.30	—
1978 D	4,280,233,400	—	0.30	—
1978 S	PROOF ONLY	—	—	2.20
1979	6,018,515,000	—	0.30	—
1979 D	4,280,233,400	—	0.30	—
1979 S Type I	PROOF ONLY	—	—	1.90
1979 S T-II	PROOF ONLY	—	—	2.50
1980	7,414,705,000	—	0.30	—
1980 D	5,140,098,660	—	0.30	—
1980 S	PROOF ONLY	—	—	1.45
1981	7,491,750,000	—	0.30	—
1981 D	5,373,235,677	—	0.30	—
1981 S	PROOF ONLY	—	—	1.25
1982 Copper Lg. Date		0.12	0.10	—
1982 Copper Sm. Date		—	0.10	—
1982 D	6,012,979,368	—	—	—
1982 Lg. Date		—	0.10	—

SMALL CENTS

DATE	MINTAGE	MS-60	MS-65	PRF-65
1982 S	PROOF ONLY	0.50	—	2.40
1982 Zinc Lg. Date		—	0.20	—
1982 ZINC Sm. Date		—	0.10	—
1983	6,467,199,428	—	—	—
1983 D	7,752,355,000	—	0.30	—
1983 Double Die rev		150	263	—
1983 S	PROOF ONLY	—	—	4.00
1984	8,151,079,000	—	0.30	—
1984 D	5,569,238,906	—	0.65	4.25
1984 Double Die		125	175	—
1984 S	PROOF ONLY	—	—	—
1985	5,648,489,887	—	0.30	—
1985 D	5,287,399,926	—	0.30	—
1985 S	PROOF ONLY	—	—	2.90
1986	4,491,395,493	—	0.55	—
1986 D	4,442,866,698	—	0.30	—
1986 S	PROOF ONLY	—	—	7.50
1987	4,682,466,931	—	0.30	—
1987 D	4,879,389,514	—	0.30	—
1987 S	PROOF ONLY	—	—	3.10
1988	6,092,810,000	—	0.30	—
1988 D	5,253,740,443	—	0.30	3.75
1988 S	PROOF ONLY	—	—	—
1989	7,261,535,000	—	0.30	—
1989 D	5,345,467,111	—	0.30	—
1989 S	PROOF ONLY	—	—	3.75
1990	6,851,765,000	—	0.30	—
1990 D	4,922,894,533	—	0.30	—
1990 S	PROOF ONLY	—	—	7.00
1991	5,165,940,000	—	0.30	—
1991 D	4,158,442,076	—	0.30	—
1991 S	PROOF ONLY	—	—	8.40
1992	4,648,905,000	—	0.30	—
1992 D	4,448,673,300	—	0.30	—
1992 S	PROOF ONLY	—	—	5.65
1993		—	0.50	—
1993 D		—	0.50	—
1993 S	PROOF ONLY	—	—	6.50
1994		—	0.30	—
1994 D		—	0.30	—
1994 S	PROOF ONLY	—	—	6.00
1995		—	0.30	—
1995 D		—	0.30	—
1995 Double Die		30	50	—
1995 S Proof Only		—	—	5.00

EDMUND'S 1996 U.S. COIN PRICES

TWO CENT PIECES

TWO CENT PIECES 1864-1873

In the long history of United States coin production, there have been some rather strange denominations, namely the two cent, three cent and the twenty cent coins. Seldom publicly supported in their time, these oddball coins disappeared from circulation relatively soon after their implementation. Over the last few years, these denominations have commanded about as much respect as they did during their production years, resulting in some negative price appreciation in all grades, now indicating that there are several attractive options here for an investor. Top quality, mint red two cent pieces in MS-65 and PR-65 are especially rare and undervalued.

TWO CENT PIECES
1864-1873

DIAMETER: 23mm
WEIGHT: 6.22 Grams
COMPOSITION: .950 Copper .050 Tin and Zinc
DESIGNER: James B. Longacre
EDGE: Plain

There are three rarities in the series. Both varieties of the 1873 piece, available only in proof condition because there were no business strikes issued that year, have performed admirably as an investment vehicle, as have all proof specimens of the two cent group. Even though this series is not a particularly popular one with collectors, coins of this quality have been in strong demand from the investment sector, usually resulting in higher and higher prices over time. The 1873, available only in tiny quantities, is now selling for less than half its 1989 price.

Another rarity, the 1872, has done better than average for the series, especially in the upper grades. With a mintage of only 65,000, this coin would be priced in the thousands of dollars if it belonged to a more heavily collected series. Someday if the two cent coins were to become popular, you would see the 1872 register impressive gains in all conditions.

The sleeper of the series is the 1864 small motto variety. At one time ranked in value alongside the 1872 and the proofs, the 1864 small motto coin has not enjoyed the same degree of appreciation, a situation which could correct itself in the future. Unblemished coins of all dates in top uncirculated condition hold much promise as well.

TWO CENT PIECES

DATE	MINTAGE	G-4	VG-8	F-12	VF-20	EF-40	AU-50	MS-60	MS-63	MS-65	PRF-65
1864 Sm. Motto	19,847,500	60	75	96	145	228	350	538	775	2125	40000
1864 Lg. Motto	Inc. Above	7.00	11	18	21	30	48	95	135	663	5400
1865	13,640,000	7.00	11	18	21	31	49	98	138	688	4000
1866	3,177,000	7.00	11	19	22	31	51	103	148	855	1675
1867	2,938,750	7.00	11	19	22	32	61	113	180	775	2200
1868	2,803,750	7.00	11	19	23	34	65	133	203	825	1650
1869	1,546,500	7.00	7.25	13	18	26	58	105	160	875	1700
1870	861,250	8.00	12	21	35	56	88	180	275	1215	1750
1871	721,250	11	15	24	40	76	125	230	333	1395	2300
1872	65,000	75	120	168	263	363	508	763	1050	2675	2500
1873	Est. 1100	—	—	900	930	960	995	1200	1400	—	2725

THREE CENT PIECES

THREE CENT PIECES 1851-1889

Three cent coins were struck in both silver and nickel, each bearing a distinctively different design.

THREE CENT PIECES (SILVER)
1851-1873

The silver three cent coin, originally called a trime, is the smallest of all United States silver coins. There are three types of trimes, occurring because of subtle design changes periodically. Type I was minted from 1851 through 1853, Type II came out in 1854 continuing until 1858, and Type III ran from 1859 to 1873.

From an investor's viewpoint, the 1855 trime holds the most promise. Turned out in a quantity of only 139,000 pieces, it is the lowest mintage for all Type I and Type II style trimes. The price of MS-65 and PR-65 trimes of the first two types have escalated solidly for decades, with only a few minor reversals.

Carefully consider Type III trimes in MS-65 and PR-65 conditions, now selling for about one-fifth their cost of five years ago. At these prices, insist only on well-struck specimens. They have low production figures, with the trimes of 1863 onward being exceedingly rare. Because of the increased value of silver in 1863, only a few thousand were minted that year and each year thereafter, while many of those were melted down for bullion or exported shortly after leaving the mint. This explains why seldom does one encounter circulated trimes dated 1863 through 1872. Type III trimes dated 1863 to 1872 have moved in well-defined price cycles. It appears that in 1996, values for coins of this description have also hit rock bottom, meaning their "up" cycle is ahead of us and not behind.

THREE CENT PIECES

VARIETY ONE - NO OUTLINES TO STAR
1851-1853

DIAMETER: 14mm
WEIGHT: .80 Grams
COMPOSITION: .750 Silver, .250 Copper
DESIGNER: James B. Longacre
EDGE: Plain

DATE	MINTAGE	G-4	VG-8	F-12	VF-20	EF-40	AU-50	MS-60	MS-63	MS-65
1851	5,477,400	13.50	15	21	27	57	108	143	240	1250
1851 O	720,000	18	20	33	55	113	205	338	468	2175
1852	18,663,500	13.50	15	21	27	54	108	143	240	1250
1853	11,400,000	13.50	15	21	27	49	113	143	278	1300

VARIETY TWO - THREE OUTLINES TO STAR
1854-1858

DIAMETER: 14mm
WEIGHT: .75 Gram
COMPOSITION: .900 Silver, .100 Copper
DESIGNER: James B. Longacre
EDGE: Plain

DATE	MINTAGE	G-4	VG-8	F-12	VF-20	EF-40	AU-50	MS-60	MS-63	MS-65	PRF-65
1854	671,000	13.50	18	25	40	96	210	303	635	4175	25000
1855	139,000	21	27	47	78	140	230	470	1063	11250	15000
1856	1,458,000	14	18	24	40	86	198	275	625	5975	—
1857	1,042,000	13.50	18	23	39	83	200	293	635	4225	11125
1858	1,604,000	13.50	18	24	40	86	185	265	613	4175	7250

EDMUND'S 1996 U.S. COIN PRICES

THREE CENT PIECES

VARIETY THREE - TWO OUTLINES TO STAR
1859-1873

DIAMETER: 14mm
WEIGHT: .75 Gram
COMPOSITION: .900 Silver, .100 Copper
DESIGNER: James B. Longacre
EDGE: Plain

DATE	MINTAGE	G-4	VG-8	F-12	VF-20	EF-40	AU-50	MS-60	MS-63	MS-65	PRF-65
1859	365,000	13.50	17	22	33	58	118	160	285	1175	2500
1860	287,000	17	18	23	32	58	118	158	288	1188	7500
1861	498,000	14	17	23	33	64	115	153	283	1175	2125
1862	343,550	17	19	24	34	60	120	158	280	1150	2200
1863	21,460	200	225	280	315	350	408	570	825	2225	1375
1864	12,470	250	275	325	375	425	458	570	888	1938	1388
1865	8,500	260	300	350	375	400	450	575	875	2475	1388
1866	22,725	225	250	280	325	375	450	593	788	2225	1388
1867	4,625	285	325	350	375	400	473	613	1005	3700	1325
1868	4,100	285	325	350	375	400	453	618	1225	5775	1325
1869	5,100	285	325	350	375	460	500	625	993	3975	1338
1870	4,000	285	325	350	375	400	460	630	875	3700	1500
1871	4,360	285	325	350	375	400	244	590	813	1950	1375
1872	1,950	325	375	450	550	650	688	850	1375	6400	1363
1873	600	—	—	750	850	950	1000	1300	1700	—	—
1873 Proof Only	Inc. Above	—	—	—	—	—	—	—	—	—	2200

THREE CENT PIECES (NICKEL)
1865-1889

DIAMETER: 17.9mm
WEIGHT: 1.94 Grams
COMPOSITION: .750 Copper, .250 Nickel
DESIGNER: James B. Longacre
EDGE: Plain

The increase in silver value in 1863 brought a new three cent coin onto the scene, composed basically of copper and nickel. Beginning in 1865, three cent nickel coins were issued until 1889. The basic demand for three cent nickel pieces has traditionally come from type set collectors. There are several coins in the series that warrant attention, these being the ones dated 1876, 1879, 1880, 1882, 1888, and 1889. Top grade uncirculated and proof

THREE CENT PIECES

examples exploded in value in the late 1970's and again in the mid to late 1980's, but have tumbled almost 80% since then. Ironically, business strikes are valued slightly above gem proof pieces of similar quality, but population reports hint that they are indeed much rarer. In light of these circumstances, a well-struck MS-65 or better represents a tremendous buy.

DATE	MINTAGE	G-4	VG-8	F-12	VF-20	EF-40	AU-50	MS-60	MS-63	MS-65	PRF-65
1865	11,382,000	7.00	7.25	7.50	9.00	15	36	84	125	688	3350
1866	4,801,000	7.00	7.25	7.50	9.00	15	36	84	125	693	1500
1867	3,915,000	7.00	7.25	7.50	9.00	15	37	85	128	700	1238
1868	3,252,000	7.00	7.25	7.50	9.15	15	38	86	128	693	1250
1869	1,604,000	7.00	7.25	7.90	9.50	16	39	86	133	738	1088
1870	1,335,000	7.00	7.75	8.25	9.75	17	41	93	163	725	1225
1871	604,000	7.00	7.75	8.90	11	19	48	103	170	763	925
1872	862,000	7.00	7.50	8.50	10	18	45	95	200	1300	1063
1873	1,173,000	7.00	7.25	8.65	11	19	41	93	168	1725	900
1874	790,000	7.00	7.50	9.00	11	20	45	108	205	1925	1063
1875	228,000	8.00	9.00	12	18	26	67	138	183	738	1925
1876	162,000	11	14	17	24	38	90	170	238	1950	738
1877	Est. 900	—	—	—	—	—	—	1000	1250	—	—
1877	Proof Only	—	—	—	—	—	—	—	—	—	1700
1878	2,350	—	—	375	400	425	450	475	500	—	—
1878	Proof Only	—	—	—	—	—	—	—	—	—	700
1879	41,200	45	50	60	68	83	128	230	350	750	625
1880	24,955	63	70	85	98	133	165	248	363	775	613
1881	1,080,575	7.00	7.25	7.40	9.50	14	37	84	158	738	580
1882	25,300	63	70	75	88	110	155	248	363	1000	608
1883	10,609	125	145	175	200	243	275	383	838	2625	605
1884	5,642	290	330	343	378	418	465	538	990	4025	610
1885	4,790	350	380	433	468	500	600	713	915	2100	628
1886	7,691	—	—	—	—	—	—	300	400	—	—
1886	Proof Only	—	—	—	—	—	—	—	—	—	625
1886/7	Proof Only	—	—	—	—	—	—	—	—	—	750
1887	Inc. Above	—	—	—	—	—	—	—	1000	1250	700
1887/6	7,961	—	—	—	—	—	—	300	450	—	—
1887/6	Proof Only	—	—	—	—	—	—	—	—	—	700
1888	41,083	35	40	43	49	65	105	225	338	725	600
1889	21,561	63	70	83	94	110	138	240	375	730	575

EDMUND'S 1996 U.S. COIN PRICES

HALF DIMES

HALF DIMES 1794-1873

Half-dimes were minted from 1794 through 1873, and carried a face value of five cents. No half-dimes were produced after 1805 until 1829. There were five basic design changes in the history of the half-dime, although technically there are eight types in all, if you consider the addition or omission of stars or arrows in the Liberty Seated theme.

Collector demand for half-dimes comes from type set numismatists. Assembling an entire set is too costly for the average collector, although there are no special or key rarities as in so many other denominations.

All early half-dimes (minted in 1805 or before) are headed on a one-way street going uphill. As all of them are rare, they are a desirable purchase in all grades listed. If affordable, zero in on coins of Fine to Extremely Fine condition.

For post-1828 half dimes in MS-65 and PR-65, the investor will be shocked to learn that nearly all of them are being sold at less than 20% of their 1989 values! They should not go lower, only higher. For those with more limited capital seeking good returns, purchase circulated half dimes in conditions Very Fine and above.

FLOWING HAIR TYPE
1794-1795

DIAMETER: 16.5mm
WEIGHT: 1.35 Grams
COMPOSITION: .8924 Silver, .1076 Copper
DESIGNER: Robert Scot
EDGE: Reeded

DATE	MINTAGE	AG-3	G-4	VG-8	F-12	VF-20	EF-40	AU-50	MS-60
1794	86,416	450	763	950	1438	2050	3425	3515	9250
1795	Inc. Above	355	558	700	963	1450	2350	3750	7525

EDMUND'S 1996 U.S. COIN PRICES

HALF DIMES

DRAPED BUST TYPE
SMALL EAGLE REVERSE
1796-1797

DIAMETER: 16.5mm
WEIGHT: 1.35 Grams
COMPOSITION: .8924 Silver, .1076 Copper
DESIGNER: Robert Scot
EDGE: Reeded

DATE	MINTAGE	AG-3	G-4	VG-8	F-12	VF-20	EF-40	AU-50	MS-60
1795	Inc. Above	535	825	1288	1675	2850	4800	7250	9000
1796	10,220	450	688	975	1375	2225	3650	4875	5650
1796 LIKERTY	Inc. Above	450	688	975	1400	2350	3825	5950	—
1797 13 Stars	44,527	570	875	1213	1900	2825	4500	6100	11500
1797 15 Stars	Inc. Above	420	650	870	1225	1900	3200	4750	5650
1797 16 Stars	Inc. Above	440	670	900	1275	1988	3125	4275	5650

DRAPED BUST TYPE
HERALDIC EAGLE REVERSE
1800-1805

DATE	MINTAGE	AG-3	G-4	VG-8	F-12	VF-20	EF-40	AU-50	MS-60
1800	24,000	253	463	600	790	1300	2225	3275	5050
1800 LIBEKTY	Inc. Above	273	493	628	835	1388	2313	3450	5050
1801	33,910	298	525	650	865	1463	2363	3650	10000
1802	13,010	5500	8625	12250	18750	32250	60000	—	—
1803	37,850	260	475	608	795	1313	2238	3325	5050
1805	15,600	345	598	713	938	1575	2875	5125	—

HALF DIMES

CAPPED BUST TYPE
1829-1837

DIAMETER: 15.5mm
WEIGHT: 1.35 Grams
COMPOSITION: .8924 Silver, .1076 Copper
DESIGNER: William Kneass
EDGE: Plain

DATE	MINTAGE	G-4	VG-8	F-12	VF-20	EF-40	AU-50	MS-60	MS-63	MS-65
1829	1,230,000	14	22	29	58	120	203	290	525	3000
1830	1,240,000	14	22	29	58	118	195	283	518	3000
1831	1,242,700	14	22	29	58	118	195	280	490	3000
1832	965,000	14	22	29	58	118	240	373	758	7000
1833	1,370,000	14	22	29	58	118	203	308	565	3500
1834	1,480,000	14	22	29	58	118	200	280	490	3000
1835 Lg Date, Lg. 5C	2,760,000	14	22	29	58	110	208	280	490	3000
1835 Lg. Date, Sm. 5C	Inc. Above	14	22	29	58	118	198	280	490	3000
1835 Sm. Date, Lg. 5c	Inc. Above	14	22	29	58	118	195	280	490	3000
1835 Sm. Date, Sm. 5C	Inc. Above	14	22	29	58	118	195	280	490	3000
1836 Lg. 5C	1,900,000	14	22	29	58	118	200	283	500	3000
1836 Sm. 5C	Inc. Above	14	22	29	58	118	200	283	500	3000
1837 Lg. 5C	2,276,000	20	32	63	150	275	358	760	500	3000
1837 Sm. 5C	Inc. Above	20	31	44	80	143	265	770	1633	8500

LIBERTY SEATED TYPE
1837-1873

VARIETY ONE - NO STARS ON OBVERSE
1837-1838

DIAMETER: 15.5mm
WEIGHT: 1.34 Grams
COMPOSITION: .900 Silver, .100 Copper
DESIGNER: Christian Gobrecht
EDGE: Reeded

DATE	MINTAGE	G-4	VG-8	F-12	VF-20	EF-40	AU-50	MS-60	MS-63	MS-65
1837 Lg. Date	Inc. Above	25	34	49	95	195	350	575	925	3500
1837 Sm. Date	Inc. Above	24	32	48	89	180	313	563	875	3500
1838 O	70,000	69	105	208	388	663	1900	2550	5300	—

HALF DIMES

VARIETY TWO - STARS ON OBVERSE
1838-1853

DIAMETER: 15.5mm
WEIGHT: 1.34 Grams
COMPOSITION: .900 Silver, .100 Copper
DESIGNER: Christian Gobrecht
EDGE: Reeded

The 1846 looks like a real sleeper in any condition. With a relatively small mintage (27,000) for post-1829 half-dimes, this coin was one of the more prized half-dimes in the 1950's and 1960's. Having achieved some healthy price hikes during the 1980's in relation to most of the other half-dimes, it still isn't what it used to be. Look for the 1846 to someday reassume its position as one of the most valuable of all late half-dimes.

For investors with big wallets, this paragraph contains interesting tidbits: some numismatic experts contend that half-dimes in nice uncirculated condition struck at the New Orleans mint during the years 1839 through 1852 are far rarer than their already expensive prices would indicate. Again, if you can purchase MS-63 to MS-65 Uncirculated half dime specimens of this type, then try to do so and take advantage of a good investment opportunity.

DATE	MINTAGE	G-4	VG-8	F-12	VF-20	EF-40	AU-50	MS-60	MS-63	MS-65
1838 O No Drapery	2,225,000	7.00	8.25	10	25	50	—	300	—	—
1838 O Sm. Stars	Inc. Above	15	25	50	75	150	—	650	—	—
1839 No Drapery		7.40	8.90	11	25	63	138	285	383	2000
1839 O No Drapery		8.75	12	17	32	70	195	413	750	2000
1839 O Rev.. 1838	1,034,039	375	575	750	1200	2250	3500	—	—	—
1840 No Drapery	1,344,085	6.40	7.50	11	21	63	130	405	438	2000
1840 Drapery Added	Inc. Above	19	31	48	80	158	263	595	1425	6500
1840 O Drapery Add.	Inc. Above	29	43	80	135	345	875	—	—	—
1840 O No Drapery	935,000	9.25	13	20	35	76	213	518	1213	10500
1841	1,150,000	5.90	7.00	9.55	21	50	95	155	280	1450
1841 O	815,000	11	17	24	40	108	250	625	1225	—
1842	815,000	5.90	7.00	9.55	21	50	95	160	285	1450
1842 O	350,000	25	38	64	233	713	1625	2950	5913	—
1843	1,165,000	5.90	7.00	9.55	19	43	95	150	280	1450
1844	430,000	6.65	8.15	10	22	55	110	213	508	2250
1844 O	220,000	63	103	210	375	900	2250	3350	4250	15000
1845	1,564,000	5.90	7.00	9.55	21	45	91	150	280	1450
1845 /1845	Inc. Above	8.00	11	15	30	75	200	225	—	5000
1846	27,000	165	245	415	700	1350	2875	—	—	—
1847	1,274,000	6.40	7.40	9.55	19	49	94	190	320	2250

EDMUND'S 1996 U.S. COIN PRICES

HALF DIMES

DATE	MINTAGE	G-4	VG-8	F-12	VF-20	EF-40	AU-50	MS-60	MS-63	MS-65
1848 Med. Date	668,000	6.90	8.15	10	26	52	109	190	340	2250
1848 Lg. Date	Inc. Above	13	19	29	45	88	203	395	900	2250
1848 O	600,000	12	16	26	43	94	210	493	863	8750
1849/8	1,309,000	13	17	28	49	100	183	445	838	5000
1849/6	Inc. Above	10	14	23	42	76	160	375	650	5000
1849	Inc. Above	6.40	7.90	10	18	44	95	378	600	5000
1849 O	140,000	22	40	73	203	450	850	1600	5250	16000
1850	955,000	5.90	7.00	9.55	18	42	135	205	318	2750
1850 O	690,000	12	16	23	50	105	293	700	1375	4000
1851	781,000	5.90	7.05	9.55	18	46	103	233	485	2250
1851 O	860,000	9.20	14	24	35	74	170	595	1113	2250
1852	1,000,500	6.40	7.40	11	18	42	98	155	283	1450
1852 O	260,000	21	33	65	115	253	650	1200	2750	11000
1853	135,000	16	20	32	56	138	225	343	658	2150
1853 O	160,000	133	203	288	500	1175	2900	—	—	—

VARIETY THREE - ARROWS AT DATE
1853-1855

DIAMETER: 15.5mm
WEIGHT: 1.24 Grams
COMPOSITION: .900 Silver, .100 Copper
DESIGNER: Christian Gobrecht
EDGE: Reeded

DATE	MINTAGE	G-4	VG-8	F-12	VF-20	EF-40	AU-50	MS-60	MS-63	MS-65	PRF-65
1853	13,210,000	6.20	7.25	9.15	16	45	93	175	420	2150	14250
1853 O	2,200,000	6.55	7.90	12	22	51	129	300	1000	—	—
1854	5,740,000	6.20	7.40	9.25	16	45	111	225	608	4550	14250
1854 O	1,560,000	6.85	8.40	12	20	55	163	508	1125	—	—
1855	1,750,000	6.20	7.25	10	19	48	113	225	543	5000	14250
1855 O	600,000	14	18	25	50	110	250	725	1550	—	—

HALF DIMES

VARIETY TWO - RESUMED
1856-1859

DATE	MINTAGE	G-4	VG-8	F-12	VF-20	EF-40	AU-50	MS-60	MS-63	MS-65	PRF-65
1856	4,880,000	5.75	6.65	9.00	18	40	89	175	255	1550	22500
1856 O	1,100,000	7.90	11	16	32	70	200	500	938	1800	—
1857	1,280,000	5.75	6.65	8.90	16	42	88	170	253	1550	5000
1857 O	1,380,000	7.40	10	13	27	60	165	353	500	—	—
1858	3,500,000	5.75	6.65	8.90	18	42	80	143	253	1550	6150
1858 Inverted Date	Inc. Above	25	36	55	110	200	318	588	750	—	—
1858 Doubled Date	Inc. Above	—	38	50	83	143	243	355	788	1300	—
1858 O	1,660,000	—	6.90	8.50	12	29	64	170	253	420	—
1859	340,000	8.50	12	17	32	69	140	213	413	3000	3820
1859 O	560,000	12	14	18	38	88	175	300	450	—	2900
1859 Obv. of 1859, Rev. 1860		—	—	—	—	—	—	—	—	—	17500
1860 Obv. of 1859, Rev. 1860		—	—	—	—	—	—	4000	—	8500	—

VARIETY FOUR - LEGEND ON OBVERSE
1860-1873

DIAMETER: 15.5mm
WEIGHT: 1.24 Grams
COMPOSITION: .900 Silver, .100 Copper
DESIGNER: Christian Gobrecht
EDGE: Reeded

If you take pleasure in collecting half-dimes for your type set, maybe you should consider some of the investment angles as you plot a course of action. First of all, there is a group of very rare half-dimes minted in Philadelphia from 1863 to 1867 that appreciated enormously throughout most of the 1980's, but have fallen off in the 1990's. Try to acquire at least one of these coins in any collectible grade, for in all likelihood they will resume their steep rise in the coming years. If you have an opportunity to purchase MS-63 to MS-65 Uncirculated half-dimes of this caliber, then go for it. Although values have increased somewhat recently, this could be just the beginning of what is to come.

EDMUND'S 1996 U.S. COIN PRICES

HALF DIMES

DATE	MINTAGE	G-4	VG-8	F-12	VF-20	EF-40	AU-50	MS-60	MS-63	MS-65	PRF-65
1860	799,000	6.10	7.25	11	21	36	69	140	225	1150	1750
1860 O	1,060,000	9.00	11	16	24	43	86	253	433	3550	—
1860 Obv. of 1859, Rev. 1860		—	—	—	—	—	—	1900	3500	8500	—
1861	3,361,000	6.15	7.00	9.00	16	30	62	138	223	1150	—
1861 /0	Inc. Above	20	30	51	81	135	313	508	1000	—	—
1862	1,492,550	6.10	7.00	8.95	17	31	62	138	218	1150	—
1863	18,460	125	163	208	268	360	475	675	1063	3250	2273
1863 S	100,000	15	21	34	58	115	258	750	1088	—	2250
1864	48,470	225	308	373	483	610	688	900	1875	4500	—
1864 S	90,000	25	36	50	84	193	400	838	1338	—	—
1865	13,500	188	253	330	408	488	675	1038	1400	4700	2250
1865 S	120,000	13	17	26	43	95	333	825	1425	—	2250
1866	10,725	175	223	305	400	508	600	875	1300	4700	—
1866 S	120,000	13	17	26	50	98	280	788	1288	—	—
1867	8,625	338	383	445	523	593	725	1043	1425	4700	2250
1867 S	120,000	13	18	29	54	186	558	350	975	—	—
1868	89,200	30	53	88	143	215	305	538	1050	5000	2250
1868 S	280,000	7.45	8.80	12	27	60	145	320	900	—	—
1869	208,600	6.90	8.30	18	27	51	110	250	600	4900	2250
1869 S	230,000	8.45	11	15	29	60	145	320	675	—	—
1870	536,600	6.45	7.70	9.50	15	32	95	205	343	4400	1200
1870 S	Unique	—	—	—	—	—	425000	—	—	—	—
1871	1,873,960	6.30	7.15	8.95	14	28	64	140	393	4400	1200
1871 S	161,000	12	18	31	44	75	130	308	675	3800	—
1872	2,947,950	6.25	7.00	8.50	14	27	63	138	375	—	1200
1872 S MM in Wreath	837,000	6.40	7.30	9.25	14	29	63	140	403	4400	—
1872 S MM Below Wreath	Inc. Above	6.40	7.30	9.25	14	29	63	138	418	2400	—
1873	712,600	6.25	7.50	9.25	16	30	73	163	390	4450	2250
1873 S	324,000	8.40	11	15	23	43	71	168	398	4000	—

NICKELS

NICKEL FIVE CENT PIECES 1866 TO DATE

SHIELD TYPE
1866-1883

DIAMETER: 20.5mm
WEIGHT: 5 Grams
COMPOSITION: .750 Copper
.250 Nickel
DESIGNER: James B. Longacre
EDGE: Plain

FIRST REVERSE
RAYS BETWEEN STARS
1866-1867

SECOND REVERSE
WITHOUT RAYS
1867-1883

The Shield nickel was the first non-silver five cent coin, approved as a substitute for the silver half-dime in 1866 when silver prices reveled in a state of chaos. The introduction of the "nickel" brought on the demise of the silver five cent piece. The Shield nickel was produced every year following its initial release until 1883.

Few of the Shield nickels in heavily circulated conditions have provided satisfactory returns as investments. As usual, Uncirculated and Proof grades performed very well. Current MS-65 and Pr-65 examples are truly advantageous to the buyer, being offered at an 80% discount from their peak of six years ago.

The rarest business strikes in the Shield nickel are reflected in the 1879, 1880, and 1881 coins. These prices multiplied in value at least tenfold from 1975 to the early 1980's. There's every reason to expect them to take off again in rampant fashion sometime in the 1990's. The values of these coins in all conditions cannot go much lower than they presently are.

DATE	MINTAGE	G-4	VG-8	F-12	VF-20	EF-40	AU-50	MS-60	MS-63	MS-65	PRF-65
1866	14,742,500	13	15	20	34	91	143	225	370	2000	3700
1867 No Rays	28,890,500	8.75	9.75	12	15	28	53	88	165	695	1200
1867 With Rays	2,019,000	14	17	25	45	123	218	290	525	3800	40750
1868	28,817,000	9.00	10	12	15	30	53	93	178	700	1150
1869	16,395,000	9.50	10.50	12	15	31	52	90	170	650	940
1870	4,806,000	9.75	11	14	21	42	62	105	263	1025	1200
1871	561,000	26	40	56	83	120	175	285	500	1400	1000
1872	6,036,000	9.00	10	13	19	39	68	125	253	890	825
1873	4,550,000	9.00	10	13	20	40	65	123	260	778	1000
1874	3,538,000	9.40	11	13	23	44	73	133	253	1125	650
1875	2,097,000	11	14	21	38	61	86	155	305	2025	1125
1876	2,530,000	10	13	20	33	54	85	133	253	1225	1000
1877	Est. 500						PROOF ONLY				1700

EDMUND'S 1996 U.S. COIN PRICES

NICKELS

DATE	MINTAGE	G-4	VG-8	F-12	VF-20	EF-40	AU-50	MS-60	MS-63	MS-65	PRF-65
1878	2,350	500	525	550	600	650	675	—	—	—	—
1878	Proof only	—	—	—	—	—	—	—	—	—	800
1879	29,100	220	265	315	400	465	525	600	750	2000	825
1880	19,995	270	325	363	443	550	650	850	1275	3600	1000
1881	72,375	138	178	233	275	375	448	565	728	1250	650
1882	11,476,600	9.00	9.75	12	15	28	50	89	165	693	650
1883	1,456,919	10	12	15	19	30	56	89	163	688	650
1883/2	Inc. Above	35	63	100	145	180	220	275	670	2600	—

LIBERTY HEAD TYPE
1883-1913

DIAMETER: 21.2mm
WEIGHT: 5 Grams
COMPOSITION: .750 Copper
.250 Nickel
DESIGNER: Charles E. Barber
EDGE: Plain

VARIETY ONE WITHOUT CENTS 1883 ONLY

VARIETY ONE WITH CENTS 1883-1913

Liberty nickels, also known as the "V" nickels, entered the scene in 1883 and were regularly produced until 1912. There are a large number of Liberty nickels that could fetch a tidy profit in the near future if bought today. The 1885 piece is without a doubt the key date in the set, but had not advanced in value over the last several years until now. Look for continued growth in the near future.

The 1912-S has by far the lowest mintage of any regular Liberty nickel, with only 238,000 pieces issued. After increasing in value incredibly in the 1950's and 60's, the only San Francisco mint Liberty nickel struggled for much of the next fifteen years. After some good years in the 1980's, it has been dormant since. Appreciation in all grades reminiscent of the 50's and 60's may occur soon, as investors and collectors notice what a true 20th century rarity the 1912-S Liberty nickel really is. For the buyer looking for serious bargains, take a close look at all MS-65 and PR-65 Liberty nickels. Retail values have plummeted considerably in many cases, indicating that at this time they are underpriced in relation to their actual scarcity. These coins are true sleepers, just waiting for the alarm clock to sound!

Low population reports for nickels from the 1890's give important insight as to a good place to begin searching.

NICKELS

DATE	MINTAGE	G-4	VG-8	F-12	VF-20	EF-40	AU-50	MS-60	MS-63	MS-65	PRF-65
1883 No Cents	5,479,519	2.70	3.00	3.30	4.75	6.50	12	28	37	325	600
1883 With Cents	16,032,983	6.25	7.75	13	19	32	55	76	98	435	550
1884	11,273,942	8.00	9.75	14	21	40	73	123	198	735	500
1885	1,476,490	220	245	315	388	580	663	838	970	2100	875
1886	3,330,290	61	73	138	180	243	320	453	600	1675	700
1887	15,263,652	6.25	7.75	14	16	37	64	89	133	645	500
1888	10,720,483	10.50	11	18	28	50	92	113	708	635	500
1889	15,881,361	4.40	6.25	13	15	32	63	91	128	533	500
1890	16,259,272	5.00	6.25	14	18	35	64	96	143	763	500
1891	16,834,350	3.75	5.00	11	14	33	63	88	120	708	500
1892	11,699,642	3.75	5.15	11	16	33	66	96	128	648	500
1893	13,370,195	3.50	4.50	11	15	30	60	89	125	550	500
1894	5,413,132	5.25	7.75	33	58	115	145	165	188	710	500
1895	9,979,884	2.25	3.65	9.75	14	33	63	87	140	798	780
1896	8,842,920	3.75	5.25	12	18	38	67	92	173	1075	500
1897	20,428,735	1.90	2.25	5.00	7.50	20	54	80	123	1035	500
1898	12,532,087	1.50	2.35	4.90	7.25	20	55	81	128	688	500
1899	26,029,031	1.00	1.25	4.65	6.25	18	51	79	103	550	500
1900	27,255,995	1.00	1.20	4.15	5.50	16	42	71	95	435	500
1901	26,480,213	1.00	6.70	4.00	5.50	16	41	70	98	438	500
1902	31,480,579	1.00	1.20	4.00	5.50	16	41	70	98	470	500
1903	28,006,725	1.00	1.20	4.00	5.50	16	41	71	95	438	500
1904	21,404,984	1.00	1.25	4.25	5.75	16	42	71	100	438	725
1905	29,827,276	1.00	1.20	4.00	5.50	16	41	69	95	443	500
1906	38,613,725	1.00	1.20	4.00	5.50	16	41	70	98	443	500
1907	39,214,800	1.00	1.20	4.00	5.50	16	41	69	95	450	500
1908	22,686,177	1.00	1.20	4.00	5.75	16	41	70	98	588	500
1909	11,590,526	1.20	1.50	4.75	6.75	18	55	80	113	563	500
1910	30,169,353	1.00	1.20	3.95	5.00	16	38	68	95	450	500
1911	39,559,372	1.00	1.20	3.95	5.00	15	38	68	95	438	500
1912	26,236,714	1.00	1.20	3.95	5.50	15	38	68	98	445	500
1912 D	8,474,000	1.00	1.35	4.45	9.25	38	90	168	263	713	—
1912 S	238,000	40	44	75	230	408	510	683	850	1900	—
1913	5			May 1996 -- Eliasberg Sale $1.485 million							

EDMUND'S 1996 U.S. COIN PRICES

NICKELS

INDIAN HEAD OR BUFFALO TYPE
1913-1938

FIRST REVERSE BUFFALO ON MOUND 1913 ONLY

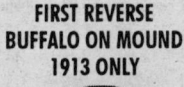

SECOND REVERSE BUFFALO ON LINE 1913-1938

DIAMETER: 21.2mm
WEIGHT: 5 Grams
COMPOSITION: .750 Copper
.250 Nickel
DESIGNER: James Earle Fraser
EDGE: Plain

Buffalo nickels, sometimes called the Indian head nickels, were minted from 1913 to 1938. This series is characterized by frequent poor strikes and changes in surface design, making grading more difficult than usual. As always, grading is critical, but in many instances with Buffalo nickels, values literally multiply each grade up after Very Fine, so be sure to absorb as much information as you can regarding the grading of these coins.

Buffalo nickels belong to a highly volatile market. They have been bouncing back and forth in price in all conditions for many years. It is especially important with Buffalo nickels to study each date separately, because these coins change in value independently of each other, more so than other series of United States coins. Although interest in the series has been increasing, there are many fine opportunities at surprisingly affordable prices. Among the best are scarce dates grading in the Extremely Fine to Almost Uncirculated range.

One of the classic American coins is the 1937-D three-legged Buffalo nickel variety, apparently due to an overpolished or clogged die. We've seen all grades increase sharply in value over the last year, but as a long term investment, a buyer cannot go wrong in acquiring this rarity, owing to its tremendous following from collectors. Beware of altered coins.

Another Buffalo head nickel popular with collectors is the 1918/7-D issue. Already this coin will set you back hundreds (if not thousands) of dollars, but we can look for consistent pressure from collectors to keep values moving in a positive direction. Because the 1918/7-D is so difficult to find in Extremely Fine and better, many buyers will pay a premium above book value to land one.

A darkhorse candidate is the 1938-D/S variety. This was the first mint mark overstrike ever discovered on a United States coin and has some worthwhile potential because of that distinction. Priced anywhere from $6.00 in Good to around $100 in MS-65, the 1938-D/S fell steadily from 1965 to 1992, and is now finally on the upswing. Being the first of its kind, dramatic rises will occur when collectors realize the obvious significance of this coin. Try to purchase the highest quality possible. At these low prices this is one bargain too good to pass up.

NICKELS

Carefully study the values of the MS-60 Uncirculated coins. Many of them have declined in value since 1980 and are now poised for near term price hikes. Unlike so many other series, MS-65 Buffalos are not priced out of sight as yet. In fact, there have been some price corrections recorded in the last several years. You'll discover some Buffalo nickels in MS-65 can now be had for under $100, indicating that strong price surges can be expected within the next few years. If you can afford to do so, purchase early Buffalos that grade higher than MS-65. Grading service population reports suggest these nickels are extremely rare, but their present day price tags do not agree. Additionally, take a close look at PR-65 gems; they have collapsed almost 70% since 1989.

DATE	MINTAGE	G-4	VG-8	F-12	VF-20	EF-40	AU-50	MS-60	MS-63	MS-65	PRF-65
1913 D Line Type	4,156,000	36	41	52	56	71	108	155	230	868	—
1913 D Mound Type	5,337,000	7.25	8.65	10	13	22	38	50	68	213	—
1913 Line Type	29,858,700	4.50	5.25	6.50	8.00	13	19	99	48	325	1350
1913 Mound Type	30,993,520	4.65	5.40	6.00	7.70	11	19	31	47	90	2400
1913 S Line Type	1,209,000	80	94	123	153	193	263	318	513	3650	—
1913 S Mound Type	2,105,000	11	13	18	24	39	50	64	125	713	—
1914	20,665,738	5.30	6.15	7.25	9.25	16	26	43	66	383	1100
1914 D	3,912,000	30	42	49	65	98	130	195	310	1300	—
1914 S	3,470,000	6.00	7.50	12	19	33	49	110	313	2400	—
1915	20,987,270	3.10	3.65	5.30	7.00	13	24	44	69	303	1100
1915 D	7,569,500	7.15	11	21	36	52	71	160	303	2563	—
1915 S	1,505,000	13	17	31	68	130	205	428	765	2625	—
1916	63,498,066	1.15	1.50	2.25	3.75	6.15	15	39	62	313	2000
1916 Double Die Obv.	Inc. Above	1950	3175	5100	7575	10375	14250	18250	50000	100000	—
1916 D	13,333,000	6.00	8.25	12	23	47	70	133	255	3475	—
1916 S	11,860,000	4.00	5.25	10	20	44	71	148	328	3125	—
1917	51,424,029	1.15	1.70	2.65	5.75	11	26	43	93	588	—
1917 D	9,910,800	5.65	8.25	18	44	86	130	275	593	2875	—
1917 S	4,193,000	5.65	8.65	19	45	110	193	333	663	3450	—
1918	32,086,314	1.30	1.90	2.95	7.65	17	33	51	208	2025	—
1918 D	8,362,000	5.50	7.50	18	64	150	248	345	733	3925	—
1918 D/17	362,000	342	517	900	2138	4250	6600	22580	32000	195000	—
1918 S	4,882,000	4.40	6.40	16	60	145	116	403	1750	15625	—
1919	60,868,000	1.10	1.40	1.90	3.75	9.00	22	41	75	500	—

EDMUND'S 1996 U.S. COIN PRICES

NICKELS

DATE	MINTAGE	G-4	VG-8	F-12	VF-20	EF-40	AU-50	MS-60	MS-63	MS-65	PRF-65
1919 D	8,006,000	6.25	10	21	75	173	258	483	950	4300	—
1919 S	7,521,000	4.25	6.50	15	63	160	248	468	1025	11000	—
1920	63,093,000	0.95	1.25	1.90	3.50	9.50	24	43	84	758	—
1920 D	9,418,000	5.00	7.00	17	73	200	290	448	1188	5575	—
1920 S	9,689,000	2.50	4.40	9.50	50	138	193	350	1175	18000	—
1921	10,663,000	1.40	1.90	3.15	7.25	20	41	84	135	713	—
1921 S	1,557,000	17	26	50	290	638	825	1163	2050	4750	—
1923	35,715,000	0.95	1.20	1.75	3.90	7.40	18	35	80	570	—
1923 S	6,142,000	2.40	3.65	8.00	83	175	220	338	693	9000	—
1924	21,620,000	0.95	1.25	1.90	4.75	9.15	28	47	89	613	—
1924 D	5,258,000	2.70	4.10	8.65	56	143	203	330	665	3725	—
1924 S	1,437,000	5.75	8.25	35	425	963	1250	1663	2550	5750	—
1925	25,565,100	0.85	1.10	1.75	3.75	8.00	21	31	73	350	—
1925 D	4,450,000	5.15	7.40	22	61	163	213	353	663	3650	—
1925 S	6,256,000	2.50	5.65	11	53	143	208	470	1800	33750	—
1926	44,693,000	0.60	0.80	1.25	2.25	6.50	17	28	44	145	—
1926 D	5,638,000	3.50	6.25	19	62	120	163	205	468	3425	—
1926 S	970,000	7.00	9.25	26	293	768	1143	2288	4175	23500	—
1927	37,981,000	0.60	0.80	1.20	2.15	6.00	18	27	53	185	—
1927 D	5,730,000	1.40	2.15	5.50	14	41	68	128	250	2850	—
1927 S	3,430,000	1.10	1.60	2.90	18	63	110	400	1600	16250	—
1928	23,411,000	0.55	0.75	1.15	2.25	5.75	17	26	43	328	—
1928 D	6,436,000	1.25	1.75	3.40	5.25	16	28	35	69	1050	—
1928 S	6,936,000	0.85	1.20	1.75	3.60	11	30	125	545	4875	—
1929	36,446,000	0.55	0.75	1.15	2.15	6.50	15	23	39	288	—
1929 D	8,370,000	1.00	1.30	2.25	5.50	13	28	41	81	1375	—
1929 S	7,754,000	0.70	0.85	1.25	2.15	9.00	19	37	70	423	—
1930	22,849,000	0.50	0.70	1.00	2.40	5.25	15	23	43	103	—
1930 S	5,435,000	0.55	0.75	1.15	2.15	8.00	23	33	75	513	—
1931 S	1,200,000	3.25	3.90	4.40	5.25	11	27	39	68	200	—
1934	20,213,003	0.55	0.60	0.75	2.10	5.25	13	23	45	305	—
1934 D	7,480,000	0.60	0.75	1.40	4.00	9.40	22	38	86	1550	—
1935	58,264,000	0.45	0.50	0.60	1.15	3.05	7.90	17	30	85	—
1935 D	12,092,000	0.60	0.85	1.50	3.75	8.75	25	32	61	443	—
1935 S	10,300,000	0.50	0.55	0.65	1.45	4.25	12	24	43	190	—
1936	119,001,420	0.45	0.50	0.60	1.15	2.80	6.90	14	26	68	1000
1936 D	24,814,000	0.50	0.55	0.65	1.25	4.25	10	16	28	78	—
1936 S	14,930,000	0.45	0.55	0.65	1.30	3.50	12	18	29	82	—
1937	79,485,769	0.45	0.50	0.60	1.15	2.75	6.50	12	20	32	950
1937 D	17,826,000	0.50	0.55	0.65	1.30	3.25	8.15	14	21	40	—
1937 D 3 Leg	Inc. Above	125	210	268	313	950	578	1313	3500	13625	—
1937 S	5,635,000	0.50	0.55	0.65	1.30	3.15	8.50	14	21	41	—
1938 D	7,020,000	0.45	0.50	0.60	1.30	2.95	7.75	12	15	28	—
1938 D/D		2.25	4.25	5.75	8.00	11	13.50	16	24	90	—
1930 D/S	Inc. Above	5.90	7.75	9.50	13	19	24	35	47	103	—

NICKELS

JEFFERSON TYPE
1938 TO DATE

DIAMETER: 21.2mm
WEIGHT: 5 Grams
COMPOSITION: 1938-1942, 1946-Date:
.750 Copper, .250 Nickel
1942-1945: .560 Copper
.350 Silver, .090 Manganese
DESIGNER: Felix Schlag
EDGE: Plain
PURE SILVER CONTENT: 1942-1945: .05626 Tr. Oz.

The familiar Jefferson nickel has been with us now since 1938. Once popularly collected, Jefferson nickels have been in the doldrums for many years, with complete sets now available for little more than what they were selling for 25 years ago; therefore, Jefferson nickels are especially attractive to low budget collectors, with virtually no downside risk.

For a modern series, the Jefferson nickel group includes a large number of error varieties. The most widely identified error coins are the 1939 doubled MONTICELLO, 1943-P 3/2, 1949-D/S, and the 1954-S/D. Although interesting pieces indeed, they have never taken off in value (with the exception of the 1939 doubled MONTICELLO), but with the inevitable return of interest in the Jeffersons, you can look for these coins to have a bright future ahead. At these low current prices, push for the absolute highest obtainable grade.

As modest as prices are today, Jefferson nickels grading no less than MS-65 are a good buy. As investment pieces, obtain PR-65 or better issues from 1938 to 1955. You should also be very selective. Look for sharp strikes, particularly at the center of the reverse. Examine the steps of Monticello under magnification. Only on well struck coins can you plainly see all six steps leading up to the door of Jefferson's home. The "Full Step" occurrence has not currently gained full widespread acceptance as a grading criterion contributing to increased value, but there is a definite shift in that direction. Insist on acquiring only Full Step Jeffersons today and tomorrow you'll probably be rewarded with an impressive premium for your foresight.

DATE	MINTAGE	G-4	VG-8	F-12	VF-20	EF-40	AU-50	MS-60	MS-63	MS-65	PRF-65
1938	19,515,365	—	0.30	0.45	0.75	1.10	1.70	2.90	2.75	7.00	43
1938 D	5,376,000	0.60	0.90	1.00	1.30	1.70	2.40	3.65	4.00	11	—
1938 S	4,105,000	1.15	1.30	1.65	1.95	2.25	2.95	3.65	4.50	13	—
1939	120,627,535	—	0.08	0.18	0.25	0.45	0.75	1.35	2.50	4.00	45
1939 D	3,514,000	2.50	2.90	3.50	4.50	7.15	18	26	40	65	—
1939 Double Monticello	Inc. Above	—	18	31	48	70	123	225	350	750	—
1939 S	6,630,000	0.40	0.65	0.80	1.25	2.65	7.50	15	20	35	—

NICKELS

DATE	MINTAGE	G-4	VG-8	F-12	VF-20	EF-40	AU-50	MS-60	MS-63	MS-65	PRF-65
1940	176,499,158	—	—	0.10	0.20	0.25	0.70	0.90	35	2.05	42.50
1940 D	43,540,000	—	0.13	0.20	0.30	0.45	1.55	2.40	2.75	4.15	—
1940 S	39,690,000	—	0.14	0.20	0.30	0.55	1.25	2.35	3.35	4.25	—
1941	203,283,720	—	—	0.10	0.20	0.25	0.40	0.75	1.25	1.60	48
1941 D	53,432,000	—	0.10	0.15	0.30	0.45	1.60	2.35	3.50	4.85	—
1941 S	43,445,000	—	0.10	0.15	0.30	0.50	2.25	3.25	4.00	5.90	—
1942	49,818,600	—	0.10	0.15	0.20	0.45	0.85	2.50	4.25	6.15	45
1942 D	19,938,000	—	0.35	0.45	0.95	2.40	7.50	18	21	35	—

WARTIME ALLOY, LARGE MINTMARK ABOVE DOME
1942-1945

The Jefferson nickels minted during World War II had 35% silver content. During the last big silver boom, war nickels suffered heavy melting, which someday could result in war nickel shortages. With the dead Jefferson nickel market, this scenario hasn't yet manifested itself, but with heightened popularity in the series, this situation will change.

DATE	MINTAGE	G-4	VG-8	F-12	VF-20	EF-40	AU-50	MS-60	MS-63	MS-65	PRF-65
1942 P	57,900,000	0.40	0.50	0.75	0.90	1.45	4.25	6.65	8.00	16	100
1942 S	32,900,000	0.40	0.55	1.00	1.30	1.90	3.75	7.00	8.00	20	—
1943 D	15,294,000	0.60	0.70	0.95	1.25	1.65	2.05	2.65	3.50	8.75	—
1943 P	271,165,000	0.30	0.40	0.75	0.85	1.30	1.90	3.40	4.00	7.25	—
1943 P 3/2	Inc. Above	20	35	49	68	93	150	243	300	538	—
1943 S	104,060,000	0.40	0.50	0.75	0.85	1.30	1.90	3.20	5.00	9.00	—
1944 D	32,309,000	0.40	0.55	0.85	1.00	1.80	3.00	7.75	9.50	12	—
1944 P	119,150,000	0.30	0.45	0.75	0.90	1.35	2.00	3.15	4.00	7.65	—
1944 S	21,640,000	0.45	0.75	0.95	1.25	1.95	3.25	4.65	5.35	12	—
1945 D	37,158,000	0.40	0.65	0.95	1.20	1.50	2.05	2.95	3.75	6.75	—
1945 P	119,408,100	0.30	0.45	0.75	0.90	1.65	2.15	3.35	4.50	8.15	—
1945 S	58,939,000	0.30	0.40	0.65	0.75	1.10	1.25	2.20	3.25	7.15	—

PRE-WAR COMPOSITION RESUMED
1946 TO DATE

The key coin in the Jefferson nickel series has been the 1950-D. A well-storied item in its own right, the 1950-D was the rave of the numismatic world twenty-five years ago. Even non-collectors were scouring through pocket change searching for the highly publicized coin. In spite of a series-low mintage of 2,630,030, the 1950-D nickel has done nothing for over twenty years, and may never return to its former glory days. However, at these extremely low prices, this coin is a handsome and affordable addition to anyone's collection.

NICKELS

DATE	MINTAGE	VG-8	F-12	VF-20	EF-40	AU-50	MS-60	MS-63	MS-65	PRF-65
1946	161,116,000	—	0.07	0.15	0.20	0.35	0.45	0.65	1.85	—
1946 D	45,292,200	0.07	0.10	0.20	0.35	0.45	0.65	0.90	5.50	—
1946 S	13,560,000	0.10	0.20	0.30	0.40	0.50	0.55	0.55	2.85	—
1947	95,000,000	—	0.07	0.15	0.20	0.30	0.50	0.75	2.00	—
1947 D	37,822,000	0.06	0.08	0.20	0.35	0.60	0.70	1.20	1.50	—
1947 S	24,720,000	·0.06	0.08	0.15	0.25	0.35	0.45	0.45	1.35	—
1948	89,348,000	—	0.07	0.15	0.20	0.30	0.40	0.55	1.20	—
1948 D	44,734,000	0.07	0.10	0.30	0.40	0.70	0.95	1.35	1.95	—
1948 S	11,300,000	0.10	0.20	0.30	0.45	0.60	0.75	0.60	1.75	—
1949	60,652,000	0.08	0.15	0.20	0.30	0.55	0.70	0.75	2.25	—
1949 D	36,498,000	0.07	0.10	0.30	0.45	0.60	0.90	1.50	2.65	—
1949 D/S	Inc. Above	—	30	38	68	108	155	185	363	—
1949 S	9,716,000	0.30	0.40	0.55	1.15	1.35	1.60	1.45	3.75	—
1950	9,847,386	0.20	0.35	0.40	0.60	0.85	1.35	0.90	18.97	—
1950 D	2,630,030	4.90	5.00	5.20	5.40	5.55	6.15	6.50	9.75	—
1951	28,609,500	—	0.07	0.30	0.40	0.60	0.90	1.40	12.08	37
1951 D	20,460,000	0.25	0.20	0.35	0.50	0.80	0.95	1.00	2.10	—
1951 S	7,776,000	0.30	0.35	0.50	0.75	1.00	1.65	2.25	4.50	—
1952	64,069,980	—	0.07	0.10	0.15	0.40	0.80	0.95	10.50	29
1952 D	30,638,000	—	0.07	0.20	0.30	0.70	1.00	1.25	2.55	—
1952 S	20,572,000	0.07	0.10	0.15	0.25	0.40	0.65	1.00	1.70	—
1953	46,772,800	—	0.07	0.10	0.20	0.25	0.30	0.35	9.50	28
1953 D	59,878,600	—	0.07	0.15	0.20	0.20	0.25	0.35	0.85	—
1953 S	19,210,900	0.08	0.15	0.20	0.25	0.30	0.40	0.75	2.00	—
1954	47,917,350	—	0.07	0.08	0.10	0.15	0.20	0.35	6.50	18
1954 D	117,136,560	—	0.07	0.08	0.10	0.15	0.25	0.35	0.90	—
1954 S	29,384,000	—	0.07	0.08	0.15	0.25	0.30	0.40	1.10	—
1954 S/D	Inc. Above	—	3.50	7.75	13	19	26	53	93	—
1955	8,266,200	0.20	0.30	0.35	0.40	0.45	0.60	0.75	4.80	11
1955 D	74,464,100	—	0.07	0.08	0.10	0.15	0.20	0.30	0.80	—
1955 D/S		—	3.00	8.50	15	25	34	52.50	122	69
1956	35,885,384	—	—	—	—	0.20	0.20	0.25	0.55	3.25
1956 D	67,222,940	—	—	—	—	0.15	0.20	0.25	0.55	—
1957	29,655,952	—	—	—	—	0.15	0.20	0.25	0.60	1.50
1957 D	136,828,900	—	—	—	—	0.15	0.20	0.25	0.60	—
1958	17,963,652	0.06	0.08	0.15	0.20	0.25	0.30	0.35	1.40	2.40
1958 D	168,249,120	—	—	—	—	0.15	0.20	0.25	0.55	—
1959	28,397,291	—	—	—	—	—	0.20	—	0.65	1.75
1959 D	160,738,240	—	—	—	—	—	0.15	—	0.50	0.50
1960	57,107,602	—	—	—	—	—	0.15	—	0.50	0.50
1960 D	192,582,180	—	—	—	—	—	0.15	—	0.50	—
1961	76,668,244	—	—	—	—	—	0.15	—	0.50	0.50
1961 D	229,342,760	—	—	—	—	—	0.15	—	0.25	—
1962	100,602,019	—	—	—	—	—	0.15	—	0.25	0.50
1962 D	280,195,720	—	—	—	—	—	0.15	—	0.25	—
1963	178,851,645	—	—	—	—	—	0.15	—	0.50	0.45

EDMUND'S 1996 U.S. COIN PRICES

NICKELS

DATE	MINTAGE	VG-8	F-12	VF-20	EF-40	AU-50	MS-60	MS-63	MS-65	PRF-65
1963 D	276,829,460	—	—	—	—	—	—	—	0.25	—
1964	1,028,622,762	—	—	—	—	—	0.25	—	—	0.40
1964 D	1,787,297,160	—	—	—	—	—	0.15	—	—	—
1965	136,131,380	—	—	—	—	—	0.15	—	—	—
1966	156,208,283	—	—	—	—	—	0.15	—	—	1.10
1967	107,325,800	—	—	—	—	—	0.15	—	—	—
1968 D	91,227,800	—	—	—	—	—	0.15	—	—	—
1968 S	103,437,510	—	—	—	—	—	0.15	—	—	0.50
1969 D	202,807,500	—	—	—	—	—	0.15	—	—	—
1969 S	123,099,631	—	—	—	—	—	0.15	—	—	0.50
1970 D	515,485,380	—	—	—	—	—	0.15	—	—	—
1970 S	241,464,814	—	—	—	—	—	0.15	—	—	0.50
1971	106,884,000	—	—	—	—	—	0.45	—	—	—
1971 D	316,144,800	—	—	—	—	—	0.20	—	—	—
1971 S	PROOF ONLY	—	—	—	—	—	—	—	—	1.25
1972	202,036,000	—	—	—	—	—	0.15	—	0.30	—
1972 D	351,694,600	—	—	—	—	—	0.15	—	0.30	—
1972 S	PROOF ONLY	—	—	—	—	—	—	—	—	1.30
1973	384,396,000	—	—	—	—	—	0.13	—	0.25	—
1973 D	261,405,400	—	—	—	—	—	0.13	—	0.25	—
1973 S	PROOF ONLY	—	—	—	—	—	—	—	—	1.10
1974	601,752,000	—	—	—	—	—	0.13	—	0.25	—
1974 D	277,373,000	—	—	—	—	—	0.20	—	0.45	—
1974 S	PROOF ONLY	—	—	—	—	—	—	—	—	1.15
1975	181,772,000	—	—	—	—	—	0.25	—	0.55	—
1975 D	401,875,300	—	—	—	—	—	0.20	—	0.40	—
1975 S	PROOF ONLY	—	—	—	—	—	—	—	—	1.05
1976	367,124,000	—	—	—	—	—	0.25	—	0.60	—
1976 D	563,964,147	—	—	—	—	—	0.30	—	0.95	—
1976 S	PROOF ONLY	—	—	—	—	—	—	—	—	1.00
1977	585,376,000	—	—	—	—	—	0.13	—	0.25	—
1977 D	297,313,460	—	—	—	—	—	0.28	—	0.80	—
1977 S	PROOF ONLY	—	—	—	—	—	—	—	—	0.70
1978	391,308,000	—	—	—	—	—	—	—	—	—
1978 D	313,092,780	—	—	—	—	—	0.15	—	0.15	—
1978 S	PROOF ONLY	—	—	—	—	—	—	—	—	0.60
1979	463,188,000	—	—	—	—	—	—	—	0.15	—
1979 D	325,867,672	—	—	—	—	—	0.13	—	0.15	—
1979 S T-I	PROOF ONLY	—	—	—	—	—	—	—	—	0.75
1979 S T-II	PROOF ONLY	—	—	—	—	—	—	—	—	1.45
1980 D	502,323,448	—	—	—	—	—	0.25	—	0.15	—
1980 P	593,004,000	—	—	—	—	—	0.25	—	0.15	—
1980 S	PROOF ONLY	—	—	—	—	—	—	—	—	0.70
1981 D	364,801,843	—	—	—	—	—	0.25	—	0.15	—
1981 P	657,504,000	—	—	—	—	—	0.25	—	0.15	—
1981 S T-I	PROOF ONLY	—	—	—	—	—	—	—	—	0.65

EDMUND'S 1996 U.S. COIN PRICES

NICKELS

DATE	MINTAGE	VG-8	F-12	VF-20	EF-40	AU-50	MS-60	MS-63	MS-65	PRF-65
1981 ST-II .. PROOF ONLY		—	—	—	—	—	—	—	—	1.75
1982 D 373,726,544		—	—	—	—	—	0.25	—	1.75	—
1982 P 292,355,000		—	—	—	—	—	0.14	—	0.65	—
1982 S .... PROOF ONLY		—	—	—	—	—	—	—	—	1.40
1983 D 536,726,276		—	—	—	—	—	0.55	—	1.30	—
1983 P 561,615,000		—	—	—	—	—	0.50	—	1.15	—
1983 S .... PROOF ONLY		—	—	—	—	—	—	—	—	1.75
1984 D 517,675,146		—	—	—	—	—	0.15	—	0.20	—
1984 P 746,769,000		—	—	—	—	—	0.10	—	0.60	—
1984 S .... PROOF ONLY		—	—	—	—	—	—	—	—	2.40
1985 D 459,747,446		—	—	—	—	—	0.15	—	0.20	—
1985 P 647,114,962		—	—	—	—	—	0.13	—	0.20	—
1985 S .... PROOF ONLY		—	—	—	—	—	—	—	—	2.00
1986 D 361,819,140		—	—	—	—	—	0.15	—	0.85	—
1986 P 536,883,483		—	—	—	—	—	0.10	—	0.25	—
1986 S .... PROOF ONLY		—	—	—	—	—	—	—	—	5.00
1987 D 410,590,604		—	—	—	—	—	0.25	—	0.15	—
1987 P 371,499,481		—	—	—	—	—	0.25	—	0.15	—
1987 S .... PROOF ONLY		—	—	—	—	—	—	—	—	1.75
1988 D 663,771,652		—	—	—	—	—	—	—	0.15	—
1988 P 771,360,000		—	—	—	—	—	0.25	—	0.15	—
1988 S .... PROOF ONLY		—	—	—	—	—	—	—	—	2.90
1989 D 570,842,474		—	—	—	—	—	—	—	—	—
1989 P 898,812,000		—	—	—	—	—	—	—	—	—
1989 S .... PROOF ONLY		—	—	—	—	—	—	—	—	2.25
1990 D 663,938,503		—	—	—	—	—	—	—	—	—
1990 P 661,636,000		—	—	—	—	—	—	—	—	—
1990 S .... PROOF ONLY		—	—	—	—	—	—	—	—	3.50
1991 D 436,496,678		—	—	—	—	—	—	—	—	—
1991 P 614,104,000		—	—	—	—	—	—	—	—	—
1991 S .... PROOF ONLY		—	—	—	—	—	—	—	—	3.90
1992 D 450,565,113		—	—	—	—	—	—	—	—	—
1992 P 399,552,000		—	—	—	—	—	—	—	—	—
1992 S .... PROOF ONLY		—	—	—	—	—	—	—	—	3.25
1993 D 406,084,135		—	—	—	—	—	—	—	—	—
1993 P 412,076,000		—	—	—	—	—	—	—	—	—
1993 S .... PROOF ONLY		—	—	—	—	—	—	—	—	2.75
1994 D		—	—	—	—	—	—	—	—	—
1994 P		—	—	—	—	—	—	—	—	—
1994 S .... PROOF ONLY		—	—	—	—	—	—	—	—	3.25

EDMUND'S 1996 U.S. COIN PRICES

DIMES

DIMES 1796 to DATE

Dimes have been minted continuously since 1796, providing numismatists with a vast array of dates and mint marks to study. The designs of the various dime series parallel those of the half-dimes through part of the Liberty Seated pattern. In all, there are eleven distinct types of dimes.

DRAPED BUST TYPE
1796-1807

Excellent investment potential exists in all the Draped Bust dimes, owing to the fact that these coins are very rare and have always been on a brisk rise, with little chance of coming to a permanent halt. Unfortunately, the price tags of the earlier dimes confine purchasing mainly to well-off investors.

SMALL EAGLE REVERSE
1796-1797

DIAMETER: 19mm
WEIGHT: 2.70 Grams
COMPOSITION: .8924 Silver, .1076 Copper
DESIGNER: Robert Scot
EDGE: Reeded

DATE	MINTAGE	AG-3	G-4	VG-8	F-12	VF-20	EF-40	AU-50	MS-60
1796	22,135	685	975	1475	1775	2925	4750	5875	7625
1797 13 Stars	25,261	750	988	1500	1863	3175	5350	7225	10250
1797 16 Stars	Inc. Above	700	963	1475	1800	3025	5100	6850	9750

DIMES

HERALDIC EAGLE REVERSE
1798-1807

DIAMETER: 19mm
WEIGHT: 2.70 Grams
COMPOSITION: .8924 Silver, .1076 Copper
DESIGNER: Robert Scot
EDGE: Plain

DATE	MINTAGE	AG-3	G-4	VG-8	F-12	VF-20	EF-40	AU-50	MS-60
1798	27,550	295	438	518	688	1113	1813	2625	5000
1798 /97 13 Stars	Inc. Above	1075	1650	2675	4300	6300	7500	—	—
1798 /97 16 Stars	Inc. Above	310	525	663	925	1675	2888	4050	6950
1798 Sm. 8	Inc. Above	550	688	950	1325	2275	3450	4750	9250
1800	21,760	295	438	518	675	1050	1813	3300	5100
1801	34,640	295	438	518	688	1100	2175	3600	7500
1802	10,975	450	655	938	1475	2975	5350	10250	25000
1803	33,040	295	433	508	680	1113	1913	2825	5750
1804 13 Stars	8,265	600	950	1388	2250	4500	8375	22000	—
1804 14 Stars	Inc. Above	650	1200	1700	2350	4750	8000	—	—
1805 4 Berries	120,780	260	418	488	650	900	1650	2550	3900
1805 5 Berries	Inc. Above	290	500	575	863	1238	1975	3825	4200
1807	165,000	260	418	488	655	925	1650	2575	3900

CAPPED BUST TYPE
1809-1837

DIAMETER: 18.8mm
WEIGHT: 2.70 Grams
COMPOSITION: .8924 Silver, .1076 Copper
DESIGNER: John Reich
EDGE: Reeded

  The Capped Bust type of 1809-1837 is more easily affordable in lower conditions. Capped Bust dimes in MS-60 have tumbled by as much as 50% from their 1989 levels, offering opportunities to investors of all means. Included in this group are the 1814 (small date), 1830 (over 29), and the 1835. These are being offered at basement prices, and will make a fine addition to anyone's collection.

  The most expensive coin in the series is the 1822. With a history of large price leaps followed by long periods of inactivity, the 1822 is fully priced at

DIMES

the moment. On the other hand, it is a sure bet if purchased with long term investment in mind. Take a close look at the 1809, 1811/9 (as all 1811's are), and the 1828 large date variety. In 1965, these issues were valued near the top of the heap of Capped dimes, alongside the 1822, and own similar appreciation records until recently. The 1822 has advanced enormously in value, while the other three have not. It is only a matter of time before the "left behind" Capped Dimes catch up with their 1822 brother and take on "normal" price differentials again.

Capped Bust dimes in MS-65 are extremely rare and expensive, having withered the stormy waters of recent years. If purchased with long range planning in mind, they offer potential second to none.

VARIETY ONE - LARGE SIZE
1809-1828

DATE	MINTAGE	G-4	VG-8	F-12	VF-20	EF-40	AU-50	MS-60	MS-63	MS-65
1809	51,065	98	188	350	575	963	1650	4475	7200	22500
1811/09	65,180	54	88	175	350	763	1425	4300	7000	22500
1814 Sm. Date	421,500	35	60	98	205	450	788	1450	1850	8000
1814 Lg. Date	Inc. Above	18	26	48	125	335	580	950	1800	8000
1820 Lg. O	942,587	18	26	48	125	335	580	950	1850	8000
1820 Sm. O	Inc. Above	16	25	39	115	325	588	913	1850	8000
1821 Lg. Date	1,186,512	15	23	38	96	313	568	850	1850	8000
1821 Sm. Date	Inc. Above	19	27	48	120	340	638	1050	1850	8000
1822	100,000	305	468	788	1263	2325	4350	8000	—	—
1822 Lg. E's	440,000	16	22	35	90	298	570	683	1375	8000
1822 Sm. E's	Inc. Above	17.50	25	45	125	380	625	800	1850	8000
1823/22 Lg. E's	440,000	16	22	35	90	298	570	850	1850	8000
1823/22 Sm. E's	Inc. Above	17.50	25	45	125	380	625	800	1850	8000
1824/22	510,000	25	34	65	230	450	1075	2163	4000	—
1825	Inc. Above	14	20	34	88	293	638	900	3000	8000
1827	1,215,000	14	20	34	88	293	638	900	2600	8000
1828 Lg. Date	125,000	30	45	70	193	500	875	2150	—	—

DIMES

VARIETY TWO - DIAMETER SLIGHTLY REDUCED
1828-1837

DATE	MINTAGE	G-4	VG-8	F-12	VF-20	EF-40	AU-50	MS-60	MS-63	MS-65
1828 Sm. Date	Inc. Above	21	36	50	113	325	558	1263	2200	—
1829	Inc. Above	28	45	68	113	305	563	1120	2275	—
1829 Lg. 10C	770,000	26	38	59	95	325	550	1263	1400	8000
1829 Med.. 10C	Inc. Above	17.50	25	35	85	265	425	625	1400	8000
1829 Sm. 10C	Inc. Above	15	21	31	68	185	383	788	1400	8000
1830 Lg. 10C	510,000	13	16	22	56	225	353	608	1400	8000
1830 Sm. 10C	Inc. Above	15	19	25	63	200	415	625	1400	8000
1830/29	Inc. Above	28	45	68	113	305	563	1120	2275	—
1831	771,350	13	16	22	55	170	313	588	1050	5500
1832	522,500	13	16	22	55	170	318	600	1050	5500
1833	485,000	13	16	22	55	170	313	593	1050	5500
1834 Lg. 4	635,000	13	16	22	55	170	313	588	1050	5500
1835	1,410,000	13	16	22	55	170	313	600	1050	—
1836	1,190,000	13	16	22	55	170	313	600	1050	5500
1837	1,042,000	13	16	22	55	170	313	1025	5500	—

LIBERTY SEATED TYPE
1837-1891

The Liberty Seated dime was first introduced in 1837 along with the Liberty Seated half-dime. There are many dimes among the Liberty Seated series that have fallen in the last few years and are currently undervalued, including slabbed coins in MS-60 to MS-65 Uncirculated condition. On a general note, the reader should not equate the precipitous plunge of Liberty Seated material with that of generic coins. High grade Liberty Seated coins and their contemporaries, unlike generic coins, are legitimately scarce. At today's depressed prices, they have excellent potential and should be among the best performers in the next market boom. This fact will be borne out repeatedly in the pages to follow.

A few typical examples of MS-60 Liberty Seated dimes costing anywhere from 10% to 30% less now than a few years ago are the 1837, 1838-O, 1838 (small stars), and the 1853 (no arrows). It is interesting to note that the Liberty Seated 1837 in MS-60 has actually dipped below its 1975 levels! Seldom will a 19th century coin of mid-range scarcity be found with the uncirculated value equaling less than that of two decades ago.

DIMES

VARIETY ONE - NO STARS ON OBVERSE
1837-1838

DIAMETER: 17.9mm
WEIGHT: 2.67 Grams
COMPOSITION: .900 Silver, .100 Copper
DESIGNER: Christian Gobrecht
EDGE: Reeded

DATE	MINTAGE	G-4	VG-8	F-12	VF-20	EF-40	AU-50	MS-60	MS-63	MS-65
1837 Lg. Date	Inc. Above	26	38	73	263	500	725	1175	1825	6500
1837 Sm. Date	Inc. Above	26	38	73	263	500	675	1175	1825	6500
1838 O	406,034	35	50	93	305	618	1125	2925	7200	21000

VARIETY TWO - STARS ON OBVERSE
1838-1853

DIAMETER: 17.9mm
WEIGHT: 2.67 Grams
COMPOSITION: .900 Silver, .100 Copper
DESIGNER: Christian Gobrecht
EDGE: Reeded

DATE	MINTAGE	G-4	VG-8	F-12	VF-20	EF-40	AU-50	MS-60	MS-63	MS-65
1838 Sm. Stars	1,992,500	19	29	46	75	158	398	1063	2450	—
1838 Lg. Stars	Inc. Above	9.00	10	15	23	59	160	428	1025	8500
1838 Part Drapery	Inc. Above	17	24	44	83	170	300	913	1550	—
1839	1,053,115	7.15	9.65	15	28	60	158	263	738	2500
1839 O	1,323,000	7.65	12	21	40	85	283	775	1400	—
1839 O Rev. 18380	Inc. Above	120	193	313	475	688	—	—	—	—
1840	1,358,580	7.00	9.50	15	23	53	153	263	718	2500
1840 Drapery	Inc. Above	25	43	80	135	288	825	1750	1925	—
1840 O	1,175,000	8.40	15	22	40	86	250	1225	—	—
1841	1,622,500	6.00	7.65	12	20	44	153	260	593	2550
1841 O	2,007,500	8.00	11	15	28	60	250	1500	—	—
1841 O Lg. O	Inc. Above	600	900	1200	2500	—	—	—	—	—
1842	1,887,500	6.00	7.75	12	18	40	148	258	588	2550
1842 O	2,020,000	8.00	12	16	38	125	950	2475	5750	—
1843	1,370,000	6.00	7.90	11	18	40	150	260	638	2550

DIMES

DATE	MINTAGE	G-4	VG-8	F-12	VF-20	EF-40	AU-50	MS-60	MS-63	MS-65
1843 /1843		15	20	30	70	125	200	400	—	—
1843 O	150,000	34	58	128	238	688	1775	—	—	—
1844	72,500	100	150	213	388	850	1850	3000	—	—
1845	1,755,000	6.00	7.25	11	19	40	115	243	600	2550
1845 /1845	Inc. Above	10	18	38	60	155	415	—	—	—
1845 O	230,000	20	33	59	165	538	1263	—	—	—
1846	31,300	70	103	158	293	813	1875	—	—	—
1847	245,000	12	18	31	60	123	345	813	—	—
1848	451,500	7.75	11	17	34	74	170	775	1875	7050
1849	839,000	6.65	9.00	13	22	51	133	438	1425	7050
1849 O	300,000	9.00	16	35	88	235	875	2750	5500	—
1850	1,931,500	6.25	7.40	11	21	49	118	243	593	2550
1850 O	510,000	8.90	13	32	68	143	363	1150	—	—
1851	1,026,500	6.00	7.00	11	18	48	115	338	950	—
1851 O	400,000	9.15	14	29	73	153	455	1625	—	—
1852	1,535,500	6.00	7.00	11	17	43	113	260	588	2550
1852 O	430,000	13	21	34	81	173	463	1825	3200	—
1853	95,000	60	83	105	170	308	450	788	1713	9000

VARIETY THREE - ARROWS AT DATE
1853-1855

DIAMETER: 17.9mm
WEIGHT: 2.49 Grams
COMPOSITION: .900 Silver, .100 Copper
DESIGNER: Christian Gobrecht
EDGE: Reeded

DATE	MINTAGE	G-4	VG-8	F-12	VF-20	EF-40	AU-50	MS-60	MS-63	MS-65	PRF-65
1853	12,078,010	5.90	6.90	8.50	14	41	118	315	730	3750	38000
1853 O	1,100,000	6.25	11	16	39	99	368	850	2525	—	—
1853 v3	12,078,010	5.90	6.90	8.50	14	41	118	315	775	2500	38000
1854	4,470,000	5.90	7.00	8.90	14	41	120	320	713	3750	38000
1854 O	1,770,000	5.85	6.75	8.75	22	70	183	593	1570	—	—
1855	2,075,000	5.95	7.00	9.00	14	49	145	400	760	4400	38000

EDMUND'S 1996 U.S. COIN PRICES

DIMES

VARIETY TWO - RESUMED
1856-1860

DATE	MINTAGE	G-4	VG-8	F-12	VF-20	EF-40	AU-50	MS-60	MS-63	MS-65	PRF-65
1856 Sm. Date	5,780,000	6.00	7.15	9.50	14	34	115	238	903	7050	38000
1856 Lg. Date	Inc. Above	8.25	10	14	23	58	168	375	975	—	—
1856 O	1,180,000	6.90	9.00	14	25	73	205	550	1600	—	—
1856 S	70,000	105	155	238	425	888	1700	3250	7750	—	—
1857	5,580,000	6.00	6.90	8.90	12	32	95	245	565	2500	4000
1857 O	1,540,000	6.75	8.40	12	23	60	175	320	905	—	—
1858	1,540,000	5.95	6.65	8.90	15	36	103	243	568	2500	4000
1858 O	290,000	14	20	35	66	138	313	743	1400	—	—
1858 S	60,000	78	125	173	283	563	1150	2225	4500	—	—
1859	430,000	6.40	7.75	11	23	53	143	340	958	7000	4000
1859 O	480,000	7.40	11	17	29	73	205	433	1000	2800	—
1859 S	60,000	93	138	238	388	875	1825	—	—	—	—
1860 S	140,000	27	34	47	108	275	750	2150	—	7000	—

VARIETY FOUR - LEGEND ON OBVERSE
1860-1873

DIAMETER: 17.9mm
WEIGHT: 2.49 Grams
COMPOSITION: .900 Silver, .100 Copper
DESIGNER: Christian Gobrecht
EDGE: Reeded

DATE	MINTAGE	G-4	VG-8	F-12	VF-20	EF-40	AU-50	MS-60	MS-63	MS-65	PRF-65
1860	607,000	7.95	12	17	26	41	77	180	590	—	1400
1860 O	40,000	300	475	775	1350	2625	4725	8000	—	—	—
1861	1,884,000	5.75	7.75	11	14	32	65	138	335	—	1400
1861 S	172,500	46	74	123	225	363	800	1700	—	—	—
1862	847,550	5.90	8.00	11	15	36	65	178	400	—	1400
1862 S	180,750	33	50	86	163	308	730	1600	2850	—	—
1863	14,460	235	363	463	583	700	813	1138	1825	—	1400
1863 S	157,500	28	33	50	89	185	413	1375	2550	—	—
1864	11,470	218	313	400	488	600	738	1325	1400	2750	1400
1864 S	230,000	21	28	39	80	153	358	1238	2150	1800	—
1865	10,500	238	355	455	555	660	938	1150	1500	—	1400
1865 S	175,000	23	30	49	89	218	688	2250	—	—	—
1866	8,725	255	375	538	663	800	1075	1500	1875	3300	1750
1866 CC Double Obv.	Inc. Above	15	25	40	125	250	400	700	800	110000	—
1866 S	135,000	31	42	66	116	238	513	1700	—	—	—

EDMUND'S 1996 U.S. COIN PRICES

DIMES

DATE	MINTAGE	G-4	VG-8	F-12	VF-20	EF-40	AU-50	MS-60	MS-63	MS-65	PRF-65
1867	6,625	325	463	638	788	950	1263	1575	1675	—	1750
1867 S	140,000	31	38	63	95	198	438	1700	—	—	—
1868	464,600	9.50	12	20	32	65	155	325	775	—	1400
1868 S	260,000	13	19	28	58	113	248	633	—	—	—
1869	256,600	13	18	29	54	110	203	593	1200	5500	1400
1869 S	450,000	11	13	19	39	80	148	425	1088	—	—
1870	71,500	7.90	9.00	13	27	60	130	263	500	—	1400
1870 S	50,000	203	278	363	450	580	900	1950	2950	5500	—
1871	907,710	6.75	7.90	9.65	18	39	130	305	800	—	1400
1871 CC	20,100	800	1063	1375	2400	4250	6875	12500	—	—	—
1871 S	320,000	14	20	31	71	135	350	793	1500	—	—
1872	2,396,450	6.00	7.25	8.90	15	32	93	168	315	—	1400
1872 CC	35,480	350	538	800	1325	2600	5000	23500	—	—	—
1872 S	190,000	25	40	71	123	220	438	1188	2500	—	—
1873 Closed 3	1,568,600	8.00	11	15	24	45	94	190	360	—	1400
1873 Open 3	Inc. Above	15	21	35	54	103	218	625	—	—	—
1873 CC	12,400	Only one specimen known, sold May 1996 $550,000									

VARIETY FIVE - ARROWS AT DATE
1873-1874

DIAMETER: 17.9mm
WEIGHT: 2.50 Grams
COMPOSITION: .900 Silver, .100 Copper
DESIGNER: Christian Gobrecht
EDGE: Reeded

DATE	MINTAGE	G-4	VG-8	F-12	VF-20	EF-40	AU-50	MS-60	MS-63	MS-65	PRF-65
1873	2,378,500	7.75	12	23	46	145	308	468	1000	4500	5000
1873 CC	18,791	638	863	1488	3150	4800	8250	22500	50000	—	—
1873 S	455,000	11	16	23	60	165	310	1100	2300	—	—
1874	2,940,700	7.50	12	20	46	145	298	470	1050	4500	5000
1874 CC	10,817	1700	2675	4125	6125	11250	19000	35000	—	—	—
1874 S	240,000	18	31	53	103	240	450	1163	2150	—	—

DIMES

VARIETY FOUR - RESUMED
1875-1891

DATE	MINTAGE	G-4	VG-8	F-12	VF-20	EF-40	AU-50	MS-60	MS-63	MS-65	PRF-65
1875	10,350,700	5.65	6.50	8.25	11	24	60	128	290	2250	4600
1875 CC Above Bow	4,645,000	6.50	8.75	15	24	48	108	218	750	2700	—
1875 CC Below Bow	Inc. Above	6.50	8.40	13	22	42	118	228	375	3000	—
1875 S Above Bow	9,070,000	6.75	9.00	12	18	33	93	185	200	3100	—
1875 S Below Bow	Inc. Above	5.65	6.40	7.90	11	21	60	128	200	1100	—
1876	11,461,150	5.65	6.40	7.90	11	22	59	120	193	1100	1250
1876 CC	8,270,000	5.75	6.65	8.25	11	24	49	130	273	200	110000
1876 CC Doubled Obv.	Inc. Above	15	25	40	125	250	400	700	750	800	110000
1876 S	10,420,000	5.90	6.90	11	18	35	60	128	203	1100	—
1877	7,310,510	5.65	6.40	8.00	12	21	59	118	203	1100	12.50
1877 CC	7,700,000	5.75	6.90	8.50	15	28	70	173	220	1900	—
1877 S	2,340,000	7.00	7.90	10	17	34	74	140	200	—	—
1878	1,678,800	5.75	6.90	10	17	27	59	148	270	1100	1250
1878 CC	200,000	43	59	95	153	245	458	750	2800	3900	—
1879	15,100	158	190	233	268	333	383	548	690	4300	4400
1880	37,335	105	140	173	215	248	325	453	700	4300	4400
1881	24,975	118	153	183	240	318	393	568	685	4300	4400
1882	3,911,100	5.65	6.40	8.00	12	21	58	118	195	1100	1200
1883	7,675,712	5.65	6.40	8.00	12	22	58	118	195	1100	1250
1884	3,366,380	5.65	6.40	8.00	12	21	58	118	195	1100	1250
1884 S	564,969	14	18	27	38	81	200	525	2175	—	—
1885	2,533,427	5.65	6.40	8.00	12	21	58	118	200	1100	1250
1885 S	43,690	343	463	725	1325	1875	3175	5250	14000	—	—
1886	6,377,570	5.65	6.40	7.75	11	21	58	118	195	1100	1250
1886 S	206,524	35	44	60	90	130	225	583	1100	—	—
1887	11,283,939	5.65	6.40	7.75	11	21	58	118	195	1100	1250
1887 S	4,454,450	5.65	6.40	7.90	12	21	59	120	270	1100	—
1888	5,496,487	5.65	6.40	7.75	11	21	58	118	198	1100	1250
1888 S	1,720,000	5.80	6.60	8.75	13	34	90	218	418	—	—
1889	7,380,711	5.65	6.40	7.75	11	21	58	118	195	1100	1250
1889 S	972,678	8.50	12	23	38	70	180	470	950	4500	—
1890	9,911,541	5.65	6.40	7.90	11	21	58	118	195	1100	1250
1890 S	1,423,076	9.75	13	22	36	65	143	343	650	4900	—
1891	15,310,600	5.65	6.40	7.75	11	21	58	118	195	1100	1250
1891 O	4,540,000	5.75	6.65	8.25	12	24	65	310	290	2250	—
1891 O/Horz. O	Inc. Above	100	120	150	225	275	400	—	—	—	—
1891 S	5,196,116	5.65	6.50	8.15	12	29	70	328	350	4400	—

EDMUND'S 1996 U.S. COIN PRICES

DIMES

BARBER TYPE
1892-1916

DIAMETER: 17.9mm
WEIGHT: 2.50 Grams
COMPOSITION: .900 Silver, .100 Copper
DESIGNER: Charles E. Barber
EDGE: Reeded
PURE SILVER CONTENT: .07234 Tr. Oz.

The Barber dime series went into production in 1892 and ran through 1916, in conjunction with a matching design on the front side of the quarter and half dollar. There is a wide spectrum of exciting opportunities awaiting Barber dime buyers, regardless of whether you have a little or a lot to spend.

A good profit opportunity exists in MS-65 and PR-65, whose trends are down an incredible 85% from those seen during the 1988-1989 explosion. Even pieces of stunning quality, such as PR-66+, once commanding price tags approaching $10,000, can be obtained for under $2000. All of them are bona fide rarities.

Better date Barber dimes, such as the 1895 and 1901-S, have maintained a contrarian status over the last couple of years, performing superbly in a generally depressed environment. This is true in grades as low as Fine, pointing squarely to collector resurgence.

DATE	MINTAGE	G-4	VG-8	F-12	VF-20	EF-40	AU-50	MS-60	MS-63	MS-65	PRF-65
1892	12,121,245	2.80	4.95	14	18	24	55	105	173	700	1450
1892 O	3,841,700	5.40	9.75	24	32	37	62	150	315	1200	—
1892 S	990,710	33	61	135	170	190	213	348	875	3600	—
1893	3,340,792	5.40	9.75	15	22	37	59	135	195	630	1450
1893 O	1,760,000	16	28	95	113	130	145	255	498	3600	—
1893 S	2,491,401	6.90	15	22	35	46	118	230	618	2400	—
1894	1,330,972	8.50	19	84	104	123	145	270	488	1175	1450
1894 O	720,000	34	70	168	210	283	588	1198	2475	8300	—
1894 S	24	40000	—	—	—	—	—	65000	95000	—	275000
1895	690,880	58	94	293	385	433	500	598	1063	2400	2000
1895 O	440,000	173	300	675	988	1738	2250	2725	4813	10000	—
1895 S	1,120,000	20	32	98	140	168	228	420	1088	6200	—
1896	2,000,762	7.00	17	37	54	68	100	158	370	1560	1450
1896 O	610,000	43	80	220	278	375	525	775	1875	6000	—
1896 S	575,056	42	68	193	250	338	418	618	1325	3600	—
1897	10,869,264	2.35	2.95	5.30	8.75	22	59	110	163	700	1450
1897 O	666,000	37	66	220	280	358	498	725	1415	5400	—
1897 S	1,342,844	8.50	20	66	83	105	193	355	968	4800	—
1898	16,320,735	1.55	1.80	5.40	9.00	20	50	98	155	700	1450
1898 O	2,130,000	4.75	13	72	92	131	195	438	1150	4300	—
1898 S	1,702,507	4.10	9.50	20	32	43	113	305	975	5300	—

EDMUND'S 1996 U.S. COIN PRICES

DIMES

DATE	MINTAGE	G-4	VG-8	F-12	VF-20	EF-40	AU-50	MS-60	MS-63	MS-65	PRF-65
1899	19,580,846	1.65	1.80	5.20	8.15	20	54	98	155	700	1450
1899 O	2,650,000	4.25	9.00	58	79	125	208	418	1075	5750	—
1899 S	1,867,493	4.25	8.90	14	20	34	84	293	650	3500	—
1900	17,600,912	1.70	2.25	5.25	8.00	20	46	98	155	900	1450
1900 O	2,010,000	6.65	14	79	103	190	343	688	1275	6000	—
1900 S	5,168,270	2.75	3.95	8.65	12	24	71	163	445	1920	—
1901	18,680,478	1.65	1.80	4.90	7.65	20	45	98	160	1170	1450
1901 O	5,620,000	2.70	3.75	12	19	46	115	355	923	2900	—
1901 S	593,022	38	60	235	318	415	593	850	1725	4750	—
1902	21,380,777	1.65	1.85	4.20	7.15	21	45	98	155	700	1450
1902 O	4,500,000	2.70	4.50	13	21	44	118	375	838	3350	—
1902 S	2,070,000	4.50	8.90	42	58	76	150	333	763	4080	—
1903	19,500,755	1.65	1.80	4.20	7.35	20	45	98	173	1100	1450
1903 O	8,180,000	2.15	3.15	8.75	14	26	87	240	568	5050	—
1903 S	613,300	32	60	303	438	718	788	1075	1675	4550	—
1904	14,601,027	1.65	2.10	5.15	8.50	20	46	110	158	2700	1450
1904 S	800,000	21	37	108	195	323	480	1025	3075	—	—
1905	14,552,350	1.65	1.80	4.20	7.00	20	53	98	155	700	1450
1905 O	3,400,000	2.65	5.25	28	38	50	115	228	430	2900	—
1905 S	6,855,199	2.30	4.00	7.40	16	32	75	195	383	1150	—
1906	19,958,406	1.55	1.70	3.50	6.50	20	45	98	155	700	1450
1906 D	4,060,000	2.55	3.75	8.00	13	26	74	143	305	2200	—
1906 O	2,610,000	4.15	8.50	41	60	73	133	205	338	1250	—
1906 S	3,136,640	2.45	4.65	12	19	37	96	228	428	1350	—
1907	22,220,575	1.55	1.75	3.40	6.50	20	46	98	155	700	1450
1907 D	4,080,000	2.35	3.55	8.50	13	34	85	240	620	4150	—
1907 O	5,058,000	1.85	3.30	29	40	48	77	205	338	1625	—
1907 S	3,178,470	2.40	4.10	8.25	15	37	95	313	555	3100	—
1908	10,600,545	1.60	1.75	3.25	42	20	45	98	155	700	1450
1908 D	7,490,000	1.70	2.40	5.75	9.25	26	56	133	223	1550	—
1908 O	1,789,000	3.05	7.25	40	56	71	130	265	618	2275	—
1908 S	3,220,000	2.35	4.05	8.75	14	28	89	250	620	2300	—
1909	10,240,650	1.70	2.05	3.25	6.50	20	45	98	160	700	1700
1909 D	954,000	4.20	8.40	57	77	106	193	433	1105	2750	—
1909 O	2,287,000	2.35	4.20	8.40	17	30	87	175	455	1400	—
1909 S	1,000,000	4.20	9.75	74	98	140	278	498	1088	3600	—
1910	11,520,551	1.60	2.05	6.75	10	21	46	98	155	700	1450
1910 D	3,490,000	2.35	4.15	7.75	14	35	87	190	440	2400	—
1910 S	1,240,000	2.80	6.50	47	62	80	163	318	603	1975	—
1911	18,870,543	1.40	1.70	3.25	6.50	20	45	98	155	700	1700
1911 D	11,209,000	1.40	1.70	3.95	7.50	21	49	105	163	700	—
1911 S	3,520,000	1.85	3.15	7.50	14	29	84	148	255	840	—
1912	19,350,000	1.40	1.70	3.25	6.65	20	46	98	155	700	1450
1912 D	11,760,000	1.40	1.70	4.10	7.40	21	49	103	160	850	—
1912 S	3,420,000	1.50	2.40	6.15	10	25	71	163	288	1200	—
1913	19,760,622	1.40	1.70	3.15	6.50	20	46	98	155	700	1450

EDMUND'S 1996 U.S. COIN PRICES

DIMES

DATE	MINTAGE	G-4	VG-8	F-12	VF-20	EF-40	AU-50	MS-60	MS-63	MS-65	PRF-65
1913 S	510,000	7.50	14	65	105	173	270	368	525	13253	—
1914	17,360,655	1.40	1.80	3.25	6.50	20	46	98	155	700	1700
1914 D	11,908,000	1.40	1.70	4.00	6.90	21	49	100	163	700	—
1914 S	2,100,000	2.00	2.65	6.00	12	28	76	148	305	1200	—
1915	5,620,450	1.40	1.70	3.85	7.50	21	46	98	158	850	2000
1915 S	960,000	2.15	4.75	25	40	49	130	243	463	2300	—
1916	18,490,000	1.40	1.80	4.50	6.90	21	47	98	155	700	—
1916 S	5,820,000	1.50	2.05	5.65	7.15	21	49	103	165	780	—

MERCURY TYPE
1916-1945

DIAMETER: 17.9mm
WEIGHT: 2.50 Grams
COMPOSITION: .900 Silver, .100 Copper
DESIGNER: Adolph A. Weinman
EDGE: Reeded
PURE SILVER CONTENT: .07234 Tr. Oz.

One of the most popular collector coins has been the Mercury dime. To assemble a complete set a collector must locate pieces dating from 1916 to 1945. In reality, the woman figure on the coin's obverse is a rendition of Miss Liberty, with wings crowning her cap to symbolize freedom of thought. The American public incorrectly saw Miss Liberty and her wings as the Greek god Mercury, hence the dime became regularly known as the "Mercury" dime.

In the latter part of the 1980's the series stagnated, with values of MS-60 and below plunging dramatically. Those same coins have rebounded nicely in the 1990's, but it is still not too late to add them to your collection at bargain prices. It would be to your advantage to land as many MS-65's as possible, since many of them are seriously undervalued and have fantastic investment potential.

For only a few hundred dollars, you can obtain proof Mercury dimes. Doing so may be a challenge, as they were produced from 1936 to 1942, in relatively small quantities (less than 80,000 total). Indeed, these are scarce "type" coins, but they are not priced as such. Just five years ago, these numismatic classics were retailing for about $1500 in PR-66.

The undisputed key Mercury is the 1916-D. Aside from concern over purchasing an altered coin, don't worry about losing ground with a 1916-D Mercury. It will be in demand from collectors for a very long time to come.

Well struck Mercury dimes sometimes have a distinct separation of the horizontal bands on the fasces design on the reverse, described as "Full Split Bands" (abbreviated FSB). Prices for FSB Uncirculated dimes are routinely listed beside normal Uncirculated dimes and always carry a

DIMES

premium. Buy FSB Mercury dimes if the premium to be paid isn't too far above the value of similar quality Uncirculated dimes without the FSB. Be sure the bands are not only clearly separated, but are also fully raised and rounded. Many beginners mistake flattened split bands for truly full split bands, which may be a costly error.

DATE	MINTAGE	VG-8	F-12	VF-20	EF-40	AU-50	MS-60	MS-63	MS-65	MS-67	FSB-65	PRF-65
1916	22,180,080	3.00	4.50	6.65	10	18	26	44	49	—	113	—
1916 D	264,000	620	1125	1725	2475	3725	4400	4925	11250	—	14500	—
1916 S	10,450,000	4.25	5.90	9.40	16	21	35	58	273	—	525	—
1917	55,230,000	1.90	2.50	5.00	7.00	13	26	54	145	—	308	—
1917 D	9,402,000	4.90	8.50	17	38	68	125	338	1763	—	6100	—
1917 S	27,330,000	2.20	3.15	5.50	9.25	26	51	163	508	—	1583	—
1918	26,680,000	2.50	5.15	11	24	39	69	108	370	—	663	—
1918 D	22,674,800	2.65	4.15	9.25	21	43	100	273	865	—	11125	—
1918 S	19,300,000	2.45	4.00	6.50	14	29	78	225	950	—	5925	—
1919	35,470,000	2.00	3.15	5.25	8.50	20	32	90	355	—	538	—
1919 D	9,939,000	4.50	6.50	15	35	64	168	438	1650	—	7175	—
1919 S	8,850,000	3.30	5.50	13	29	70	175	433	1050	—	4750	—
1920	59,030,000	1.85	2.65	4.50	6.75	15	26	55	233	—	358	—
1920 D	19,171,000	2.90	3.90	6.25	15	36	95	283	1150	—	3125	—
1920 S	13,820,000	2.55	4.00	6.75	14	31	73	265	1163	—	5438	—
1921	1,230,000	29	68	170	425	763	1063	1325	2600	—	4725	—
1921 D	1,080,000	51	98	210	488	818	1163	1488	2650	—	4950	—
1923	50,130,000	1.90	2.65	3.90	6.50	13	23	38	108	—	210	—
1923 S	6,440,000	2.75	4.65	9.25	36	72	143	353	1500	—	4500	—
1924	24,010,000	1.85	2.65	5.00	9.00	20	34	75	203	—	483	—
1924 D	6,810,000	2.85	5.10	11	37	65	140	313	1238	—	3200	—
1924 S	7,120,000	2.50	3.50	8.50	33	72	128	503	1775	—	6650	—
1925	25,610,000	1.85	2.40	3.90	7.25	18	30	66	218	—	513	—
1925 D	5,117,000	4.75	9.25	27	88	178	280	605	1575	—	5775	—
1925 S	5,850,000	2.40	3.75	7.50	35	91	148	450	2125	—	4375	—
1926	32,160,000	1.65	2.15	3.90	5.65	14	23	45	243	—	568	—
1926 D	6,828,000	2.50	3.75	6.40	16	35	71	193	520	—	2225	—
1926 S	1,520,000	8.00	16	35	183	433	735	1288	2975	—	5100	—
1927	28,080,000	1.60	2.15	3.90	5.50	12	19	41	178	—	325	—
1927 D	4,812,000	3.75	5.00	12	40	91	195	445	1275	—	5350	—
1927 S	4,770,000	2.25	3.15	5.50	13	39	113	328	1013	—	4700	—
1928	19,480,000	1.60	2.15	3.90	5.75	14	21	44	128	—	245	—
1928 D	4,161,000	4.00	5.75	16	35	78	130	293	855	—	2525	—
1928 S	7,400,000	2.20	2.90	4.50	13	29	69	175	465	—	1500	—
1929	25,970,000	1.55	2.20	3.50	4.75	9.25	18	28	58	—	183	—
1929 D	5,034,000	3.05	4.50	7.50	12	21	28	35	83	—	128	—
1929 S	4,730,000	1.70	2.15	3.90	5.25	16	36	45	135	—	325	—
1930	6,770,000	1.60	2.20	3.75	5.40	14	22	43	145	—	270	—
1930 S	1,843,000	3.25	4.25	6.25	12	39	68	84	150	—	255	—
1931	3,150,000	2.40	3.00	4.50	10	20	35	54	153	—	450	—

DIMES

DATE	MINTAGE	VG-8	F-12	VF-20	EF-40	AU-50	MS-60	MS-63	MS-65	MS-67	FSB-65	PRF-65
1931 D	1,260,000	6.25	9.90	16	30	50	72	100	198	—	265	—
1931 S	1,800,000	3.15	4.25	6.25	12	36	64	86	205	—	1425	—
1934	24,080,000	1.05	1.50	2.65	4.50	8.50	15	18	29	—	44	—
1934 D	6,772,000	1.80	2.65	4.50	9.25	19	29	39	69	—	233	—
1935	58,830,000	0.90	1.25	1.75	3.25	6.00	10	15	26	—	34	—
1935 D	10,477,000	1.65	2.75	4.75	9.40	19	31	37	58	—	318	—
1935 S	15,840,000	1.25	1.55	2.45	4.40	12	23	25	35	—	153	—
1936	87,504,130	0.95	1.25	1.80	2.75	4.90	8.25	15	24	—	34	875
1936 D	16,132,000	1.30	1.75	3.00	6.40	14	21	25	38	—	105	—
1936 S	9,210,000	1.30	1.55	2.40	4.00	8.00	17	19	28	—	37	—
1937	56,865,756	0.95	1.25	1.70	2.55	4.75	9.50	14	24	—	35	300
1937 D	14,146,000	1.30	1.65	2.50	4.40	8.25	20	22	35	—	51	—
1937 S	9,740,000	1.30	1.65	2.50	4.40	7.25	17	22	30	—	92	—
1938	22,198,728	0.95	1.25	1.80	2.95	5.25	12	15	22	—	33	215
1938 D	5,537,000	1.65	1.95	3.15	5.50	9.75	15	18	27	—	38	—
1938 S	8,090,000	1.35	1.60	2.10	3.40	7.25	15	19	29	—	49	—
1939	67,749,321	0.95	1.25	1.65	2.50	4.25	9.00	13	23	—	69	210
1939 D	29,394,000	1.20	1.50	1.90	2.75	5.00	11	14	23	—	33	—
1939 S	10,540,000	1.50	1.90	2.40	4.15	8.75	22	25	35	—	370	—
1940	65,361,827	0.75	0.95	1.10	2.15	3.90	6.25	9.00	21	—	30	185
1940 D	21,198,000	0.75	1.00	1.20	2.00	6.00	7.75	13	23	—	33	—
1940 S	21,560,000	0.75	1.00	1.20	1.70	4.40	7.90	12	23	—	38	—
1941	175,106,557	0.75	0.95	1.10	1.50	3.25	5.50	9.00	19	—	24	160
1941 D	45,634,000	0.75	1.00	1.20	1.70	6.00	7.50	12	22	—	25	—
1941 S	43,090,000	0.75	1.00	1.20	1.70	4.00	9.50	13	21	—	31	—
1942	205,432,329	0.75	0.95	1.10	1.50	3.25	5.25	9.00	19	36	25	160
1942/41 D	Unknown	185	250	375	525	975	1750	2850	5750	—	—	8500
1942/41	Unknown	175	225	250	318	445	1550	3175	6550	9675	—	—
1942 D	60,740,000	0.75	1.00	1.20	1.70	4.00	7.75	13	23	—	30	—
1942 S	49,300,000	0.75	1.00	1.25	1.75	4.00	9.50	14	23	—	48	—
1943	191,710,000	0.75	0.95	1.10	1.50	3.40	6.00	9.00	18	—	24	—
1943 D	7,194,900	0.75	1.00	1.20	1.70	3.75	7.75	12	23	—	28	—
1943 S	60,400,000	0.75	1.00	1.20	1.70	4.40	9.50	13	21	—	33	—
1944	231,410,000	0.75	0.95	1.05	1.40	3.25	5.25	12	19	—	57	—
1944 D	62,224,000	0.75	1.00	1.20	1.70	3.75	7.75	13	21	—	28	—
1944 S	49,490,000	0.75	1.00	1.20	1.70	3.65	8.75	13	22	—	32	—
1945	159,130,000	0.75	0.95	1.05	1.40	3.40	5.50	9.00	22	—	3563	—
1945 D	40,245,000	0.75	1.00	1.20	1.70	4.25	7.50	10	21	—	29	—
1945 S	41,920,000	0.75	1.00	1.20	1.75	3.75	7.75	13	20	—	52	—
1945 S Micro S	Inc. Above	1.60	1.95	3.00	4.65	11	18	26	59	—	418	—

EDMUND'S 1996 U.S. COIN PRICES

DIMES

ROOSEVELT TYPE
1946-DATE

DIAMETER: 17.9mm
WEIGHT: 1946-1964: 2.50 Grams
1965 To Date: 2.27 Grams
COMPOSITION:
1946-1964: .900 Silver, .100 Copper
1965 To Date: Copper Clad Issue
.750 Copper, .250 Nickel Outer Layers
Pure Copper Inner Core
DESIGNER: John R. Sinnock
EDGE: Reeded
PURE SILVER CONTENT:
1946-1964: .07234 Tr. Oz.

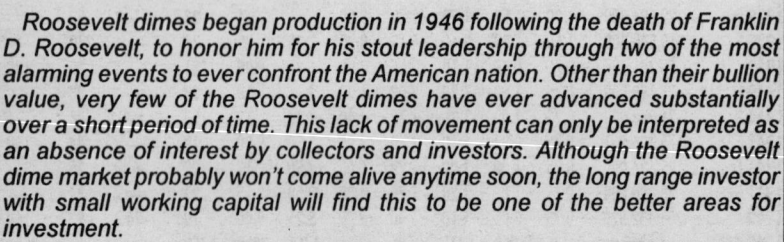

Roosevelt dimes began production in 1946 following the death of Franklin D. Roosevelt, to honor him for his stout leadership through two of the most alarming events to ever confront the American nation. Other than their bullion value, very few of the Roosevelt dimes have ever advanced substantially over a short period of time. This lack of movement can only be interpreted as an absence of interest by collectors and investors. Although the Roosevelt dime market probably won't come alive anytime soon, the long range investor with small working capital will find this to be one of the better areas for investment.

Even in the uppermost grades, Roosevelt dimes are easily affordable. Purchase a complete set of Roosevelt dimes, including proofs, in nothing less than MS-60 condition, although MS-65 coins have greater potential. With such a minor price difference, you really shouldn't pass up the MS-65 dimes, as there could be a much greater gap between the two grades in ten years or so, which is the route so many other series have gone in the past. Buy them now and put them away for long term growth.

DATE	MINTAGE	VG-8	F-12	VF-20	EF-40	AU-50	MS-60	MS-63	MS-65	PRF-65
1946	225,250,000	0.40	0.50	0.65	0.70	0.80	0.70	1.20	3.65	—
1946 D	61,043,500	0.40	0.55	0.65	0.75	0.90	0.80	1.30	5.75	—
1946 S	27,900,000	0.40	0.55	0.65	1.00	1.30	1.85	2.65	7.90	—
1947	121,520,000	0.40	0.55	0.65	0.80	0.95	1.25	1.35	4.65	—
1947 D	46,835,000	0.50	0.65	0.70	1.15	1.50	1.90	2.20	11	—
1947 S	34,840,000	0.55	0.70	0.75	0.95	1.20	2.00	2.25	9.25	—
1948	74,950,000	0.40	0.55	0.65	0.95	1.35	3.00	5.00	13	—
1948 D	52,841,000	0.50	0.65	0.70	1.30	1.75	2.50	3.75	10	—
1948 S	35,520,000	0.40	0.55	0.60	0.95	1.20	1.90	2.50	11	—

DIMES

DATE	MINTAGE	VG-8	F-12	VF-20	EF-40	AU-50	MS-60	MS-63	MS-65	PRF-65
1949	30,940,000	1.00	1.25	1.40	1.90	4.25	9.00	12	26	—
1949 D	26,034,000	0.45	0.65	0.85	1.45	2.65	4.25	5.25	13	—
1949 S	13,510,000	0.90	1.40	1.90	3.15	6.90	14	17	49	—
1950	50,181,500	0.40	0.55	0.75	1.10	1.25	1.70	2.10	6.30	25
1950 D	46,803,000	0.40	0.55	0.70	0.85	1.00	1.25	2.05	6.30	—
1950 S	20,440,000	0.95	1.20	1.45	2.05	5.50	9.00	10	29	—
1951	102,937,602	0.40	0.55	0.65	0.80	0.90	0.85	1.30	3.55	23
1951 D	565,229,000	0.40	0.55	0.60	0.80	0.90	1.15	1.35	3.75	—
1951 S	31,630,000	0.60	1.00	1.10	1.40	3.15	4.75	6.50	19	—
1952	99,122,073	0.40	0.55	0.65	0.90	1.00	1.20	1.65	3.65	23
1952 D	122,100,000	0.40	0.55	0.65	0.80	0.90	0.90	1.25	4.05	—
1952 S	44,419,500	0.55	1.00	1.05	1.15	1.30	1.95	4.50	10	—
1953	53,618,920	0.40	0.50	0.60	0.90	1.00	1.05	1.45	3.95	21
1953 D	136,433,000	0.40	0.50	0.65	0.75	0.85	0.75	1.15	3.65	—
1953 S	39,180,000	0.40	0.45	0.60	0.75	0.85	0.65	1.15	2.80	—
1954	114,243,503	0.40	0.50	0.60	0.70	0.80	0.90	1.50	3.35	9.50
1954 D	106,397,000	0.40	0.50	0.60	0.75	0.80	0.70	1.05	2.70	—
1954 S	22,860,000	0.45	0.50	0.60	0.70	0.70	0.65	0.95	2.70	—
1955	12,828,381	0.60	0.65	0.70	0.80	0.85	0.85	1.05	4.00	8.00
1955 D	13,959,000	0.50	0.55	0.65	0.70	0.75	0.73	0.95	2.85	—
1955 S	18,510,000	0.50	0.55	0.65	0.70	0.75	0.73	0.90	3.40	—
1956	109,309,384	0.40	0.50	0.60	0.70	0.75	0.73	0.95	2.45	3.00
1956 D	108,015,100	0.40	0.50	0.60	0.70	0.75	0.73	1.00	2.25	—
1957	101,407,952	0.40	0.50	0.60	0.70	0.75	0.73	0.95	2.25	2.25
1957 D	113,354,330	0.40	0.50	0.60	0.70	0.75	0.75	1.10	3.45	—
1958	32,785,652	0.45	0.55	0.65	0.70	0.75	0.68	0.95	2.90	2.75
1958 D	136,564,600	0.40	0.50	0.60	0.70	0.75	0.68	0.95	2.65	—
1959	86,929,291	0.40	0.50	0.60	0.70	0.75	0.68	0.95	2.05	1.75
1959 D	164,919,790	0.40	0.50	0.60	0.70	0.75	0.68	0.95	2.20	—
1960	72,081,602	0.40	0.45	0.55	0.65	0.75	0.68	0.85	2.00	1.45
1960 D	200,160,400	0.40	0.45	0.55	0.65	0.75	0.68	0.85	1.95	—
1961	96,758,244	0.40	0.45	0.55	0.65	0.75	0.68	0.90	1.85	1.30
1961 D	209,146,550	0.40	0.45	0.55	0.65	0.75	0.68	0.85	1.85	—
1962	75,668,019	0.40	0.45	0.55	0.65	0.75	0.68	0.85	1.85	1.30
1962 D	334,948,380	0.40	0.45	0.55	0.65	0.75	0.68	0.90	2.05	—
1963	126,725,645	0.40	0.45	0.55	0.65	0.75	0.68	0.85	1.80	1.25
1963 D	421,476,530	0.40	0.45	0.55	0.65	0.75	0.68	0.85	1.80	—
1964	933,310,762	0.40	0.45	0.55	0.65	0.75	0.68	0.85	1.80	1.25
1964 D	1,357,517,180	0.40	0.45	0.55	0.65	0.75	0.68	0.85	1.80	—

DIMES

COPPER-NICKEL CLAD COINAGE

DATE	MINTAGE	MS-60	MS-63	MS-65	PRF-65
1965	1,652,140,570	0.23	—	0.55	—
1966	1,382,734,540	—	—	0.50	—
1967	2,244,007,320	0.23	—	0.50	—
1968	424,470,000	0.23	—	0.50	—
1968 D	480,748,280	0.23	—	0.50	—
1968 S	PROOF ONLY	—	—	—	0.70
1969	145,790,000	0.35	—	0.90	—
1969 D	563,323,870	0.25	—	0.55	—
1969 S	PROOF ONLY	—	—	—	0.70
1970	345,570,000	0.23	—	0.50	—
1970 D	754,942,100	0.23	—	0.50	—
1970 S	PROOF ONLY	—	—	—	33
1971	162,690,000	0.27	—	0.55	—
1971 D	377,914,240	0.23	—	0.45	—
1971 S	PROOF ONLY	—	—	—	40
1972	431,540,000	0.27	—	0.50	—
1972 D	330,290,000	0.25	—	0.50	—
1972 S	PROOF ONLY	—	—	—	0.90
1973	315,670,000	0.23	—	0.45	—
1973 D	455,032,426	0.23	—	0.45	—
1973 S	PROOF ONLY	—	—	—	0.65
1974	470,248,000	0.23	—	0.45	—
1974 D	571,083,000	0.23	—	0.45	—
1974 S	PROOF ONLY	—	—	—	0.75
1975	585,673,900	0.25	—	0.50	—
1975 D	313,705,300	0.25	—	0.45	—
1975 S	PROOF ONLY	—	—	—	0.80
1976	568,760,000	0.25	—	0.60	—
1976 D	695,222,774	0.25	—	0.60	—
1976 S	PROOF ONLY	—	—	—	0.75
1977	796,930,000	0.20	—	0.45	—
1977 D	376,607,228	0.21	—	0.50	—
1977 S	PROOF ONLY	—	—	—	0.65
1978	663,980,000	0.20	—	0.45	—
1978 D	282,847,540	0.21	—	0.45	—
1978 S	PROOF ONLY	—	—	—	30
1979	315,440,000	0.20	—	0.45	—
1979 D	390,921,184	0.20	—	0.45	—
1979 S	PROOF ONLY	—	—	—	0.65
1980 D	719,354,321	0.20	—	0.35	—
1980 P	735,170,000	0.20	—	0.35	—
1980 S	PROOF ONLY	—	—	—	0.65
1981 D	712,284,143	0.20	—	0.35	—
1981 P	676,650,000	0.20	—	0.35	—

DIMES

DATE	MINTAGE	MS-60	MS-63	MS-65	PRF-65
1981 S	PROOF ONLY	—	—	—	0.75
1982 D	542,713,584	0.30	—	0.30	—
1982 P	519,475,000	0.85	—	1.50	—
1982 S	PROOF ONLY	—	—	—	0.85
1983 D	730,129,224	0.28	—	0.70	—
1983 P	647,025,000	0.30	—	0.75	—
1983 S	PROOF ONLY	—	—	—	1.20
1984 D	704,803,976	0.20	—	0.35	—
1984 P	856,669,000	0.20	—	0.25	—
1984 S	PROOF ONLY	—	—	—	1.55
1985 D	587,979,970	0.20	—	0.30	—
1985 P	705,200,962	0.21	—	0.35	—
1985 S	PROOF ONLY	—	—	—	1.05
1986 D	473,329,970	0.20	—	0.50	—
1986 P	682,649,693	0.20	0.75	0.45	—
1986 S	PROOF ONLY	—	—	—	2.00
1987 D	653,203,402	0.20	—	0.20	—
1987 P	762,709,481	0.20	—	0.20	—
1987 S	PROOF ONLY	—	—	—	1.40
1988 D	962,385,489	0.20	—	0.20	—
1988 P	1,030,550,000	0.20	—	0.20	—
1988 S	PROOF ONLY	—	—	—	1.65
1989 D	896,535,597	0.20	—	0.20	—
1989 P	1,298,400,000	0.20	—	0.20	—
1989 S	PROOF ONLY	—	—	—	1.35
1990 D	839,995,824	0.20	—	0.20	—
1990 P	1,034,340,000	0.20	—	0.20	—
1990 S	PROOF ONLY	—	—	—	2.65
1991 D	601,241,114	0.20	—	0.20	—
1991 P	927,220,000	0.20	—	0.20	—
1991 S	PROOF ONLY	—	—	—	3.15
1992 D	616,273,932	0.20	—	0.20	—
1992 P	593,500,000	0.20	—	0.20	—
1992 S	PROOF ONLY	—	—	—	2.55
1993 D	750,110,166	0.20	—	0.20	—
1993 P	766,180,000	0.20	—	0.20	—
1993 S		—	—	—	—
1994 D		0.20	—	—	—
1994 P		0.20	—	0.20	—
1994 S	PROOF ONLY	—	—	—	3.25
1994 S Silver Proof		—	—	—	—
1995 D		0.20	—	0.35	—
1995 P		0.20	—	0.35	—
1995 S	PROOF ONLY	—	—	—	—
1995 S Silver Proof		—	—	—	—

EDMUND'S 1996 U.S. COIN PRICES

TWENTY CENT PIECES

TWENTY CENT PIECES 1875-1878

The twenty cent coin is the shortest-lived denomination of all United States coins, being minted for circulation in 1875 and 1876. In 1877 and 1878 production was limited only to Proofs. The series died a premature death because the American people complained it resembled too closely the quarter dollar.

TWENTY CENT PIECES
1875-1878

DIAMETER: 22mm
WEIGHT: 5 Grams
COMPOSITION: .900 Silver
.100 Copper
DESIGNER: William Barber
EDGE: Plain

Investors should choose coins grading Extremely Fine to MS-65. These coins have displayed consistent value growth for much of the past three decades, but at the moment, prices are only at about 70% of what they were just a few years ago. Proof examples formerly costing $20,000 can be purchased for under $10,000. Now is a great time to add one of these oddities to your collection or portfolio.

DATE	MINTAGE	G-4	VG-8	F-12	VF-20	EF-40	AU-50	MS-60	MS-63	MS-65	PRF-65
1875	39,700	45	50	73	99	175	330	600	1050	5125	8250
1875 CC	133,290	50	55	76	118	220	430	715	1475	6700	—
1875 S	1,155,000	45	50	69	94	153	280	463	863	4263	45000
1876	15,900	90	100	133	190	323	483	718	1250	5550	6500
1876 CC	10,000	—	—	—	—	17500	25000	47500	77500	225000	—
1877 Proof only	510	—	—	—	1600	1700	1900	2200	2900	—	8000
1878 Impaired Proof	Inc. Above	—	—	—	1300	1500	1800	1900	2500	—	—
1878 Proof only	600	—	—	—	1300	1500	1800	1900	2500	—	8000

QUARTERS

QUARTER DOLLARS 1796 TO DATE

The quarter dollar has been a part of our coinage system intermittently since 1796. All told, there are thirteen types of quarters to collect.

DRAPED BUST TYPE
SMALL EAGLE REVERSE
1796

DIAMETER: 27.5mm
WEIGHT: 6.74 Grams
COMPOSITION: .8924 Silver
.1076 Copper
DESIGNER: Robert Scot
EDGE: Reeded

The first type of American Quarter is a one-year only design, the 1796 Draped Bust with small eagle. Like so many other American coins of the 18th century, the 1796 quarter has done extremely well as an investment. Should you happen to be an investor geared toward long term growth who has thousands of dollars to spend, this issue may be tailored for you. Since the 1796 quarter in lower grades had been red-hot for almost fifteen years, we have witnessed a cooling-off period in the 1990's similar to that of the late 1960's. However, any owner of a 1796 quarter can expect it to resume its upward climb in the not too distant future.

DATE	MINTAGE	AG-3	G-4	VG-8	F-12	VF-20	EF-40	AU-50	MS-60
1796	6,146	2800	3875	5750	8575	13375	16000	18500	25750

EDMUND'S 1996 U.S. COIN PRICES

QUARTERS

DRAPED BUST TYPE
HERALDIC EAGLE REVERSE
1804-1807

DIAMETER: 27.5mm
WEIGHT: 6.74 Grams
COMPOSITION: .8924 Silver
.1076 Copper
DESIGNER: Robert Scot
EDGE: Reeded

The Draped Bust quarters with the heraldic (large) eagle of 1804 to 1807 have seen some serious price corrections across the board since the middle 1980's. Judging from value trends of the past, one can anticipate a steep rise within the next several years. There may never be a better time than now to purchase these early American quarters.

DATE	MINTAGE	AG-3	G-4	VG-8	F-12	VF-20	EF-40	AU-50	MS-60
1804	6,738	600	930	1313	2125	3750	8125	16000	22000
1805	121,394	125	195	275	413	808	1950	3225	5950
1806	206,124	125	200	263	390	775	1900	3150	4100
1806/05	Inc. Above	135	208	280	418	875	2050	3300	6075
1807	220,643	125	193	270	400	795	1913	3125	4700

QUARTERS

CAPPED BUST TYPE
1815-1838

The Liberty Capped series, minted from 1815 to 1838, presents opportunities for both the collector wanting to acquire nice coins at bargain prices, and to the investor seeking a profit. Prices in grades MS-60 to MS-65 are now only mere shadows of their 1980's glory years. Conceivably, decades could pass before we again see another period of relative weakness associated with this group. What these coins are worth today will pale in comparison to what we'll see in the next few years.

VARIETY ONE - LARGE SIZE
1815-1838

DIAMETER: 27mm
WEIGHT: 6.74 Grams
COMPOSITION: .8924 Silver
             .1076 Copper
DESIGNER: John Reich
EDGE: Reeded

If you think a purchase of this sort fits in with your plans, give some special consideration to the 1822 quarter dollar. Even though it has one of the tiniest mintages of all the Liberty Capped quarters, it is and always has been priced in the same neighborhood as its contemporaries.

DATE	MINTAGE	G-4	VG-8	F-12	VF-20	EF-40	AU-50	MS-60	MS-63	MS-65
1815	89,235	50	73	110	318	768	1513	2200	2200	22000
1818	361,174	40	59	89	263	693	1113	1550	3825	125000
1818/15		56	78	120	313	750	1525	2725	4000	22000
1819 Sm. 9	144,000	48	63	91	270	718	1138	1850	4450	12500
1819 Lg. 9	Inc. Above	48	63	91	270	718	1138	1850	4450	12500
1820 Sm. 0	127,444	50	66	99	283	738	1238	2650	5625	12500
1820 Lg. 0	Inc. Above	45	60	90	258	688	1100	1850	4325	12500
1821	216,851	45	60	90	258	688	1100	1850	3825	12500
1822	64,080	65	93	138	383	913	1475	2175	4450	12500
1822 25/50 C	Inc. Above	2075	3125	4350	5875	8625	12500	20000	—	25000
1823/22	17,800	8375	12250	17750	24750	32000	40000	—	—	—

EDMUND'S 1996 U.S. COIN PRICES

QUARTERS

DATE	MINTAGE	G-4	VG-8	F-12	VF-20	EF-40	AU-50	MS-60	MS-63	MS-65
1824 /22	168,000	85	125	195	550	1313	1975	3900	4400	12500
1825 /22	Inc. Above	143	203	438	950	1400	2075	4075	12500	—
1825 /23	Inc. Above	53	78	178	480	1070	1388	3275	3250	12500
1825 /24	Inc. Above	45	60	90	255	683	1188	2050	3850	12500
1827 Original	4,000	—	—	—	—	—	—	—	—	—
1827 Restrike	Inc. Above	—	—	—	—	—	—	—	—	—
1828	102,000	45	60	88	255	708	1188	2075	3950	12500
1828 25/50 C	Inc. Above	145	240	350	750	1450	2800	5800	6000	—

VARIETY TWO - REDUCED SIZE, NO MOTTO ON REVERSE
1831-1838

DIAMETER: 24.3mm
WEIGHT: 6.74 Grams
COMPOSITION: .8924 Silver
.1076 Copper
DESIGNER: William Kneass
EDGE: Reeded

DATE	MINTAGE	G-4	VG-8	F-12	VF-20	EF-40	AU-50	MS-60	MS-63	MS-65
1831 Sm. Letters	398,000	36	43	54	85	215	600	875	2200	13000
1831 Lg. letters	Inc. Above	45	50	60	90	240	750	900	2450	13000
1832	320,000	36	43	54	85	215	608	933	2425	13000
1833	156,000	39	45	58	94	258	675	1225	2925	17000
1834	286,000	37	43	55	85	220	610	900	2250	13000
1835	1,952,000	36	43	54	85	215	600	875	2250	13000
1836	472,000	36	43	54	85	215	638	1050	2775	13000
1837	252,400	36	43	54	85	215	605	913	2250	13000
1838	832,000	36	43	56	86	218	610	925	2275	13000

QUARTERS

LIBERTY SEATED TYPE
1838-1891

The long-running Liberty Seated pattern was in use from 1838 to 1891. There are so many opportunities here for investors to capitalize upon, that space allows discussion of only a small percentage of the best prospects. We find a steep fall off from prices realized in the 1980's. Today's prices for high grade material would suggest that these are little more than common stuff, but this is not the case. The present situation is merely a temporary aberration certain to correct itself in the not too distant future.

Most of the Liberty Seated quarters in MS-65 and PR-65 are so badly undervalued that they almost cry out for proper consideration, especially the Philadelphia minted quarters of the 1880's. Not only have they dipped in value throughout the 1990's, they are also priced in the ballpark with other Liberty Seated quarters of the identical type in similar conditions, having an original mintage up to 1400 times greater. If that's not enough to grab your attention, take a peek at their appreciation records. At times in the past, quarters of the 1880's were worth much more than what the more common quarters of the 1870's sold for. In short, this equal treatment of these very rare quarters probably will not continue much longer.

VARIETY ONE
NO MOTTO ABOVE EAGLE
1838-1853

DIAMETER: 24.3mm
WEIGHT: 6.68 Grams
COMPOSITION: .900 Silver
.100 Copper
DESIGNER: Christian Gobrecht
EDGE: Reeded

DATE	MINTAGE	G-4	VG-8	F-12	VF-20	EF-40	AU-50	MS-60	MS-63	MS-65
1838 No Drapery	Inc. Above	9.25	15	28	64	230	500	963	10467	—
1839 No Drapery	491,146	9.25	15	27	57	203	473	850	1790	25000
1840	188,127	23	31	48	76	185	350	725	2850	—
1840 O	Inc. Above	9.25	16	28	73	265	488	1075	3525	—
1840 O No Drapery	425,200	9.25	20	35	75	350	600	1100	3750	—
1841	120,000	45	59	84	128	233	435	813	2900	—
1841 O	452,000	14	24	40	70	155	340	738	1850	—
1842 Sm. Date	88,000	—	—	—	—	—	25000	50000	—	—
1842 Lg. Date	Inc. Above	78	106	163	238	400	888	3100	8000	—

EDMUND'S 1996 U.S. COIN PRICES

QUARTERS

DATE	MINTAGE	G-4	VG-8	F-12	VF-20	EF-40	AU-50	MS-60	MS-63	MS-65
1842 O Sm. Date	769,000	393	513	913	1600	3600	9050	16500	—	—
1842 O Lg. Date	Inc. Above	11	17	31	65	165	663	2900	8500	—
1843	645,600	9.40	14	20	38	71	240	505	2238	—
1843 O	968,000	16	27	48	100	218	800	—	—	—
1844	421,200	10	14	20	39	73	185	370	725	3500
1844 O	740,000	12	18	34	59	135	383	1575	4750	—
1845	922,000	8.65	14	23	38	75	210	483	1413	3500
1846	510,000	11	17	30	50	91	218	493	1725	3500
1847	734,000	8.65	12	23	39	70	185	438	1238	8000
1847 O	368,000	21	38	70	104	250	680	1163	3200	7000
1848	146,000	28	40	76	138	210	413	1263	3200	—
1849	340,000	14	22	39	69	123	333	1000	—	—
1849 O	Inc. w/1850 O	368	578	963	1550	3175	6750	—	—	—
1850	190,800	23	40	58	84	158	313	938	2300	—
1850 O	412,000	16	28	44	83	188	543	1450	5000	—
1851	160,000	31	48	78	140	208	358	900	1900	—
1851 O	88,000	163	265	358	595	1175	2625	—	4650	—
1852	177,060	33	44	78	130	193	380	875	1550	—
1852 O	96,000	170	250	350	613	1200	3000	5250	13500	—

VARIETY TWO - ARROWS AT DATE
RAYS AROUND EAGLE
1853

DIAMETER: 24.3mm
WEIGHT: 6.22 Grams
COMPOSITION: .900 Silver
.100 Copper
DESIGNER: Christian Gobrecht
EDGE: Reeded

DATE	MINTAGE	G-4	VG-8	F-12	VF-20	EF-40	AU-50	MS-60	MS-63	MS-65
1853	15,210,020	8.50	13	22	38	158	343	850	2500	17500
1853/54	Inc. Above	35	52.50	145	225	475	1100	2350	6350	—
1853 O	1,332,000	10	21	28	66	238	1475	2400	2900	7500
1853 Recut Date	44,200	223	295	413	613	813	1500	2625	2900	5500

QUARTERS

VARIETY THREE - ARROWS AT DATE, NO RAYS
1854-1855

Variety Three PRF-65 quarters (arrows at date, no rays) are much rarer than generally recognized and possess exciting potential.

DATE	MINTAGE	G-4	VG-8	F-12	VF-20	EF-40	AU-50	MS-60	MS-63	MS-65	PRF-65
1854	12,380,000	8.50	12	21	30	120	255	475	1200	7500	—
1854 O	1,484,000	9.00	15	28	48	130	315	1288	2000	—	—
1854 O Huge O	Inc. Above	90	145	200	350	675	—	—	—	—	—
1855	2,857,000	8.25	12	21	25	68	255	498	1375	7500	17500
1855 O	176,000	31	48	98	250	613	1550	2550	8000	—	—
1855 S	396,400	28	41	65	143	375	1150	1850	4750	—	—

VARIETY ONE RESUMED
1856-1866

DATE	MINTAGE	G-4	VG-8	F-12	VF-20	EF-40	AU-50	MS-60	MS-63	MS-65	PRF-65
1856	7,264,000	8.00	13	21	28	53	138	303	813	3500	15000
1856 O	968,000	11	16	24	43	105	413	1025	2750	—	—
1856 S	286,000	40	59	90	210	453	1038	2750	5000	—	—
1856 S/S	Inc. Above	46	68	140	270	763	1625	—	—	—	—
1857	9,644,000	8.25	13	21	26	49	133	280	568	3000	15000
1857 O	1,180,000	10	14	24	40	78	663	1950	—	—	—
1857 S	82,000	68	108	180	290	510	1063	2900	5500	—	—
1858	7,368,000	8.25	13	21	26	49	155	283	575	3000	11500
1858 O	520,000	11	17	30	49	100	373	1200	5250	—	—
1858 S	121,000	46	73	133	240	550	1775	—	—	—	—
1859	1,344,000	9.40	14	21	28	64	168	553	1500	—	7000
1859 O	260,000	16	24	34	51	100	413	1175	—	—	—
1859 S	80,000	88	120	200	308	963	4875	—	—	—	4000
1860	805,400	8.50	12	21	28	63	145	633	650	11500	—
1860 O	388,000	12	19	36	49	93	263	988	2200	—	—
1860 S	56,000	160	250	400	763	3125	9500	—	—	—	—
1861	4,854,600	8.25	13	21	27	50	155	285	583	3000	4000
1861 S	96,000	58	80	148	265	613	3300	—	—	—	—
1862	932,550	9.50	15	23	32	59	163	320	600	3000	4000
1862 S	67,000	51	71	140	238	495	1200	2750	4750	—	—
1863	192,060	27	38	51	74	160	300	650	1450	—	7000
1864	94,070	49	60	98	143	235	415	888	1400	—	9250
1864 S	20,000	238	400	520	925	1775	3125	—	—	—	—
1865	59,300	55	70	120	155	268	383	850	1350	11500	7000
1865 S	41,000	70	108	180	268	450	1275	2425	5000	—	—
1866	UNIQUE	—	—	—	—	—	—	—	—	—	—

EDMUND'S 1996 U.S. COIN PRICES

QUARTERS

VARIETY FOUR
MOTTO ABOVE EAGLE
1866-1873

DIAMETER: 24.3mm
WEIGHT: 6.22 Grams
COMPOSITION: .900 Silver, .100 Copper
DESIGNER: Christian Gobrecht
EDGE: Reeded

DATE	MINTAGE	G-4	VG-8	F-12	VF-20	EF-40	AU-50	MS-60	MS-63	MS-65	PRF-65
1866	17,525	250	338	420	525	693	1275	2000	3250	—	6750
1866 S	28,000	190	280	443	688	1250	1950	3750	4750	—	—
1867	20,625	165	200	243	320	470	575	1138	1650	—	6750
1867 S	48,000	145	215	295	395	663	1650	3750	—	—	—
1868	30,000	96	130	200	258	353	470	1063	1750	—	6750
1868 S	96,000	53	70	125	205	508	1200	2550	6000	—	—
1869	16,600	215	275	355	438	600	950	1575	3450	—	6750
1869 S	76,000	65	100	163	270	500	1213	2450	3750	—	—
1870	87,400	44	57	88	140	243	350	975	—	—	6550
1870 CC	8,340	1600	2625	4550	8250	14250	25000	—	—	—	—
1871	119,160	31	40	54	108	188	300	800	950	—	6550
1871 CC	10,890	1200	2150	3300	4800	10250	18000	—	—	—	—
1871 S	30,900	263	333	433	575	838	1550	3375	6500	—	—
1872	182,950	30	39	51	91	150	280	1000	3200	5100	4050
1872 CC	22,850	375	575	1000	1800	3450	7000	—	—	—	—
1872 S	83,000	375	550	1100	1750	3350	5200	7500	15000	—	—
1873 Closed 3	212,600	150	235	338	443	618	938	2900	—	—	8000
1873 Open 3	Inc. Above	30	35	51	93	160	300	668	1750	—	—
1873 CC	4,000	—	—	—	—	—	—	—	450000	—	—

QUARTERS

VARIETY FIVE
ARROWS AT DATE
1873-1874

DIAMETER: 24.3mm
WEIGHT: 6.25 Grams
COMPOSITION: .900 Silver, .100 Copper
DESIGNER: Christian Gobrecht
EDGE: Reeded

DATE	MINTAGE	G-4	VG-8	F-12	VF-20	EF-40	AU-50	MS-60	MS-63	MS-65	PRF-65
1873	1,271,700	11	16	29	53	188	365	675	1475	3500	5500
1873 CC	12,462	1400	2575	3525	6250	10000	20000	—	—	—	—
1873 S	156,000	25	38	75	153	303	600	1150	3050	—	—
1874	471,900	15	25	39	68	193	363	750	1750	3500	5500
1874 S	392,000	19	30	50	120	235	475	825	1813	—	—

VARIETY FOUR RESUMED
1875-1891

DATE	MINTAGE	G-4	VG-8	F-12	VF-20	EF-40	AU-50	MS-60	MS-63	MS-65	PRF-65
1875	4,293,500	8.15	12	19	26	55	108	290	490	—	3050
1875 CC	140,000	50	83	158	288	463	693	1338	2250	—	—
1875 S	680,000	31	41	61	100	173	295	613	1650	—	—
1876	17,817,150	8.15	12	19	26	51	108	288	490	—	3050
1876 CC	4,994,000	8.45	14	21	32	63	173	363	975	3900	—
1876 CC Fine Reed		9.00	15	22	35	70	210	375	—	—	—
1876 S	8,596,000	8.20	12	19	26	60	128	225	485	1450	—
1877	10,911,710	8.15	12	19	26	51	108	223	470	1450	2000
1877 CC	4,192,000	8.25	14	23	33	65	170	308	595	—	—
1877 Over Horiz S	Inc. Above	25	43	70	130	213	313	700	2250	—	—
1877 S	8,996,000	8.15	12	20	28	52	110	228	485	1450	—
1878	2,260,800	8.25	13	22	33	56	133	300	520	—	3050
1878 CC	996,000	17	26	39	60	103	220	443	975	4100	—
1878 S	140,000	75	140	225	295	500	775	1500	3350	—	—
1879	14,700	138	170	208	250	330	393	485	800	2000	2000
1880	14,955	143	173	210	253	335	395	483	775	2500	2000
1881	12,975	140	175	213	260	328	393	498	800	1400	2000
1882	16,300	150	185	218	268	340	428	575	810	2000	2000
1883	15,439	150	185	218	268	338	418	573	825	—	2000
1884	8,875	178	223	270	340	405	448	625	900	23000	2000
1885	14,530	145	180	213	258	335	393	520	800	—	2000
1886	5,886	245	290	343	433	563	775	975	1100	—	2000

EDMUND'S 1996 U.S. COIN PRICES

QUARTERS

DATE	MINTAGE	G-4	VG-8	F-12	VF-20	EF-40	AU-50	MS-60	MS-63	MS-65	PRF-65
1887	10,710	185	210	250	305	380	458	600	840	—	2000
1888	10,833	155	190	230	278	343	458	575	825	2200	2000
1888 S	1,216,000	8.75	13	21	28	57	138	298	613	1450	
1889	12,711	153	195	235	280	353	440	575	775	1500	2000
1890	80,590	50	56	83	110	188	293	450	875	2150	
1891	3,920,600	8.15	12	20	27	51	125	228	475	1725	2000
1891 O	68,000	130	165	263	450	688	1550	2950	—	—	
1891 S	2,216,000	8.65	12	21	32	55	123	303	560	4400	—

BARBER TYPE
1892-1916

DIAMETER: 24.3mm
WEIGHT: 6.25 Grams
COMPOSITION: .900 Silver, .100 Copper
DESIGNER: Charles E. Barber
EDGE: Reeded
PURE SILVER CONTENT: .18084 Tr. Oz.

Barber quarters were coined between the years 1892 to 1916 inclusive. The items that appear most attractive in the Barber quarter series appear to be in the Extremely Fine to MS-65 grade range, especially rare dates coveted most by collectors. These coins are widely admired, but have not participated in any major price run-ups in recent memory. Another large surge of collector interest is imminent. High quality buyers looking for deep discounts should make their move soon. MS-65 and PR-65 material is retailing for a paltry 20% of 1989 values. Respected authors conclude that Barber quarter beauties will be at the forefront of the next big boom in the coin world.

Budget wary individuals will find solace in key date Barber quarters in lower grades. These dates can be identified as the 1896-S, the 1901-S, and the 1913-S. These issues have experienced some new gains recently, and there is every reason to expect that this is just the beginning of another period of consistent growth, just as was exhibited throughout much of the last 40 years.

The 1914-S is starting to come alive, but it's not too late to cash in on its up-and-coming status. This issue has the fourth lowest coinage of the Barber quarter series, with only 264,000 pieces released from the San Francisco mint. Nevertheless, it is valued at only $78 in Very Good and $120 in Fine, which is a severe underestimation for a coin of this rarity. The 1914-S will probably appreciate steadily in the years to come, eventually assuming a position more appropriate in relation to the key dates in the series. Dealers who specialize in Barbers expect this rise to come faster and be stronger than most other coins of comparable condition.

QUARTERS

DATE	MINTAGE	G-4	VG-8	F-12	VF-20	EF-40	AU-50	MS-60	MS-63	MS-65	PRF-65
1892	8,237,245	4.00	4.75	19	28	65	115	168	278	1300	1850
1892 O	2,640,000	5.15	8.25	21	33	74	145	263	345	975	—
1892 S	964,079	13	25	35	52	118	255	405	863	6300	—
1893	5,484,838	3.85	5.05	20	28	65	115	203	305	1700	1850
1893 O	3,396,000	4.20	6.80	22	38	70	143	263	550	1800	—
1893 S	1,454,535	6.00	9.65	29	47	104	268	410	1050	7100	—
1894	3,432,972	4.15	4.75	20	31	73	120	198	390	1275	1850
1894 O	2,852,000	4.25	7.25	26	37	75	175	308	965	3000	—
1894 S	2,648,821	5.15	6.50	26	40	75	165	305	788	4100	—
1895	4,440,880	4.35	5.20	20	28	65	115	198	445	1700	1850
1895 O	2,816,000	4.90	7.00	27	41	84	210	368	870	2800	—
1895 S	1,764,681	5.75	11	28	46	81	205	355	905	3500	—
1896	3,874,762	4.15	5.05	21	28	65	115	208	378	1550	1850
1896 O	1,484,000	4.90	10	50	185	305	585	810	1863	8100	—
1896 S	188,039	220	315	570	863	1450	2825	4050	7550	9890	—
1897	8,140,731	3.45	5.10	20	31	65	113	168	275	1300	1850
1897 O	1,414,800	6.40	14	63	163	320	563	825	1700	3700	—
1897 S	542,229	11	23	89	145	288	530	813	1738	6300	—
1898	11,100,735	2.80	4.60	19	28	63	110	168	268	1300	1850
1898 O	1,868,000	4.95	13	37	78	160	350	545	1325	8600	—
1898 S	1,020,592	4.30	9.00	24	43	73	175	373	1113	5200	—
1899	12,624,846	2.80	4.60	19	28	61	110	165	268	1300	2200
1899 O	2,644,000	4.75	10	24	41	84	233	373	800	5200	—
1899 S	708,000	7.50	15	28	47	78	180	340	950	3350	—
1900	10,016,912	3.30	4.70	18	28	61	110	165	268	1300	2200
1900 O	3,416,000	5.10	10	30	49	89	245	408	1050	3700	—
1900 S	1,858,585	4.95	8.00	24	38	65	115	300	953	5800	—
1901	8,892,813	4.75	5.70	18	28	61	110	165	268	1900	1900
1901 O	1,612,000	16	33	63	155	300	568	720	1950	5750	—
1901 S	72,664	1575	2425	3575	5200	6825	8800	11125	16750	40250	—
1902	12,197,744	3.45	4.05	18	28	61	110	165	268	1300	2275
1902 O	4,748,000	3.95	6.75	27	48	92	188	418	1250	5700	—
1902 S	1,524,612	7.50	13	26	46	77	198	400	823	3600	—
1903	9,670,064	3.45	4.05	19	28	61	110	165	355	2600	1850
1903 O	3,500,000	4.95	6.40	25	41	77	188	375	1038	6800	—
1903 S	1,036,000	7.50	16	30	54	98	223	380	830	2100	—
1904	9,588,813	3.40	4.45	19	28	61	110	165	330	1550	1850
1904 O	2,456,000	5.10	8.50	33	63	155	338	688	1275	2750	—
1905	4,968,250	4.00	5.15	20	31	64	110	183	315	1675	1850
1905 O	1,230,000	6.25	10	31	60	125	260	405	1125	5700	—
1905 S	1,884,000	5.25	9.25	26	43	80	190	335	1088	4100	—
1906	3,656,435	3.40	4.45	19	28	61	110	165	268	1300	1850
1906 D	3,280,000	3.60	4.45	21	35	65	145	215	425	3600	—
1906 O	2,056,000	3.45	4.70	27	37	75	173	238	458	1350	—

EDMUND'S 1996 U.S. COIN PRICES

QUARTERS

DATE	MINTAGE	G-4	VG-8	F-12	VF-20	EF-40	AU-50	MS-60	MS-63	MS-65	PRF-65
1907	7,192,575	2.80	3.50	18	28	61	110	165	268	1300	1850
1907 D	2,484,000	3.55	4.25	22	36	75	168	280	825	2650	—
1907 O	4,560,000	2.80	3.75	20	34	63	130	230	495	2750	—
1907 S	1,360,000	4.20	5.30	30	43	99	198	363	955	3600	—
1908	4,232,545	2.80	3.45	18	28	61	110	183	283	1300	4050
1908 D	5,788,000	3.55	4.40	19	28	66	115	193	370	1500	—
1908 O	6,244,000	2.80	3.80	19	29	68	118	190	300	1300	—
1908 S	784,000	8.15	15	47	96	208	380	613	1250	7200	—
1909	9,268,650	2.80	3.55	18	147	61	110	165	268	1300	1850
1909 D	5,114,000	3.55	4.40	19	29	64	158	213	343	1800	—
1909 O	712,000	7.90	15	45	100	190	343	608	1363	7800	—
1909 S	1,348,000	3.00	4.45	21	33	70	173	270	825	3000	—
1910	2,244,551	3.50	4.20	22	31	65	125	178	293	1425	1850
1910 D	1,500,000	4.15	5.75	25	40	83	178	303	958	1400	—
1911	3,720,543	3.40	4.20	19	28	69	110	178	275	1350	1850
1911 D	933,600	4.25	6.75	68	168	273	408	563	1225	5000	—
1911 S	988,000	3.75	5.05	30	41	105	198	285	653	1425	—
1912	4,400,700	2.80	3.55	17	28	61	110	165	268	1300	1850
1912 S	708,000	3.75	5.05	30	44	87	210	348	930	3000	—
1913	484,613	8.75	15	50	143	373	535	915	1238	4700	2500
1913 D	1,450,800	4.50	5.65	24	37	79	145	238	370	1325	—
1913 S	40,000	373	600	1638	2450	3163	3725	4275	6000	10000	—
1914	6,244,610	3.60	4.05	15	26	61	110	165	275	1300	2200
1914 D	3,046,000	3.45	4.20	17	27	64	113	170	288	1300	—
1914 S	264,000	53	78	120	168	343	533	803	1313	3250	—
1915	3,480,450	3.60	4.05	16	26	61	110	168	275	1300	2500
1915 D	3,694,000	3.45	4.10	17	26	63	110	165	273	1300	—
1915 S	704,000	3.85	5.40	21	37	76	175	260	513	1400	—
1916	1,788,000	3.45	4.10	18	27	64	113	163	268	1300	—
1916 D	6,540,800	3.35	4.00	16	26	63	115	165	275	1300	—

QUARTERS

STANDING LIBERTY TYPE
1916-1930

In 1916, when the Barber quarter entered into permanent retirement, the stylish Standing Liberty quarter made its debut. There were several modifications made in the following year because of public outrage to Miss Liberty's unclothed top on the premiere design. There were also three stars added below the eagle on the reverse. And so, there are two varieties of the Standing Liberty quarter to be had: Variety I being the "obscene" design of 1916-1917, and Variety II, with clothing and extra stars, from 1917 to the termination of the series in 1930.

VARIETY ONE
1916-1917

DIAMETER: 24.3mm
WEIGHT: 6.25 Grams
COMPOSITION: .900 Silver, .100 Copper
DESIGNER: Herman A. MacNeil
EDGE: Reeded
PURE SILVER CONTENT: .18084 Tr. Oz.

One of two key coins in the series without question is the 1916 issue. Having a mintage of only 52,000, this coin is the most difficult link in completing the set, which has long been a favorite with collectors. Numismatic popularity explains why the 1916 Standing Liberty quarter has been such a consistent winner over time with only a few minor reversals. Prices will likely never be lower than they are at the present time, but with bargain prices starting at "only" $1000 in Good condition, this investment is certainly not within reach of some buyers.

There are many excellent buys among the MS-60 to MS-65 Uncirculated pieces. In most cases MS-65 Uncirculated Standing Liberty quarters have nosedived from about $2000 in 1990 to less than $500 in 1995. The potential for this inspirational series is indeed tremendous.

DATE	MINTAGE	VG-8	F-12	VF-20	EF-40	AU-50	MS-60	MS-63	MS-65
1916	52,000	1250	1500	2175	2600	3225	4550	6300	12300
1917	8,792,000	15	20	31	59	103	150	310	475
1917 D	1,509,200	21	47	61	88	113	168	280	1250
1917 S	1,952,000	20	34	61	76	106	165	290	1050

EDMUND'S 1996 U.S. COIN PRICES

QUARTERS

VARIETY TWO
1917-1930

DIAMETER: 24.3mm
WEIGHT: 6.25 Grams
COMPOSITION: .900 Silver, .100 Copper
DESIGNER: Herman A. MacNeil
EDGE: Reeded
PURE SILVER CONTENT: .18084 Tr. Oz.

The 1918/7-S overstrike is an important coin date. Even in the lowest grades, a quarter of this description has always commanded respect. In better grades, prices absolutely go through the roof. Obtain the highest quality that you can afford, and look for collector interest to keep pushing the value of your coin up, up, and away!

DATE	MINTAGE	VG-8	F-12	VF-20	EF-40	AU-50	MS-60	MS-63	MS-65
1917	13,880,000	12	17.50	27.50	46	75	120	180	500
1917 D	6,224,400	18.50	28	37.50	57.50	85	165	295	1300
1917 S	5,522,000	20	29	38	59	87.50	165	290	1150
1918	14,240,000	15	21	31	48	72	130	190	475
1918 D	7,380,000	25	42	58	85	138	208	350	1450
1918 S	1,836,000	16	23	29	44	83	183	288	1575
1918 S/17	Inc. Above	1200	1638	2225	4150	7675	10950	22250	68500
1919	11,324,000	29	42	51	65	89	138	213	483
1919 D	1,944,000	63	105	165	250	365	500	1188	2425
1919 S	1,836,000	58	94	213	368	505	738	1463	3400
1920	27,860,000	15	19	24	35	64	128	183	470
1920 D	3,586,400	30	58	78	103	153	200	638	1850
1920 S	6,380,000	17	24	31	51	80	198	733	2425
1921	1,916,000	80	110	175	233	325	425	795	1813
1923	9,716,000	14	21	25	33	61	125	165	420
1923 S	1,360,000	140	170	298	380	463	575	835	1788
1924	10,920,000	15	18	23	39	61	123	178	418
1924 D	3,112,000	30	48	65	94	118	148	198	433
1924 S	2,860,000	18	21	28	79	168	285	750	1900

QUARTERS

RECESSED DATE STYLE
1925-1930

DATE	MINTAGE	VG-8	F-12	VF-20	EF-40	AU-50	MS-60	MS-63	MS-65
1925	12,280,000	3.00	5.00	14	26	54	115	175	443
1926	11,316,000	3.00	5.00	14	29	61	115	175	433
1926 D	1,716,000	7.00	13	23	43	79	120	178	485
1926 S	2,700,000	4.25	10	23	89	193	313	738	2200
1927	11,912,000	3.00	5.00	14	25	59	113	178	413
1927 D	976,400	7.00	16	40	76	123	150	223	453
1927 S	396,000	10	51	158	1075	2525	3450	5375	9750
1928	6,336,000	3.00	5.00	14	25	54	113	175	438
1928 D	1,627,600	5.00	8.00	19	36	70	135	180	413
1928 S	2,644,000	3.25	5.75	15	31	67	130	178	378
1929	11,140,000	3.00	5.00	14	28	53	113	175	420
1929 D	1,358,000	5.00	7.25	17	31	68	135	180	435
1929 S	1,764,000	2.75	5.40	14	31	55	123	173	355
1930	5,632,000	3.00	4.90	14	27	56	110	173	408
1930 S	1,556,000	3.25	5.15	13	28	58	123	210	425

WASHINGTON TYPE
1932 TO DATE

DIAMETER: 24.3mm
WEIGHT: 1932-1964: 6.25 Grams,
            1965 To Date: 5.67 Grams
COMPOSITION: 1932-1964: .900 Silver, .100 Copper
            1965 To Date: Copper Clad Issue
            .750 Copper, .250 Nickel Outer Layers
            Pure Copper Inner Core
DESIGNER: John Flanagan
EDGE: Reeded
PURE SILVER CONTENT - 1932-1964: .18084 Tr. Oz.

NOTE: The Washington quarters of 1976 are listed on page 175 with the other bicentennial coinage.

The familiar Washington quarter has been in circulation since 1932. Originally intended to be a one year commemorative issue to mark the 200th anniversary of the birth of our first president, the Washington quarter is somewhat popular with modern day collectors, and undoubtedly it will be in far greater demand in the future.

QUARTERS

The only true rare dates in the series are the 1932-D and 1932-S. In lower grades, don't expect any big gains within the next few years. However, prices will likely multiply in the years ahead when Washington quarters become really "hot" numismatic items. Prices have been stagnant for over twenty years now, so they're already at basement levels.

Generally it's wise to buy Washington quarters, whenever possible, in MS-65. Specimens from the 1930's and 1940's grading MS-65 or better are surprisingly scarce, and haven't even begun to fulfill their destiny, especially the pre-1940 Washingtons. Pieces dated beyond 1950 have such a small extra cost attached to top notch specimens, it's really foolish to opt for anything less than MS-65. While selecting quarters of this description, be sure to include the 1955-D. It's one of the rarest Washingtons, but presently is not priced accordingly. Set aside some high quality proof specimens too. If your motive is profit, self discipline here is important. Settle only for the finest examples of Washington quarters. As with the Roosevelt dimes, don't anticipate great things to happen in the next few years. However, you can rest assured that someday you'll be very pleased for adding these coins to your collection at today's prices.

On many Washington quarters, the reverse design and the rim have a tendency to be weakly struck. The most frequently affected dates are the 1934-D, 1935-D, 1935-S, 1936-D, 1936-S, 1937-D, 1937-S, 1939-D, and 1940-D. Always keep in mind that poor strikes are not restricted to these dates only. Professional coin analysts report that this situation is every bit as pronounced in Washington quarters as are the Full Split Bands in Mercury dimes or Full Head in Standing Liberty quarters, although it is less studied at present. Knowing this may provide you with an additional advantage when you select Washington quarters, as any future increase in collector and/or investor activity is likely to bring strike quality to the forefront. Just as with the previously mentioned denominations, there will probably be significant premiums attached to such coins.

DATE	MINTAGE	G-4	VG-8	F-12	VF-20	EF-40	AU-50	MS-60	MS-63	MS-65	MS-67	PRF-65
1932	5,404,000	1.75	2.25	2.75	4.00	8.40	14	20	28	160	—	—
1932 D	436,800	32	38	45	63	135	250	415	843	4500	—	—
1932 S	408,000	28	32	37	45	58	95	250	400	2000	—	—
1934	31,912,052	1.75	2.40	3.00	3.75	5.25	9.75	20	26	78	—	—
1934 Light Motto	31,912,052	1.75	3.20	3.75	6.00	8.00	11	26	70	275	—	—
1934 D	3,527,200	3.65	4.40	6.00	7.25	13	40	96	178	880	—	—
1935	32,484,000	1.65	2.25	3.00	3.75	5.00	9.50	19	25	73	—	—
1935 D	5,780,000	2.30	3.40	5.50	7.15	14	50	200	250	575	—	—
1935 S	5,660,000	2.20	2.90	4.25	5.00	10	25	47	70	175	—	—
1936	41,303,837	1.50	2.00	2.75	3.00	5.15	9.40	17	25	50	—	863
1936 D	5,374,000	2.55	3.15	4.65	14	32	120	278	358	600	—	—

EDMUND'S 1996 U.S. COIN PRICES

QUARTERS

DATE	MINTAGE	G-4	VG-8	F-12	VF-20	EF-40	AU-50	MS-60	MS-63	MS-65	MS-67	PRF-65
1936 S	3,828,000	2.40	2.90	4.00	6.65	11	25	47	60	100	—	—
1937	19,701,542	1.50	2.25	3.00	4.75	6.25	13	22	25	65	—	413
1937 D	7,189,600	2.35	2.75	4.00	6.50	9.00	17	34	40	60	—	—
1937 S	1,652,000	3.40	3.75	5.75	12	21	51	83	101	150	—	—
1938	9,480,045	2.40	2.80	4.25	7.75	13	25	45	54	100	—	305
1938 S	2,832,000	2.90	3.15	4.40	7.90	13	25	48	56	283	—	—
1939	33,548,795	1.50	2.25	2.90	3.40	4.50	8.00	13	19	45	—	275
1939 D	7,092,000	2.15	2.95	3.75	5.25	8.00	13	26	31	65	—	—
1939 S	2,628,000	3.15	3.50	4.50	6.00	12	29	51	64	110	—	—
1940	35,715,246	1.65	2.25	2.90	3.15	3.75	7.15	10	16	35	—	135
1940 D	2,797,600	3.15	3.60	6.15	9.25	15	29	54	62	110	—	—
1940 S	8,244,000	2.15	2.50	3.25	3.65	4.40	9.00	16	22	48	—	—
1941	79,047,287	1.00	1.25	1.80	2.15	3.00	4.00	6.25	8.00	24	—	98
1941 D	16,714,800	1.00	1.25	1.80	2.45	3.40	6.25	16	21	36	—	—
1941 S	16,080,000	1.00	1.25	1.80	2.30	3.25	6.25	15	21	65	—	—
1942	102,117,123	1.00	1.25	1.80	2.25	13	3.75	5.65	7.25	24	—	95
1942 D	17,487,200	1.35	1.65	1.95	2.45	3.35	5.15	9.00	12	36	—	—
1942 S	19,384,000	1.45	1.65	2.00	2.50	4.75	16	45	59	115	—	—
1943	99,700,000	1.00	1.25	1.80	2.30	2.50	2.90	4.65	5.90	24	—	—
1943 D	16,095,600	1.00	1.25	1.80	2.25	3.20	6.75	13	16	28	—	—
1943 S	21,700,000	1.00	1.25	1.80	2.30	4.75	12	24	31	38	—	—
1944	104,956,000	1.00	1.25	1.80	2.15	2.95	3.40	4.00	5.15	15	—	—
1944 D	14,600,800	1.00	1.25	1.80	2.15	3.00	4.90	7.90	10	23	—	—
1944 S	12,560,000	1.00	1.25	1.80	2.15	3.00	5.00	8.15	10	26	—	—
1945	74,372,000	1.00	1.25	1.80	2.15	2.80	3.20	3.75	5.15	14	—	—
1945 D	12,341,600	1.40	1.60	2.00	2.40	3.25	4.65	6.65	8.75	24	—	—
1945 S	17,004,001	1.00	1.25	1.80	2.20	3.05	4.15	5.15	6.15	18	—	—
1946	53,436,000	1.00	1.25	1.80	2.15	2.40	2.65	4.25	5.65	14	—	—
1946 D	9,072,800	1.00	1.25	1.80	2.20	2.45	2.85	3.65	4.75	12	—	—
1946 S	4,204,000	1.35	1.55	2.00	2.25	1.50	2.70	3.50	4.75	18	—	—
1947	22,556,000	1.00	1.25	1.80	2.15	2.80	3.75	5.90	7.25	12	—	—
1947 D	15,338,400	1.00	1.25	1.80	2.20	2.90	3.65	4.65	6.40	14	—	—
1947 S	5,532,000	1.00	1.25	1.80	2.20	2.55	2.75	4.15	5.25	15	—	—
1948	35,196,000	1.00	1.25	1.80	2.15	2.40	2.75	3.65	4.50	11	—	—
1948 D	16,766,800	1.00	1.25	1.80	2.20	2.55	2.85	4.25	5.75	13	—	—
1948 S	15,960,000	1.00	1.25	1.80	2.20	3.05	3.40	4.75	6.00	15	—	—
1949	9,312,000	1.00	1.25	1.80	2.45	3.50	8.00	17	22	27	—	—
1949 D	10,068,400	1.00	1.25	1.80	2.45	3.40	5.50	7.25	9.65	21	—	—
1950	24,971,512	1.00	1.05	1.80	2.40	2.80	3.30	4.00	4.90	8.50	—	58
1950 D	21,075,600	1.00	1.05	1.80	2.40	2.65	2.95	3.90	4.75	9.25	—	—
1950 D D/S	Inc. Above	21	25	34	68	135	195	243	343	695	—	—
1950 S	10,284,004	1.00	1.05	1.80	2.65	2.90	4.90	6.40	7.75	14	—	—
1950 S S/D	Inc. Above	21	25	49	74	158	258	360	423	563	—	—
1951	43,505,602	1.00	1.05	1.70	2.00	2.30	2.50	3.90	4.75	7.50	5.00	34
1951 D	35,354,800	1.00	1.05	1.70	1.00	2.30	2.50	3.10	3.90	6.75	—	—

EDMUND'S 1996 U.S. COIN PRICES

QUARTERS

DATE	MINTAGE	G-4	VG-8	F-12	VF-20	EF-40	AU-50	MS-60	MS-63	MS-65	MS-67	PRF-65
1951 S	9,048,000	1.00	1.05	1.70	2.00	3.40	7.40	11	16	22	—	—
1952	38,862,073	1.00	1.05	14	2.00	2.20	2.40	2.85	3.75	6.25	—	34
1952 D	49,795,200	1.00	1.05	1.70	2.00	2.25	1.45	3.00	3.90	7.00	—	—
1952 S	13,707,800	1.00	1.05	1.70	2.15	2.50	4.90	7.65	9.50	13	—	—
1953	18,664,920	1.20	1.25	2.25	2.10	2.25	2.55	2.95	3.65	6.65	—	22
1953 D	56,112,400	1.00	1.05	1.95	1.65	1.80	1.95	2.20	3.00	6.65	—	—
1953 S	14,016,000	1.00	1.05	1.75	2.05	2.35	2.65	3.40	4.65	8.25	—	—
1954	54,645,503	1.00	1.05	1.45	1.55	1.45	1.65	1.95	3.00	5.25	—	12
1954 D	42,305,500	1.00	1.05	1.33	1.45	1.60	1.75	1.75	2.75	5.00	—	—
1954 S	11,834,722	1.00	1.05	1.90	1.75	1.90	2.05	2.05	3.00	6.65	—	—
1955	18,558,381	1.00	1.05	1.75	1.70	1.85	2.00	1.85	3.00	6.75	—	12
1955 D	3,182,400	1.40	1.45	1.75	1.75	2.05	2.20	2.40	3.00	8.75	—	—
1956	44,813,384	1.00	1.05	1.55	1.45	1.75	1.90	1.90	2.65	5.00	—	6.25
1956 D	32,334,500	1.20	1.25	1.75	1.55	2.00	2.30	1.50	3.15	5.25	—	—
1957	47,779,952	1.00	1.05	1.55	1.60	1.50	1.90	2.30	2.90	5.75	—	3.75
1957 D	77,924,160	1.00	1.05	1.55	1.60	1.50	1.75	1.90	2.65	4.50	—	—
1958	7,235,652	1.00	1.05	1.60	1.70	1.50	1.90	2.20	3.00	5.65	—	6.25
1958 D	78,124,900	1.00	1.05	1.40	1.45	1.40	1.65	1.90	2.50	4.35	—	—
1959	25,533,291	1.00	1.05	1.50	1.60	1.45	1.75	1.85	2.50	4.50	—	4.65
1959 D	62,054,232	1.00	1.05	1.40	1.45	1.40	1.65	1.85	2.65	4.10	—	—
1960	30,855,602	1.00	1.05	1.35	1.40	1.35	1.65	2.25	2.75	4.90	—	2.90
1960 D	63,000,324	1.00	1.05	1.35	1.40	1.35	1.65	1.85	2.50	3.85	—	—
1961	40,064,244	1.00	1.05	1.40	1.45	1.40	1.55	1.75	2.50	4.75	—	2.75
1961 D	83,656,928	1.00	1.05	1.35	1.40	1.35	1.50	1.20	2.15	3.85	—	—
1962	39,374,019	1.00	1.05	1.35	1.40	1.35	1.50	1.70	2.15	3.85	—	2.75
1962 D	127,554,756	1.00	1.05	1.35	1.40	1.35	1.50	1.75	2.15	3.85	—	—
1963	77,391,645	1.00	1.00	1.30	1.35	1.35	1.50	1.65	2.00	3.65	—	2.75
1963 D	135,288,184	1.00	1.00	1.30	1.35	1.35	1.50	1.55	2.50	3.65	—	—
1964	564,341,347	1.00	1.00	1.30	1.35	1.35	1.50	1.65	2.00	3.65	—	2.75
1964·D	704,135,528	1.00	1.00	1.30	1.35	1.35	1.50	1.65	2.00	3.65	—	—

QUARTERS

COPPER-NICKEL CLAD COINAGE

DATE	MINTAGE	MS-60	MS-63	MS-65	PRF-65
1965	1,819,717,540	0.50	—	1.15	—
1966	821,101,500	0.50	—	1.15	—
1967	1,524,031,848	0.50	—	1.40	—
1968	220,731,500	0.40	—	1.05	—
1968 D	101,534,000	0.42	—	1.15	—
1968 S	PROOF ONLY	—	—	—	1.10
1969	176,212,000	0.40	—	1.15	—
1969 D	114,372,000	0.50	—	1.30	—
1969 S	PROOF ONLY	—	—	—	1.00
1970	136,420,000	0.35	—	0.75	—
1970 D	417,341,364	0.35	—	0.75	—
1970 S	PROOF ONLY	—	—	—	0.95
1971	109,284,000	0.50	—	0.80	—
1971 D	258,634,428	0.40	—	0.90	—
1971 S	PROOF ONLY	—	—	—	0.95
1972	215,048,000	—	0.65	0.70	—
1972 D	311,067,732	0.35	—	0.70	—
1972 S	PROOF ONLY	—	—	—	0.95
1973	346,924,000	0.30	—	0.70	—
1973 D	232,977,400	0.30	—	0.70	—
1973 S	PROOF ONLY	—	—	—	0.95
1974	801,456,000	0.30	—	0.70	—
1974 D	353,160,300	0.30	—	0.70	—
1974 S	PROOF ONLY	—	—	—	0.95

See pages 174-175 for 1976 bicentennial quarters

DATE	MINTAGE	MS-60	MS-63	MS-65	PRF-65
1977	468,566,000	0.30	—	0.70	—
1977 D	258,898,212	0.30	—	0.75	—
1977 S	PROOF ONLY	—	—	—	0.95
1978	521,452,000	—	—	0.40	—
1978 D	287,373,152	—	—	0.40	—
1978 S	PROOF ONLY	—	—	—	0.95
1979	515,708,000	—	0.65	0.50	—
1979 D	489,789,780	—	0.65	0.50	—
1979 S	PROOF ONLY	—	—	—	0.95
1979 S Type I	PROOF ONLY	—	—	—	0.95
1979 S Type II	PROOF ONLY	—	—	—	1.25
1980 D	518,327,487	—	—	0.50	—
1980 P	635,832,000	—	—	0.50	—
1980 S	PROOF ONLY	—	—	—	1.75
1981 D	575,722,833	—	—	0.50	—
1981 P	601,716,000	—	—	0.50	—

EDMUND'S 1996 U.S. COIN PRICES

QUARTERS

DATE	MINTAGE	MS-60	MS-63	MS-65	PRF-65
1981 S	PROOF ONLY	—	—	—	0.85
1981 T-II		—	—	—	3.00
1982 D	480,042,788	—	—	1.00	—
1982 P	500,931,000	—	—	4.50	—
1982 S	PROOF ONLY	—	—	—	2.25
1983 D	617,806,446	—	—	4.50	—
1983 P	675,535,000	—	—	5.75	—
1983 S	PROOF ONLY	—	—	—	2.40
1984 D	546,483,064	—	—	2.00	—
1984 P	676,545,000	—	—	0.85	—
1984 S	PROOF ONLY	—	—	—	1.80
1985 D	519,962,888	—	—	3.25	—
1985 P	775,818,962	—	—	2.50	—
1985 S	PROOF ONLY	—	—	—	1.40
1986 D	504,298,660	—	—	2.75	—
1986 P	551,199,333	—	—	4.00	—
1986 S	PROOF ONLY	—	—	—	2.75
1987 D	655,594,696	—	—	0.50	—
1987 P	582,499,481	—	—	0.50	—
1987 S	PROOF ONLY	—	—	—	1.45
1988 D	596,810,688	—	—	0.60	—
1988 P	562,052,000	—	—	1.50	—
1988 S	PROOF ONLY	—	—	—	1.50
1989 D	896,535,597	—	—	0.50	—
1989 P	512,868,000	—	—	0.50	—
1989 S	PROOF ONLY	—	—	—	1.45
1990 D	927,638,181	—	—	0.50	—
1990 P	613,792,000	—	—	0.50	—
1990 S	PROOF ONLY	—	—	—	3.15
1991 D	630,966,693	—	—	0.50	—
1991 P	570,968,000	—	—	0.50	—
1991 S	PROOF ONLY	—	—	—	5.00
1992 D	389,777,107	—	—	0.50	—
1992 P	384,764,000	—	—	0.50	—
1992 S	PROOF ONLY	—	—	—	3.50
1993 D	645,476,128	—	—	0.50	—
1993 P	639,276,000	—	—	0.50	—
1993 S	PROOF ONLY	—	—	—	1.75
1993 S Silver Proof		—	—	—	4.50
1994 D		—	—	0.50	—
1994 P		—	—	0.50	—
1994 S	PROOF ONLY	—	—	—	4.00
1995 D		—	—	0.50	—
1995 P		—	—	0.50	—
1995 S	PROOF ONLY	—	—	—	3.00
1995 S Silver Proof		—	—	—	4.00

EDMUND'S 1996 U.S. COIN PRICES

HALF DOLLARS

HALF DOLLARS 1794 TO DATE

Half dollars have been coined almost every year since 1794. The half dollar types of the 18th and 19th centuries closely resemble the designs of the smaller silver coins in production during the same period.

FLOWING HAIR TYPE
1794-1795

DIAMETER: 32.5mm
WEIGHT: 13.48 Grams
COMPOSITION:
        .8924 Silver,
        .1076 Copper
DESIGNER: Robert Scot
EDGE: FIFTY CENTS
      OR HALF A DOLLAR
      With Decorations Between Words

The first half dollar, the Flowing Hair type, was minted in only 1794 and 1795. Most of its demand originates from the type-collecting sector of the numismatic industry. Try to land the best grade that you can afford. As a long term investment, you really can't go astray by purchasing these particular half dollars.

DATE	MINTAGE	AG-3	G-4	VG-8	F-12	VF-20	EF-40	AU-50	MS-60
1794	23,464	618	1025	1775	2550	3775	9250	12500	20500
1795	299,680	263	400	550	888	1750	5500	7525	15666
1795 3-Leaves	Inc. Above	1163	1688	1925	4000	7625	12000	15000	26500
1795 Recut Date	Inc. Above	325	500	700	1000	2275	7000	8000	9500

EDMUND'S 1996 U.S. COIN PRICES

HALF DOLLARS

DRAPED BUST TYPE
SMALL EAGLE
REVERSE
1796-1797

DIAMETER: 32.5mm
WEIGHT: 13.48 Grams
COMPOSITION: .8924 Silver,
.1076 Copper
DESIGNER: Robert Scot
EDGE: FIFTY CENTS OR HALF A DOLLAR
With Decorations Between Words

The Draped Bust half dollars with the small eagle on the reverse, coined in 1796 and 1797, are extremely rare, and capable of bringing around $10,000 in Good condition. With this half dollar, should you be able to afford it, you're virtually assured of an investment that will steadily rise in value year after year.

DATE	MINTAGE	AG-3	G-4	VG-8	F-12	VF-20	EF-40	AU-50	MS-60
1796 15 Stars	3,918	6975	9500	11750	15750	23250	34750	56500	—
1796 16 Stars	Inc. Above	7100	10125	12375	16500	25000	39000	—	—
1797	Inc. Above	6850	9750	12000	16000	24500	36500	55000	115000

DRAPED BUST TYPE
HERALDIC EAGLE REVERSE
1801-1807

DIAMETER: 32.5mm
WEIGHT: 13.48 Grams
COMPOSITION: .8924 Silver,
.1076 Copper
DESIGNER: Robert Scot
EDGE: FIFTY CENTS
OR HALF A DOLLAR
With Decorations Between Words

EDMUND'S 1996 U.S. COIN PRICES

HALF DOLLARS

Draped Bust halves with the heraldic eagle reverse of 1801 to 1807 have been mildly progressive for a number of years now, and we'll probably see this improvement sustained. Most notable is that Extremely Fine halves did poorly from 1980 to 1990, in relation to other grades, and there are huge gaps between some Extremely Fine and MS-60 Uncirculated values. These facts are evidence that Extremely Fine half dollars of this type are seriously undervalued coins at this time.

DATE	MINTAGE	AG-3	G-4	VG-8	F-12	VF-20	EF-40	AU-50	MS-60
1801	30,289	104	190	293	513	825	2150	5900	9500
1802	29,890	95	178	245	445	788	1988	5675	13625
1803 Sm. 3	188,234	79	145	190	300	475	1150	2750	6275
1803 Lg. 3	Inc. Above	70	133	163	228	348	775	2250	5550
1805	211,722	64	133	155	235	335	813	2425	5675
1805/4	Inc. Above	113	178	275	470	750	1725	4625	11875
1806 Knobbed 6, Lg. Stars	839,576	65	125	158	1082	320	638	1950	4900
1806	Inc. Above	65	125	155	208	380	750	2100	5175
1806 Knobbed 6, Sm. Stars	Inc. Above	75	125	160	210	325	625	2150	5400
1806 Over Inverted 6	Inc. Above	98	183	245	493	938	1538	3425	8875
1806 Pointed 6, Stem Not Through Claw	Inc. Above	75	125	160	210	325	625	2150	5400
1806 Pointed 6, Stem through Claw	Inc. Above	64	120	153	198	315	625	1900	4825
1807	301,076	64	120	153	198	295	625	1900	4825

CAPPED BUST TYPE
1807-1839

The Liberty Capped half dollar was a very important coin during its heyday of 1807 to 1836. At the time, there was a severe shortage of silver dollars and gold coins in circulation, leaving this half dollar as the largest denomination readily available for major transactions. Liberty Capped half dollars were also extensively utilized to maintain bank reserves and pay foreign debts. Since the coins were simply transferred in bags to consummate business proceedings rather than handled individually, many of them remain today in better than average condition. Unfortunately, few of these coins survive today in MS-65, as 19th century bankers were required to periodically count how many half dollars they held in storage. To do so required sliding them across the accounting table, often done in a careless manner, leaving most specimens with table scratches.

HALF DOLLARS

For investment purposes, the best opportunities to seize upon appear to be in the MS-63 range. Six years ago, spectacular bidding pushed prices near the $10,000 mark. In 1996, many of the exact same coins can be garnered for $1500 to $2000. This is an obvious turn of events favorable to discount shoppers.

For relatively small spenders, circulated Capped Bust half dollars in grades VF to AU have appreciated well at times in the past, so it's a safe assumption that these collectibles will fetch a much more handsome price several years from today.

VARIETY ONE - LETTERED EDGE
1807-1836

DIAMETER: 32.5mm
WEIGHT: 13.48 Grams
COMPOSITION: .8924 Silver, .1076 Copper
DESIGNER: John Reich
EDGE: 1807-1814
FIFTY CENTS OR
HALF A DOLLAR
1814-1831, Stars Added Between
DOLLAR and FIFTY
1832-1836, Vertical Lines
added Between Words

DATE	MINTAGE	G-4	VG-8	F-12	VF-20	EF-40	AU-50	MS-60	MS-63	MS-65
1807 Sm. Stars	750,000	59	98	183	323	713	2225	3800	9750	35000
1807 50/20C	Inc. Above	42	73	115	195	413	1500	3200	8500	—
1807 Lg. Stars	Inc. Above	48	66	165	288	725	2300	4100	12500	—
1808	1,368,600	36	42	57	95	198	450	1275	2850	—
1808 /7	Inc. Above	40	50	60	125	200	500	1500	3500	—
1809	1,405,810	35	42	57	100	315	593	1325	3000	—
1810	1,276,276	32	38	47	85	195	455	1150	2950	—
1811 Sm. 8	1,203,644	31	38	47	73	153	420	788	1750	—
1811 Dt. 18.11	Inc. Above	33	41	69	120	238	533	1275	4750	—
1811 Lg. 8	Inc. Above	31	38	49	80	168	475	875	1850	—
1812	1,628,059	32	49	64	116	258	520	1168	2875	9500
1812 /11	Inc. Above	42	55	85	155	290	750	2200	—	—
1814	1,039,075	32	38	49	73	160	425	1425	2675	—
1814 Single Leaf	Inc. Above	32	38	49	73	160	425	1425	2675	—
1814 /13	Inc. Above	45	55	78	138	338	505	1475	4750	—
1815 /12	47,150	680	900	1200	1763	2750	4100	7500	24500	—

EDMUND'S 1996 U.S. COIN PRICES

HALF DOLLARS

DATE	MINTAGE	G-4	VG-8	F-12	VF-20	EF-40	AU-50	MS-60	MS-63	MS-65
1817	1,215,562	29	35	42	64	145	300	758	1875	—
1817/13	Inc. Above	80	120	178	330	588	1438	2800	12500	—
1817 Dt. 181.7	Inc. Above	37	47	70	115	195	395	700	1600	—
1817/14	5 KNOWN	—	—	35000	65000	—	—	—	—	—
1818	1,960,322	29	34	39	63	130	275	688	1750	—
1818/17	Inc. Above	29	34	39	63	130	275	688	1750	—
1819	2,208,022	27	34	37	60	130	290	725	1800	—
1819 Lg. 9	Inc. Above	29	36	45	71	148	318	775	1725	—
1819 Sm. 9	Inc. Above	32	37	53	105	230	450	1075	2450	—
1820 Sm. Date	751,122	37	47	66	130	243	438	975	2350	—
1820 Lg. Date	Inc. Above	36	46	64	125	230	413	900	2225	—
1820/19	Inc. Above	36	240	73	163	288	488	1125	2675	—
1821	1,305,797	31	36	43	70	140	343	775	1700	—
1822	1,559,573	32	34	40	65	135	250	700	1600	—
1822/21	Inc. Above	48	62	90	160	288	563	1175	2888	—
1823	1,694,200	29	33	38	65	130	270	713	1675	—
1823 Broken 3	Inc. Above	37	52	73	120	308	588	1100	2425	—
1823 Patched 3	Inc. Above	34	45	63	85	173	413	1100	2175	—
1823 Ugly 3	Inc. Above	34	43	60	90	175	420	1125	2200	—
1824	3,504,954	28	32	37	48	100	325	775	2050	—
1824/21	Inc. Above	31	37	51	95	198	325	775	2050	—
1824/Various Dates	Inc. Above	30	33	39	59	153	288	725	1625	—
1825	2,943,166	28	31	37	48	98	235	645	1450	—
1826	4,004,180	28	31	37	47	90	220	628	1438	4600
1827 Curled 2	5,493,400	30	35	43	78	130	258	650	1538	—
1827 Square 2	Inc. Above	28	31	37	49	89	223	663	1875	—
1827/26	Inc. Above	30	35	49	88	165	320	963	2700	—
1828 Curled Base 2, No Knob ...	3,075,200	27	31	35	47	86	218	613	1425	6000
1828 Curled Base2, Knobbed 2 ...	Inc. Above	35	45	60	85	150	350	750	2100	—
1828 Lg. 8's Square Base 2 ...	Inc. Above	27	32	35	46	88	248	630	1438	—
1828 Sm. 8's. Square Base 2, Lg Letters ...	Inc. Above	26	31	35	43	430	233	628	1425	15500
1828 Sm. 8's. Square Base 2, Sm Letters ...	Inc. Above	33	42	70	113	213	475	1000	2100	6000
1829	3,712,156	28	33	37	44	95	250	725	1700	—
1829/27	Inc. Above	31	38	54	73	140	313	838	2325	—
1830 Sm. O in Date	4,764,800	26	31	35	43	83	215	605	1238	6500
1830 Lg. O in Date	Inc. Above	26	31	35	43	83	218	608	1250	6500
1831	5,873,660	26	31	35	43	83	215	600	1238	6500
1832 Sm. Letters	4,797,000	26	31	35	43	83	215	600	1238	6500
1832 Lg. Letters	Inc. Above	29	36	43	75	168	373	920	2350	8500
1833	5,206,000	26	31	35	43	83	215	605	1300	6500

EDMUND'S 1996 U.S. COIN PRICES

HALF DOLLARS

DATE	MINTAGE	G-4	VG-8	F-12	VF-20	EF-40	AU-50	MS-60	MS-63	MS-65
1834 Sm. Date, Lg. Stars, Sm. Letters 6,412,004		27.50	33	36	43	89	250	700	1250	6500
1834 Sm. Date, Sm. Stars, Sm. Letters .... Inc. Above		27.50	33	36	43	89	250	700	1250	6500
1834 Lg. Date, Lg. Letters .. Inc. Above		27.50	33	36	43	89	250	700	1250	6500
1834 Lg. Date, Sm. Letters . Inc. Above		27.50	33	36	43	89	250	700	1250	6500
1835 5,352,006		26	31	35	43	83	215	600	1275	6500
1836 6,545,000		326	403	468	647	892	1858	5050	11369	6500
1836 50/00 .... Inc. Above		41	58	78	163	255	580	1500	3650	—

VARIETY TWO
REEDED EDGE
REVERSE 50 CENTS
1836-1837

DIAMETER: 30mm
WEIGHT: 13.36 Grams
COMPOSITION:
.900 Silver,
.100 Copper
DESIGNER: Christian Gobrecht
EDGE: Reeded

The half dollar was reduced in size in 1836 with the introduction of the reeded edge Liberty Cap half. The previous type had a lettered edge. The first reeded edge half dollars are much more difficult to locate in upper grades because of lesser storage in bank vaults during their time of service, and yet the values of Extremely Fine and Uncirculated specimens approximate the value of earlier Liberty Capped halves with comparable mintages. To analyze the situation further, reeded edge examples of Capped halves were priced well above the lettered edge type throughout most of the previous three decades, and this ratio should be reinstated in the not too distant future. Therefore, you should buy the best grade you can afford in the reeded edge type.

DATE	MINTAGE	G-4	VG-8	F-12	VF-20	EF-40	AU-50	MS-60	MS-63	MS-65
1836 Rev 1,200		688	838	1025	1263	1725	3250	7250	14500	—
1837 3,629,820		30	36	48	80	145	315	713	1950	12500

EDMUND'S 1996 U.S. COIN PRICES

HALF DOLLARS

**VARIETY THREE
REEDED EDGE
REVERSE HALF DOLLAR**
1838-1839

DIAMETER: 30mm
WEIGHT: 13.36 Grams
COMPOSITION: .900 Silver,
.100 Copper
DESIGNER: Christian Gobrecht
EDGE: Reeded

DATE	MINTAGE	G-4	VG-8	F-12	VF-20	EF-40	AU-50	MS-60	MS-63	MS-65
1838	3,546,000	30	35	44	68	133	373	963	2525	8500
1838 O	20	—	—	—	—	42500	75000	100000	450000	—
1839	3,334,560	30	35	43	73	145	358	800	3000	8500
1839 O	178,976	115	150	220	305	550	1100	3025	5550	—

LIBERTY SEATED TYPE
1839-1891

Six distinct types of Liberty Seated half dollars were minted between 1839 and 1891.

For common date coins of the series, all slabbed MS-65 or above specimens represent one of your best hopes for immediate advancements. In many instances, values have been slashed as much as 80% since the 1980's. If you've got extra thousands to spend, PR-65 Liberty Seated halves offer excellent possibilities, having fallen likewise from their 1989 high water mark. On the opposite side of the spectrum, individuals with less than $150 to spend should look for nice, problem-free Extremely Fine half dollars of this era. They have not yet attained the respect they deserve from the numismatic community. Investment dollars spent here should do quite well in the years ahead.

EDMUND'S 1996 U.S. COIN PRICES

HALF DOLLARS

**VARIETY ONE
NO MOTTO
ABOVE EAGLE
1839-1853**

DIAMETER: 30.6mm
WEIGHT: 13.36 Grams
COMPOSITION: .900 Silver,
.100 Copper
DESIGNER: Christian Gobrecht
EDGE: Reeded

DATE	MINTAGE	G-4	VG-8	F-12	VF-20	EF-40	AU-50	MS-60	MS-63	MS-65
1839 Drapery	Inc. Above	20	29	44	78	125	270	470	2375	—
1839 No Drapery	Inc. Above	39	58	113	258	688	1650	3175	7125	250000
1840 Med. Letters	Inc. Above	105	148	220	298	488	1150	2625	4500	—
1840 O	855,100	19	27	42	70	115	275	565	2275	—
1840 Sm. Letters	1,435,008	20	28	41	70	110	305	314	1875	8250
1841	310,000	33	44	83	145	253	463	1250	2675	—
1841 O	401,000	16	25	47	87	138	248	838	2300	—
1842 Sm. Date	2,012,764	24	35	48	73	150	375	1088	2350	12000
1842 Lg. Date	Inc. Above	16	26	41	56	83	158	838	1300	12000
1842 O Sm. Date	957,000	538	800	1325	1975	3875	12500	—	—	—
1842 O Lg. Date	Inc. Above	16	24	37	66	128	300	600	3575	—
1843	3,884,000	16	22	37	52	76	180	403	950	4500
1843 O	2,268,000	16	25	39	58	90	223	588	1725	—
1844	1,766,000	16	22	34	49	78	178	400	938	4588
1844 O	2,005,000	16	22	36	52	81	200	580	1925	4750
1845	589,000	26	37	53	89	175	343	900	—	—
1845 O	2,094,000	16	22	38	52	113	243	613	2250	—
1845 O No Drapery	Inc. Above	24	33	63	98	168	363	800	2875	—
1846 Med. Date	2,210,000	16	22	34	46	79	200	450	1600	9000
1846 Horizontal 6	Inc. Above	128	180	243	355	588	1150	2550	—	—
1846 O Med. Date	2,304,000	17	20	33	49	108	240	645	2250	12000
1846 O Tall Date	Inc. Above	130	243	335	543	950	1900	3725	—	—
1846 Tall Date	Inc. Above	20	29	52	70	123	245	593	1950	12000
1847	1,156,000	18	25	39	52	85	173	440	1475	9000
1847/1846	Inc. Above	1200	2200	3000	3750	4500	7500	—	—	—
1847 O	2,584,000	16	24	36	53	110	270	698	2200	7000
1848	580,000	32	53	75	130	228	463	1125	2575	9000
1848 O	3,180,000	17	26	38	48	113	305	763	2575	9000
1849	1,252,000	25	35	49	77	145	358	1015	2175	9000
1849 O	2,310,000	17	26	42	60	115	243	675	2300	9000
1850	227,000	185	253	333	395	550	875	1700	5125	—
1850 O	2,456,000	16	25	41	56	115	238	613	1975	9000

EDMUND'S 1996 U.S. COIN PRICES

HALF DOLLARS

DATE	MINTAGE	G-4	VG-8	F-12	VF-20	EF-40	AU-50	MS-60	MS-63	MS-65
1851	200,750	238	313	380	458	575	763	1438	2500	—
1851 O	402,000	27	37	55	88	180	343	643	1900	9000
1852	77,130	293	385	463	575	718	838	1275	2825	—
1852 O	144,000	48	85	150	300	470	825	2800	7875	14500

VARIETY TWO - ARROW AT DATE
RAYS AROUND EAGLE
1853

DIAMETER: 30.6mm
WEIGHT: 12.44 Grams
COMPOSITION: .900 Silver,
.100 Copper
DESIGNER: Christian Gobrecht
EDGE: Reeded

DATE	MINTAGE	G-4	VG-8	F-12	VF-20	EF-40	AU-50	MS-60	MS-63	MS-65
1853	3,532,708	16	27	43	85	238	470	1350	3225	21500
1853 O	1,328,000	19	28	51	125	270	825	2725	5750	21500

VARIETY THREE - ARROWS AT DATE
NO RAYS
1854-1855

DIAMETER: 30.6mm
WEIGHT: 12.44 Grams
COMPOSITION:
.900 Silver,
.100 Copper
DESIGNER: Christian Gobrecht
EDGE: Reeded

DATE	MINTAGE	G-4	VG-8	F-12	VF-20	EF-40	AU-50	MS-60	MS-63	MS-65	PRF-65
1854	2,982,000	15	22	34	46	98	245	630	2150	11500	22500
1854 O	5,240,000	15	21	33	45	95	233	500	1400	9000	—
1855	759,500	20	28	41	60	128	280	1013	2625	8000	22500
1855 O	3,688,000	16	22	34	47	96	248	688	2175	8000	—
1855 S	129,950	338	455	758	1525	2650	6350	14500	—	—	—

EDMUND'S 1996 U.S. COIN PRICES

HALF DOLLARS

VARIETY ONE RESUMED
1856-1866

DATE	MINTAGE	G-4	VG-8	F-12	VF-20	EF-40	AU-50	MS-60	MS-63	MS-65	PRF-65
1856	938,000	16	23	34	46	81	148	398	788	8500	12500
1856 O	2,658,000	14	21	31	43	79	158	428	900	12500	—
1856 S	211,000	41	53	98	208	400	1350	3000	4500	19000	—
1857	1,988,000	14	19	31	43	77	148	400	838	4500	12500
1857 O	818,000	16	23	34	57	113	263	825	1900	12500	—
1857 S	158,000	55	73	125	230	468	763	2875	5125	19000	—
1858	4,226,000	14	19	34	50	76	145	393	800	6500	9750
1858 O	7,294,000	14	19	34	43	71	145	413	1025	12500	—
1858 S	476,000	18	28	52	93	173	378	950	3225	12500	—
1859	748,000	19	28	46	61	95	205	545	1800	6600	5500
1859 O	2,834,000	14	23	39	48	80	175	453	1013	6500	—
1859 S	566,000	19	27	48	78	158	305	838	2800	12500	—
1860	303,700	17	23	40	65	115	293	750	1650	6500	5500
1860 O	1,290,000	15	21	39	50	71	183	425	1100	4500	—
1860 S	472,000	17	27	47	64	120	208	713	2400	12500	—
1861	2,888,400	14	23	33	42	71	145	388	763	4500	5500
1861 O	2,532,633	15	25	41	53	74	183	425	1075	4500	—
1861 S	939,500	16	22	37	52	100	208	938	3500	9500	—
1862	253,550	25	36	54	85	168	218	663	1675	4500	5500
1862 S	1,352,000	15	24	36	55	87	213	488	1875	9000	—
1863	503,660	18	27	44	67	133	250	605	1325	4500	5500
1863 S	916,000	17	27	41	54	108	200	435	1325	9000	—
1864	379,570	22	31	53	80	155	240	625	1550	4500	5500
1864 S	658,000	16	23	41	52	85	210	550	2425	9000	—
1865	511,900	20	27	44	65	125	260	633	1675	4500	6750
1865 S	675,000	16	23	36	55	85	263	643	2100	9000	—
1866	Unique	—	—	—	—	—	—	—	—	—	—
1866 S	1,054,000	43	70	129	233	450	998	2650	1400	5000	—

VARIETY FOUR
MOTTO ABOVE EAGLE
1866-1873

DIAMETER: 30.6mm
WEIGHT: 12.44 Grams
COMPOSITION:
.900 Silver,
.100 Copper
DESIGNER: Christian Gobrecht
EDGE: Reeded

HALF DOLLARS

DATE	MINTAGE	G-4	VG-8	F-12	VF-20	EF-40	AU-50	MS-60	MS-63	MS-65	PRF-65
1866	745,625	15	24	33	40	80	145	350	1200	4800	3750
1866 S	Inc. Above	15	24	33	40	75	145	350	1400	5000	—
1867	449,925	20	33	51	88	145	235	393	1150	4800	3750
1867 S	1,196,000	15	23	35	44	78	158	425	2250	7000	—
1868	418,200	35	48	68	133	250	338	550	1125	7100	3750
1868 S	1,160,000	15	25	37	45	103	200	525	1975	7000	—
1869	795,900	18	27	36	46	85	168	385	1188	4600	3750
1869 S	656,000	15	26	39	52	98	280	725	2175	7000	—
1870	634,900	19	27	38	59	100	175	423	1125	7000	3750
1870 CC	54,617	475	763	1375	2375	4225	8500	—	40000	—	—
1870 S	1,004,000	18	26	40	59	108	233	473	1225	7000	—
1871	1,204,560	17	24	36	49	71	155	345	1163	7000	3750
1871 CC	153,950	120	173	298	463	913	1950	4075	6000	9150	—
1871 S	2,178,000	14	22	34	43	74	185	575	1538	7000	—
1872	881,550	15	24	35	44	67	163	370	1025	4500	3750
1872 CC	272,000	50	88	173	300	638	1575	2675	5000	8800	—
1872 S	580,000	23	32	58	88	180	383	1125	2775	7000	—
1873 Closed 3	801,800	21	33	52	79	120	268	455	1063	4550	3750
1873 Open 3	Inc. Above	2325	3000	4450	6200	8500	10750	19000	40000	—	—
1873 CC	122,500	120	160	265	475	1275	2075	5050	8000	9000	3750
1873 S	5,000	43	63	103	198	2193	713	1850	5225	14000	—

VARIETY FIVE
ARROWS AT DATE
1873-1874

DIAMETER: 30.6mm
WEIGHT: 12.50 Grams
COMPOSITION: .900 Silver, .100 Copper
DESIGNER: Christian Gobrecht
EDGE: Reeded

DATE	MINTAGE	G-4	VG-8	F-12	VF-20	EF-40	AU-50	MS-60	MS-63	MS-65	PRF-65
1873	1,815,700	17	25	38	77	208	443	938	2375	14000	9000
1873 CC	214,560	100	120	225	400	800	1250	4500	—	—	—
1873 S	233,000	45	60	90	195	400	725	1600	2950	14000	—
1874	2,360,300	17	25	38	75	203	443	938	2275	14000	9000
1874 CC	59,000	63	93	161	290	763	1643	3400	8350	14000	—
1874 S	394,000	29	35	64	135	283	600	1775	3700	14000	—

HALF DOLLARS

VARIETY FOUR RESUMED
1875-1891

DATE	MINTAGE	G-4	VG-8	F-12	VF-20	EF-40	AU-50	MS-60	MS-63	MS-65	PRF-65
1875	6,027,500	14	22	31	39	64	140	368	788	3500	2550
1875 CC	1,008,000	18	36	50	78	153	283	570	1363	5450	—
1875 S	3,200,000	15	23	38	49	75	143	330	700	2700	—
1876	8,419,150	14	22	31	39	63	148	325	668	5300	3750
1876 CC	1,956,000	17	29	48	68	130	275	588	1263	4200	—
1876 S	4,528,000	14	22	31	39	64	168	363	813	2700	—
1877	8,304,510	14	22	30	42	64	153	325	670	2700	3750
1877 CC	1,420,000	18	31	44	65	123	268	615	1063	3250	—
1877 S	5,356,000	14	22	30	39	65	158	338	675	2700	—
1878	1,378,400	19	32	43	55	105	203	430	763	3650	2550
1878 CC	62,000	258	343	513	975	1675	2575	4875	12975	—	—
1878 S	12,000	6375	7875	10250	13750	18500	22000	28750	75000	—	—
1879	5,900	200	223	275	315	388	470	618	1075	2900	2550
1880	9,755	188	210	245	190	365	468	618	1075	2900	2550
1881	10,975	178	203	243	280	358	460	633	1038	2900	2550
1882	5,500	208	238	288	348	420	508	688	1175	3600	2550
1883	9,039	185	213	245	250	383	475	663	1188	2900	2550
1884	5,275	235	275	310	363	435	533	690	1250	2900	2550
1885	6,130	225	245	290	343	425	515	700	1263	2900	2550
1886	5,886	268	338	413	445	480	570	733	1243	4800	2550
1887	5,710	325	385	450	550	650	750	900	1500	2900	2550
1888	12,833	175	200	235	300	375	425	700	1100	2900	2550
1889	12,711	175	200	235	300	375	425	700	1100	2900	2550
1890	12,590	175	200	235	300	375	425	700	1100	3250	2550
1891	200,600	40	50	60	90	140	290	500	950	3250	2550

HALF DOLLARS

BARBER TYPE
1892-1915

DIAMETER: 30.6mm
WEIGHT: 12.50 Grams
COMPOSITION: .900 Silver,
              .100 Copper
DESIGNER: Charles E. Barber
EDGE: Reeded
PURE SILVER CONTENT: .36169 Tr. Oz.

The Barber half dollar bears the identical front and reverse design as the Barber quarter and was in production from 1892 to 1915, one year less than both small Barber coins. Barber halves offer an interesting mix for investors. The most shocking aspect of Barber half dollars is how poorly MS-65 and PR-65 have performed over the last five years. Almost any Barber half properly graded in these conditions is a bargain at today's prices, and is unlikely to be this affordable again.

Another area with good potential can be found in the Extremely Fine and Almost Uncirculated grades. These coins enjoyed healthy advances in the late 1980's, but have fallen off slightly in the 1990's. For the best return on your money, focus on the better date issues, such as the 1892-S or the 1897-S.

DATE	MINTAGE	G-4	VG-8	F-12	VF-20	EF-40	AU-50	MS-60	MS-63	MS-65	PRF-65
1892	935,245	9.65	25	40	77	163	270	408	713	2600	2500
1892 O	390,000	87	140	198	275	388	428	773	1425	5225	—
1892 S	1,020,028	108	68	193	263	370	573	838	1700	5225	—
1893	1,826,792	13	18	40	71	148	308	495	950	3775	2500
1893 O	1,389,000	17	25	52	118	263	355	543	1118	9600	—
1893 S	740,000	57	74	133	263	373	553	1113	2413	12000	—
1894	1,148,972	14	29	56	90	190	343	473	880	3125	2500
1894 O	2,138,000	11	15	53	102	225	348	488	1018	4500	—
1894 S	4,048,690	11	14	44	79	245	320	490	1338	9600	—
1895	1,835,218	8.25	13	43	74	170	300	480	868	3400	2500
1895 O	1,766,000	9.75	18	47	88	233	368	605	1550	6000	—
1895 S	1,108,086	17	25	62	120	263	373	538	1213	7800	—
1896	950,762	16	22	48	85	193	308	475	913	5400	3400
1896 O	924,000	19	26	74	145	335	628	1175	3275	12000	—
1896 S	1,140,948	54	71	108	183	358	600	1125	2850	10250	—
1897	2,480,731	16	8.00	27	71	128	293	418	713	3300	2500
1897 O	632,000	45	69	270	483	823	1125	1475	2950	4700	—
1897 S	933,900	81	108	250	403	625	938	1300	2975	7600	—
1898	2,956,735	6.00	7.25	25	68	128	285	393	668	2600	2500

EDMUND'S 1996 U.S. COIN PRICES

HALF DOLLARS

DATE	MINTAGE	G-4	VG-8	F-12	VF-20	EF-40	AU-50	MS-60	MS-63	MS-65	PRF-65
1898 O	874,000	14	24	87	168	380	510	838	2575	8400	—
1898 S	2,358,550	7.75	14	38	80	180	343	733	2288	9000	—
1899	5,538,846	5.75	7.25	25	69	128	285	388	673	3300	3900
1899 O	1,724,000	7.65	12	41	86	185	325	563	1145	6100	—
1899 S	1,686,411	7.65	13	43	80	183	338	548	1325	6600	—
1900	4,762,912	5.75	7.50	25	68	123	275	388	670	2600	2500
1900 O	2,744,000	7.25	11	38	86	243	343	725	2463	14500	—
1900 S	2,560,322	7.00	11	37	86	175	305	588	2025	9600	—
1901	4,268,813	5.75	7.40	25	68	123	275	378	678	4200	3250
1901 O	1,124,000	7.30	13	45	99	288	475	1225	3225	14500	—
1901 S	847,044	13	22	90	205	500	890	1475	4200	12500	—
1902	4,922,777	5.70	7.40	25	68	123	255	378	633	3400	2900
1902 O	2,526,000	6.75	10	37	72	178	348	683	2925	9900	—
1902 S	1,460,670	6.75	10	39	81	213	388	605	1800	5500	—
1903	2,278,755	6.90	8.50	29	69	145	300	448	1300	8000	3125
1903 O	2,100,000	6.15	10	38	72	173	313	633	1313	9000	—
1903 S	1,920,772	6.15	11	37	75	200	348	583	1538	5900	—
1904	2,992,670	5.70	7.40	27	68	123	275	393	838	4200	3400
1904 O	1,117,600	9.00	15	48	110	275	458	975	2600	9600	—
1904 S	553,038	13	23	113	313	580	950	1775	3675	14000	—
1905	662,727	11	13	46	80	195	305	545	1275	5400	3125
1905 O	505,000	11	20	59	125	315	558	1383	1425	6000	—
1905 S	2,494,000	5.90	8.00	34	72	173	333	563	1800	9000	—
1906	2,638,675	5.40	6.90	24	68	123	275	393	633	3400	2500
1906 D	4,028,000	5.50	7.90	26	69	138	278	408	638	4100	—
1906 O	2,446,000	5.65	7.95	33	72	158	290	573	1200	5400	—
1906 S	1,740,154	6.25	10	41	73	178	310	540	1025	5650	—
1907	2,598,575	5.40	6.90	25	68	123	275	400	620	2600	3250
1907 D	3,856,000	5.50	8.00	26	71	143	285	410	688	2600	—
1907 O	3,946,000	5.40	7.90	27	68	145	293	470	848	3400	—
1907 S	1,250,000	5.50	10	62	106	325	475	825	2550	10750	—
1908	1,354,545	5.40	6.90	30	70	148	293	425	725	3250	3250
1908 D	3,280,000	5.40	7.90	29	69	135	293	453	740	2600	—
1908 O	5,360,000	5.40	7.90	27	68	140	348	458	800	2600	—
1908 S	1,644,828	6.25	12	38	75	180	333	675	1950	5200	—
1909	2,368,650	5.40	6.90	25	68	123	255	388	633	2600	3200
1909 O	925,400	6.65	8.75	33	80	213	398	583	1263	4750	—
1909 S	1,764,000	5.65	8.00	27	73	170	325	508	1125	3350	—
1910	418,551	9.50	17	57	105	238	395	722	1188	3850	3450
1910 S	1,948,000	5.65	7.15	26	68	165	343	575	1875	4300	—
1911	1,406,543	5.40	7.15	25	68	128	288	400	645	2600	2500
1911 D	695,080	6.25	10	34	79	173	280	495	793	2600	—
1911 S	1,272,000	5.65	8.15	31	73	153	323	513	1175	4900	—
1912	1,550,700	5.40	6.90	25	68	138	288	388	620	3700	3200
1912 D	2,300,800	5.40	7.75	25	71	125	288	415	758	2600	—
1912 S	1,370,000	5.40	8.15	27	72	160	303	493	963	5300	—

EDMUND'S 1996 U.S. COIN PRICES

HALF DOLLARS

DATE	MINTAGE	G-4	VG-8	F-12	VF-20	EF-40	AU-50	MS-60	MS-63	MS-65	PRF-65
1913	188,627	18	27	81	170	320	613	930	2100	3600	3000
1913 D	534,000	6.00	8.50	34	69	435	278	473	770	4550	—
1913 S	604,000	6.25	10	37	79	185	343	605	1070	4000	—
1914	124,610	27	44	153	288	480	750	1050	1738	11000	3575
1914 S	992,000	6.25	7.75	30	68	163	328	563	1138	3400	—
1915	138,450	20	27	77	188	350	635	988	1988	4300	3250
1915 D	1,170,400	5.40	6.90	25	68	125	250	383	625	2600	—
1915 S	1,604,000	5.40	7.00	26	69	138	258	468	705	2600	—

WALKING LIBERTY TYPE
1916-1947

DIAMETER: 30.6mm
WEIGHT: 12.50 Grams
COMPOSITION: .900 Silver,
.100 Copper
DESIGNER: Adolph A. Weinman
EDGE: Reeded
PURE SILVER CONTENT: .36169 Tr. Oz.

The artistically acclaimed Walking Liberty half dollar replaced the Barber half as our nation's fifty cent piece in 1916. "Walkers," as they are referred to by insiders, have traditionally been among the most well-liked United States coins, appealing to both collectors and investors. Because of their widespread popularity, Walkers should always enjoy a strong demand. As an added incentive to the investor, quality Walkers normally carry wholesale values relatively close to retail values, translating into smaller markdowns when you sell.

In terms of availability, the Walking Liberty half can be divided into two groups. The first group, comprised of halves dating 1916 through 1933, are less common, especially in upper grades. The second group, dating 1934 to the end of the series in 1947, saw annual production figures far in excess of the earlier issues, and are more readily available in higher grades. A collector contemplating purchasing a Walker for investment purposes would be wise to keep these facts in mind.

Walking Liberty half dollars in the best conditions are more volatile in price than nearly any other series of American coins. They have been a prime target of promoters and speculators for a long time now, which explains the roller coaster effect on values. An attractive, immensely popular coin with large supplies, it's a small wonder as to why the Walkers are so heavily promoted.

HALF DOLLARS

The majority of the speculator activity seen in the last decade or so has been mainly confined to the MS-65 or better grades. In 1990-91, the market for Walkers, including common dates grading MS-65 and better, collapsed. To date, it has not yet recovered (recall from the Introduction the discussion concerning high grade "generic" pieces). To purchase a Walker matching this description at today's prices would have to be considered a steal. Can we expect future price surges similar to those of the past? Probably so, but it's really difficult to say when it might happen with so much promoter involvement. One thing is certain: if you purchase even common date MS-65 Walking Liberty halves with long term objectives in mind, you're virtually guaranteed of enviable returns.

Of all the Walking Liberty half dollars, not even the key dates have escaped severe price plunges. The drops are evident from the lowest grades to the highest grades. In most instances, we see prices drastically reduced from their 1989 highs. As an investor, though, the only halves to buy in less than Fine condition are the 1916, 1916-D, 1916-S, 1917-D (mint mark on obverse), 1917-S (mint mark on obverse), 1919, 1921, 1921-D, 1921-S, and the 1938-D. The rest of the low grade Walkers march to the tune of the metals market and shouldn't be counted on to appreciate solely on the basis of their numismatic integrity.

In grades from Extremely Fine and above, Walkers dated before 1934 appear to be sound investments. They are very scarce in problem-free condition, but are not priced as such. Some of the issues of 1934 and beyond are desirable acquisitions in Extremely Fine and Almost Uncirculated, but on the whole, you need to look at nothing less than MS-65 specimens for the best potential. The generic Walkers fall within this range (most of the halves dated in the 1940's), and as mentioned above, now is a great chance to land very high quality examples of these coins at garage sale prices!

For the first time in a long while, all pre-1934 Walkers properly graded at MS-65 Uncirculated should be considered, as prices have retreated dramatically from their 1989 record setting levels. With prices this low, you can feel safe in expecting them to rise sharply within the next few years. These increases could be very pronounced if promoters and speculators again become actively involved in the Walker market. The best possible action to take is to acquire these coins before the bandwagon pushes costs higher!

MINT MARK ON OBVERSE

DATE	MINTAGE	G-4	VG-8	F-12	VF-20	EF-40	AU-50	MS-60	MS-63	MS-65
1916	608,000	19	24	52	108	145	190	243	388	1538
1916 D	1,014,400	11	17	31	69	128	173	265	488	2000
1916 S	508,000	56	63	120	280	475	598	798	1528	4650
1917 D	765,400	12	15	30	84	150	210	430	1100	6500
1917 S	952,000	13	21	44	235	633	1100	1825	4150	12325

HALF DOLLARS

MINT MARK ON REVERSE

DATE	MINTAGE	G-4	VG-8	F-12	VF-20	EF-40	AU-50	MS-60	MS-63	MS-65	PRF-65
1917	12,292,000	7.00	7.50	9.75	19	32	60	91	210	863	—
1917 D	1,940,000	8.50	11	21	59	173	385	678	1965	15500	—
1917 S	5,554,000	6.00	8.00	14	25	48	120	280	1500	9750	—
1918	6,634,000	7.25	8.75	17	42	115	218	390	888	3200	—
1918 D	3,853,040	8.00	9.25	19	49	140	318	725	1888	19080	—
1918 S	10,282,000	7.00	7.75	13	27	53	130	338	1600	16125	—
1919	962,000	10.50	15	31	128	358	573	958	2425	4213	—
1919 D	1,165,000	9.50	13	32	143	485	1063	2400	5650	45670	—
1919 S	1,552,000	8.50	11	25	120	575	1275	2000	5325	10125	—
1920	6,372,000	7.00	7.75	11	23	58	103	248	663	5525	—
1920 D	1,551,000	8.50	9.40	26	128	328	670	1163	3113	9300	—
1920 S	4,624,000	7.00	7.75	14	44	175	343	738	1975	8725	—
1921	246,000	52	82	175	540	1388	2125	2850	4050	9800	—
1921 D	208,000	83	120	243	698	1875	2625	3050	4463	13750	—
1921 S	548,000	18	21	62	570	4125	6425	8600	16500	40750	—
1923 S	2,178,000	8.50	9.25	17	44	205	520	1100	2938	13625	—
1927 S	2,392,000	6.00	6.65	11	26	83	283	650	1500	8375	—
1928 S	1,940,000	6.00	6.90	11	29	100	305	608	1950	5600	—
1929 D	1,001,200	6.25	6.75	9.90	18	68	150	255	625	2050	—
1929 S	1,902,000	5.50	6.25	9.40	16	65	163	300	698	2333	—
1933 S	1,786,000	5.50	6.65	8.75	12	43	168	478	950	3313	—
1934	6,964,000	2.65	2.75	2.85	4.25	11	24	47	82	303	—
1934 D	2,361,400	3.25	4.00	5.50	7.75	24	53	103	238	988	—
1934 S	3,652,000	3.00	3.40	4.15	6.00	24	69	223	598	2575	—
1935	9,162,000	2.65	2.75	2.85	4.25	8.25	20	42	55	258	—
1935 D	3,003,800	3.25	3.75	4.75	7.75	23	52	110	220	1118	—
1935 S	3,854,000	3.10	3.40	4.00	5.65	24	64	125	260	1900	—
1936	12,617,901	2.50	2.75	3.15	4.25	7.75	19	36	49	135	2500
1936 D	4,252,400	2.95	3.25	4.00	5.50	16	45	68	103	345	—
1936 S	3,884,000	3.00	3.25	3.75	5.60	17	45	98	178	510	—
1937	9,527,728	2.65	2.75	3.15	4.25	8.00	19	35	47	190	850
1937 D	1,676,000	7.25	6.75	8.40	11	28	84	153	185	475	—
1937 S	2,090,000	6.00	5.90	6.65	8.00	17	57	100	155	470	—
1938	4,118,152	3.00	3.25	4.25	6.25	10	35	55	85	250	580
1938 D	491,600	18	18	25	44	95	243	375	480	925	—
1939	6,820,808	2.65	2.65	3.15	4.50	8.75	19	38	48	135	525
1939 D	4,267,800	2.95	3.25	3.50	5.25	9.75	23	41	50	140	—
1939 S	2,552,000	6.30	6.25	7.15	8.40	13	43	95	113	195	—
1940	9,167,279	2.65	2.65	3.35	4.75	7.50	12	30	36	113	450
1940 S	4,550,000	2.65	3.15	3.50	5.25	10	19	38	54	390	—
1941	24,207,412	2.65	2.65	3.10	4.15	6.40	8.25	25	35	105	435
1941 D	11,248,400	2.65	2.80	3.25	4.25	6.00	14	39	44	118	—

EDMUND'S 1996 U.S. COIN PRICES

HALF DOLLARS

DATE	MINTAGE	G-4	VG-8	F-12	VF-20	EF-40	AU-50	MS-60	MS-63	MS-65	PRF-65
1941 S	8,098,000	2.65	2.80	3.40	4.65	7.00	23	73	115	1050	—
1942	47,839,120	2.65	2.65	3.10	4.15	5.65	8.25	25	35	105	435
1942 D	10,973,800	2.65	2.80	3.25	4.25	6.00	16	39	57	188	—
1942 S	12,706,000	2.65	2.80	3.25	4.65	7.00	19	36	48	403	—
1943	53,190,000	2.65	2.65	3.10	4.15	5.65	8.25	25	35	105	—
1943 D	11,346,000	2.65	2.80	3.25	4.25	6.00	19	45	62	145	—
1943 S	13,450,000	2.65	2.80	3.40	4.50	6.00	20	34	46	310	—
1944	28,206,000	2.65	2.80	3.30	4.40	5.50	7.50	32	—	100	—
1944 D	9,769,000	2.65	2.80	3.25	4.25	6.00	17	32	40	115	—
1944 S	8,904,000	2.65	2.80	3.25	4.40	6.15	19	34	47	548	—
1945	31,502,000	2.65	2.65	3.10	4.15	5.65	8.25	24	35	108	—
1945 D	9,966,800	2.65	2.80	3.25	4.25	6.00	14	34	38	108	—
1945 S	10,156,000	2.65	2.80	3.25	5.40	15	13	32	38	148	—
1946	12,118,000	2.65	2.65	3.10	4.25	5.75	12	31	36	128	—
1946 D	2,151,000	4.50	4.50	5.90	8.90	11	19	33	38	105	—
1946 S	3,724,000	2.65	2.80	3.25	4.50	5.50	16	32	36	113	—
1947	4,094,000	2.65	3.10	3.40	4.75	7.50	18	33	39	158	—
1947 D	3,900,600	2.65	2.90	3.40	4.75	7.50	18	33	39	128	—

FRANKLIN TYPE
1948-1963

DIAMETER: 30.6mm
WEIGHT: 12.50 Grams
COMPOSITION: .900 Silver,
.100 Copper
DESIGNER: John R. Sinnock
EDGE: Reeded
PURE SILVER CONTENT: .36169 Tr. Oz.

The Ben Franklin half dollar made its appearance in 1948 and continued its run until 1963, with the introduction of the Kennedy half dollar in 1964. What we find in this series as a whole are coins that for many years never earned proper respect from collectors or investors, considered as nothing more than bullion coins. Collectors are just now beginning to acknowledge Franklin halves as worthy keepsakes, leaving foresighted investors with plenty of chances to locate very nice coins at minimal expenditures.

Many Franklins in MS-65 Uncirculated condition increased 14 times their value from 1987 to 1990, but have dipped now to well below that level. True, in 1990 the prices may have been artificially high, but presently there is little downside risk to adding gem Franklins to your numismatic holdings. One can expect, if nothing else, some speculative attention to return to MS-65

HALF DOLLARS

Franklins, and those who act knowledgeably today, most certainly for pre-1959 production, should experience enviable gains.

Whatever uncirculated condition half you are able to buy, make the attempt to select well struck specimens having "Full Bell Lines" on the Liberty Bell reverse (abbreviated FBL). Most coin experts, but not all, believe this quality is every bit as important as the Full Split Bands in the Mercury dime series, and are happy to pay hefty premiums to obtain them. On the other hand, you won't have to spend too much extra for a FBL half in some instances. If buying a FBL Franklin half dollar, it would be generally safer to buy one with a lower premium attached to it.

The Ben Franklin half dollar in MS-65 Proof condition is also far more affordable than a few years ago. Any of these coins, properly graded, would be an excellent acquisition on your part. Some attention should be given to "cameo" proofs. These are proofs that were the very first strikes off new proof dies, and exhibit frosted surface features similar to current day proofs. Some numismatists contend cameo proofs are 30 times scarcer overall than ordinary proof Franklins, but are not priced as such.

For the very small budget investor who cannot afford the gem material, the Franklin half still holds out some hope. A collection of very inexpensive, well-worn specimens stands to benefit from an improvement in the metals market, it nothing else. As more collectors get interested in this obsolete series, we'll see more demand and hence more appreciation of these coins. Moreover, Franklins are not as plentiful as one might think, not even in lower grades, because of the huge melting losses over the years. No one has an inventory on the actual number of survivors, but we'll get a clearer picture of the situation when future buyers compete for the remaining supply of Franklins. There is one thing we do know: you will probably never be able to purchase Ben Franklin halves this cheaply again.

DATE	MINTAGE	G-4	VG-8	F-12	VF-20	EF-40	AU-50	MS-60	MS-63	MS-65	PRF-65
1948	3,006,814	2.75	3.50	3.40	4.00	6.75	8.50	18	23	68	—
1948 D	4,028,600	4.50	4.25	4.25	4.75	7.15	8.15	9.25	16	150	—
1949	5,614,000	3.50	3.75	3.75	5.00	8.50	13	39	50	93	—
1949 D	4,120,600	—	3.50	3.75	5.05	10	17	39	48	1163	—
1949 S	3,744,000	—	3.75	4.40	5.90	11	25	54	65	145	—
1950	7,793,509	—	—	3.35	3.90	6.90	9.75	30	43	115	270
1950 D	8,031,600	—	—	3.30	3.85	6.65	8.65	22	28	455	—
1951	16,859,602	—	—	3.00	3.60	5.50	6.50	12	18	76	198
1951 D	9,475,200	—	—	3.20	3.90	4.65	11	30	40	235	—
1951 S	13,696,000	—	—	3.50	4.00	4.75	15	27	42	70	—
1952	21,274,073	—	—	2.50	3.00	3.50	4.00	8.00	13	55	133
1952 D	25,395,600	—	—	2.70	3.15	3.70	4.25	6.00	8.00	100	—
1952 S	5,526,000	—	—	3.05	4.00	4.75	15	37	42	68	—
1953	2,796,920	3.75	4.00	4.15	4.75	5.50	9.00	12	19	115	74
1953 D	20,900,400	—	—	2.50	2.95	3.45	9.00	7.00	11	100	—
1953 S	4,148,000	—	—	3.50	4.00	4.40	8.75	15	20	58	—

EDMUND'S 1996 U.S. COIN PRICES

HALF DOLLARS

DATE	MINTAGE	G-4	VG-8	F-12	VF-20	EF-40	AU-50	MS-60	MS-63	MS-65	PRF-65
1954	13,421,503	—	—	2.50	2.95	3.85	4.50	5.75	12	63	54
1954 D	25,445,580	—	—	2.50	2.70	3.45	4.25	6.15	10	100	—
1954 S	4,993,400	—	—	3.00	3.45	3.90	5.40	6.50	11	40	—
1955	2,876,381	4.50	5.00	6.00	6.40	6.75	7.40	8.40	11	35	45
1956	4,701,384	—	—	3.10	3.70	4.50	5.25	6.75	11	32	14
1957	6,361,952	—	—	2.95	3.45	3.85	4.25	6.90	11	32	14
1957 D	19,966,850	—	—	2.90	3.35	2.75	3.15	5.75	9.50	32	—
1958	4,917,652	—	—	2.65	3.00	3.75	4.40	5.00	9.50	32	14
1958 D	23,962,412	—	—	2.00	2.40	2.65	3.00	3.90	8.00	32	—
1959	7,349,291	—	—	2.00	2.40	2.65	3.00	5.00	8.00	100	13
1959 D	13,053,750	—	—	2.00	2.40	2.65	3.25	5.25	8.15	90	—
1960	7,715,602	—	—	2.25	2.40	2.65	3.00	4.25	7.25	100	13
1960 D	18,215,812	—	—	2.40	2.40	2.65	3.00	5.15	6.90	500	—
1961	11,318,244	—	—	2.00	2.40	2.55	2.75	4.50	7.00	150	9.50
1961 D	20,276,442	—	—	2.25	2.40	2.55	2.75	4.50	7.00	375	—
1962	12,932,019	—	—	2.00	2.40	2.55	2.75	3.90	6.75	140	9.50
1962 D	35,473,281	—	—	2.25	2.40	2.55	3.00	4.15	6.90	300	—
1963	25,239,645	—	—	2.00	2.40	2.55	2.75	3.15	6.00	75	9.50
1963 D	67,069,292	—	—	2.00	2.40	2.50	2.65	3.15	6.00	75	—

KENNEDY TYPE
1964 TO DATE

DIAMETER: 30.6mm
WEIGHT: 1964: 12.50 Grams
1965-1970: 11.50 Grams
1971 To Date: 11.34 Grams
COMPOSITION: 1964: .900 Silver, .100 Copper
1965-1970: Silver Clad
overall composition
.400 Silver, .600 Copper
1971 To Date: Copper Clad Issue
.750 Copper, .250 Nickel Outer Layers
Pure Copper Inner Core
DESIGNERS: Gilroy Roberts
Frank Gasparro
EDGE: Reeded
PURE SILVER CONTENT:
1964: .36169 Tr. Oz.
1965-1970: .14792 Tr. Oz.

NOTE: The Kennedy half dollars of 1976 are listed on page 175 with the other bicentennial coinage.

HALF DOLLARS

The first Kennedy half dollars were issued in 1964 in honor of the slain president. Throughout its history, the speculator influence has been very minimal, leaving ground floor opportunities for investors with virtually no downside risk.

SILVER COINAGE 1964

The 1964 pieces are the only Kennedy halves to contain 90% silver. Today, MS-65 Uncirculated 1964 Kennedys are selling for only slightly above their bullion value. Although no United States coin has ever been hoarded more than the 1964 issues, they are certainly poised for future price appreciation when collector interest and bullion prices are triggered. You shouldn't have any difficulty in obtaining MS-65 (or better) examples

DATE	MINTAGE	MS-60	MS-65	PRF-65
1964	277,254,766	2.40	7.50	8.00
1964 D	156,205,446	2.40	9.25	—

SILVER CLAD COINAGE 1965-1970

The rarest Kennedy half is the 1970-D, with a mintage of 2.15 million, very low by modern day standards. Priced at only $12 in MS-60 and $17 in MS-65, this coin is destined to multiply in value when Kennedys become widely collected. Just as the rarest coin in other series jumped in value when they became popular, we can rightfully expect a similar occurrence here.

The second scarcest Kennedy half is the 1970-S proof edition, having a production total of slightly over 2.6 million. This coin is priced well below its earlier highs and should be considered a sleeper with encouraging investment potential.

DATE	MINTAGE	MS-60	MS-65	PRF-65
1965	65,879,366	1.15	4.25	—
1966	108,984,932	1.10	4.20	—
1967	295,046,978	1.00	5.65	—
1968 D	246,951,930	1.00	4.15	—
1968 S	3,041,506	—	—	3.00
1969 D	129,881,800	1.00	3.50	4.00
1969 S	2,934,631	—	—	3.00
1970 D	2,150,000	9.50	27	—
1970 S	2,632,810	—	—	7.25

HALF DOLLARS

COPPER-NICKEL CLAD COINAGE

DATE	MINTAGE	MS-60	MS-65	PRF-65
1971	155,164,000	1.25	3.25	—
1971 D	302,097,424	1.00	2.25	—
1971 S	Proof Only	—	—	2.90
1972	153,180,000	1.50	3.25	—
1972 D	141,890,000	1.50	3.25	—
1972 S	Proof Only	—	—	2.75
1973	64,964,000	1.20	3.25	—
1973 D	83,171,400	0.95	3.00	—
1973 S	Proof Only	—	—	1.75
1974	201,596,000	0.95	2.40	—
1974 D	79,066,300	1.05	3.00	—
1974 S	Proof Only	—	—	1.65

See pages 174-175 for 1976 bicentennial half dollars

DATE	MINTAGE	MS-60	MS-65	PRF-65
1977	43,598,000	1.85	3.65	—
1977 D	31,449,106	1.85	3.25	—
1977 S	Proof Only	—	—	1.65
1978	14,350,000	1.15	3.50	—
1978 D	13,765,799	1.50	3.50	—
1978 S	Proof Only	—	—	1.65
1979	68,312,000	0.95	2.50	—
1979 D	15,815,422	0.95	2.65	—
1979 S	Proof Only	—	—	1.75
1980 D	33,456,449	0.90	2.40	—
1980 P	44,134,000	0.90	2.40	—
1980 S	Proof Only	—	—	1.50
1981 D	27,839,533	0.95	2.25	—
1981 P	29,544,000	1.00	2.50	—
1981 S	Proof Only	—	—	1.50
1982 D	13,140,102	1.10	2.00	—
1982 P	10,819,000	1.10	1.50	—
1982 S	Proof Only	—	—	2.65
1983 D	32,472,244	1.05	1.50	—
1983 P	34,139,000	1.05	1.50	—
1983 S	Proof Only	—	—	3.15
1984 D	26,262,158	1.25	1.50	—
1984 P	26,029,000	1.25	1.50	—
1984 S	Proof Only	—	—	5.75
1985 D	19,814,034	1.25	1.25	—
1985 P	18,706,962	1.25	1.25	—
1985 S	Proof Only	—	—	3.50
1986 D	15,336,145	1.35	1.50	—

EDMUND'S 1996 U.S. COIN PRICES

HALF DOLLARS

DATE	MINTAGE	MS-60	MS-65	PRF-65
1986 P	13,107,633	1.60	2.00	—
1986 S	Proof Only	—	—	15
1987 D	2,890,758	2.15	4.50	—
1987 P	2,890,758	2.15	4.50	—
1987 S	Proof Only	—	—	3.25
1988 D	12,000,096	1.00	2.50	—
1988 P	13,626,000	0.90	2.50	—
1988 S	Proof Only	—	—	6.25
1989 D	23,000,216	0.90	2.50	—
1989 P	24,542,000	1.00	2.50	—
1989 S	Proof Only	—	—	4.15
1990 D	20,096,242	0.90	1.50	—
1990 P	22,278,000	0.90	1.50	—
1990 S	Proof Only	—	—	4.50
1991 D	15,054,678	0.90	1.50	—
1991 P	14,874,000	0.90	1.50	—
1991 S	Proof Only	—	—	15
1992 D	17,000,106	0.90	1.00	—
1992 P	17,628,000	0.90	1.00	—
1992 S	Proof Only	—	—	15
1993 D		0.90	1.00	—
1993 P		0.90	1.00	—
1993 S	Proof Only	—	—	13
1994 D		0.90	1.00	—
1994 P		0.90	1.00	—
1994 S	Proof Only	—	—	11
1995 P		0.90	1.00	—
1995 D		0.90	1.00	—
1995 S	Proof Only	—	—	11
1995 S	Silver Proof	—	—	11

SILVER DOLLARS

SILVER DOLLARS 1794 TO DATE

Silver dollars were a part of the American coinage system from 1794 to 1981, with several lengthy breaks interspersed. The dollar unit has always been the foundation upon which the face values of all other United States coins are based. In all, there are eleven different types of silver dollars to collect; some don't cost very much, while others are very expensive. Nevertheless, solid investment opportunities abound in all types of silver dollars for the buyer who knows how to analyze market trends.

FLOWING HAIR TYPE 1794-1795

DIAMETER: 39-40mm
WEIGHT: 26.96 Grams
COMPOSITION: .8924 Silver, .1076 Copper
DESIGNER: Robert Scot
EDGE: HUNDRED CENTS ONE DOLLAR OR UNIT With Decorations Between Words

The Flowing Hair silver dollar saw production in 1794 and 1795. The 1794 is a consistent gainer suitable for big-time investors. Only twice over the last 40 years has there been a let-down in performance; once in the late 1960's and again in the late 1980's and early 1990's. Watch for the 1794 dollar to take off again toward many years of sustained growth.

Both varieties of the 1795 Flowing Hair dollar are currently valued well below their 1983 highs, and probably will not fall much further. Although not nearly as expensive as the 1794, you'll still require over $750 to purchase a specimen in Good condition. That's a considerable sum of money to spend, but for a collectible of this caliber, it's really a bargain. Don't fret about high price tags for better quality material. They're undervalued as well, and will make a proud addition to anyone's holdings.

DATE	MINTAGE	AG-3	G-4	VG-8	F-12	VF-20	EF-40	AU-50	MS-60
1794	1,758	4550	8250	13500	18750	27000	41500	82500	200000
1795 2 Leaves	203,033	475	738	888	1525	2300	4775	7875	29500
1795 3 Leaves	Inc. Above	463	725	875	1500	2275	4725	7825	29500

SILVER DOLLARS

DRAPED BUST TYPE SMALL EAGLE REVERSE 1795-1798

DIAMETER: 39-40mm
WEIGHT: 26.96 Grams
COMPOSITION: .8924 Silver,
.1076 Copper
DESIGNER: Robert Scot
EDGE: HUNDRED CENTS ONE DOLLAR OR UNIT With Decorations Between Words

The Draped Bust silver dollar with the small eagle reverse had a short lifespan, running from 1795 to 1798. There are many interesting varieties to study as the dies were engraved by hand. These silver dollars have followed almost identically the value trends of the 1795 Flowing Hair dollars, translating into more good buys for the investor or collector. This series contains a number of issues that are more easily affordable to the buying public than the previous silver dollars, although they're by no means inexpensive.

DATE	MINTAGE	AG-3	G-4	VG-8	F-12	VF-20	EF-40	AU-50	MS-60
1795	Inc. Above	368	595	775	1023	1638	3525	6700	18500
1796 Sm. Date, Sm. Letters	72,920	388	650	813	1100	1800	3625	7000	15500
1796 Lg. Date, Sm. Letters	Inc. Above	365	600	770	1035	1663	3475	6500	15500
1796 Sm. Date, Lg. Letters	Inc. Above	363	608	763	1023	1638	3425	6450	15500
1797 9 Stars Left, 7 Stars, Sm. Letters	7,776	850	1300	1825	2650	4175	8100	13500	22000
1797 10 Stars Left, 6 Stars Right	Inc. Above	310	535	720	985	1563	3363	6375	15500
1797 9 Stars Left, 7 Stars Right, Lg. Letters	Inc. Above	310	535	720	985	1563	3375	6425	15500
1798 13 Stars	327,536	470	788	988	1375	2200	4150	11875	18000
1798 15 Stars	Inc. Above	605	963	1375	1925	2850	6075	13750	18000

SILVER DOLLARS

DRAPED BUST TYPE HERALDIC EAGLE REVERSE 1798-1804

DIAMETER: 39-40mm
WEIGHT: 26.96 Grams
COMPOSITION: .8924 Silver,
.1076 Copper
DESIGNER: Robert Scot
EDGE: HUNDRED CENTS ONE DOLLAR OR UNIT With Decorations Between Words

The large eagle reverse type of the Draped Bust motif was struck from 1798 to 1804. At the conclusion of this series, the dollar denomination entered into a period of hibernation which eventually stretched to 32 years. The latest value trends of these silver dollars cannot be categorically lumped into one overall summary; the price movements vary by date and condition. However, judging from the 40 year track record of these coins, you should be guaranteed of future appreciation no matter which one you decide upon.

DATE	MINTAGE	AG-3	G-4	VG-8	F-12	VF-20	EF-40	AU-50	MS-60	PRF-65
1798 Knob 9	Inc. Above	225	375	450	575	850	1675	3500	7500	—
1798 10 Arrows	Inc. Above	200	355	425	550	700	1300	3500	7500	—
1798 Close Date	Inc. Above	200	355	425	550	700	1300	3500	7500	
1798 Wide Date, 13 Arrows										
	Inc. Above	200	355	425	550	700	1300	3500	7500	—
1798 13 Star Rev.	423,515	200	355	425	550	700	1300	3500	15000	
1798 15 Star Rev.	Inc. Above	240	400	500	850	1150	2000	5000	15000	
1799 Irregular Date, 13 Star Reverse										
	Inc. Above	200	355	425	550	690	1250	3500	7500	
1799 Irregular Date, 15 Star Reverse										
	Inc. Above	200	355	425	550	690	1250	3500	7500	
1799 Normal Date	Inc. Above	163	340	425	538	670	1175	3325	7500	
1799 Stars-8 Left, 5 Right	Inc. Above	215	398	478	700	975	1750	3550	7500	
1800	229,920	170	345	425	538	675	1213	3325	7500	
1800 Dotted Date	Inc. Above	175	353	430	543	708	1250	19475	7500	
1800 10 Arrows	Inc. Above	200	355	425	550	690	1300	3500	7500	
1800 12 Arrows	Inc. Above	200	355	425	550	690	1300	3500	7500	
1800 AMERICAI	Inc. Above	183	355	443	568	775	1538	3650	7500	
1801	54,454	213	375	458	593	783	1775	3875	7500	
1801 Restrike	Unknown	—	—	—	—	—	—	—	—	

SILVER DOLLARS

DATE	MINTAGE	AG-3	G-4	VG-8	F-12	VF-20	EF-40	AU-50	MS-60	PRF-65
1802 /1 Narrow Date	41,650	140	335	430	535	705	1500	4000	—	—
1802 /1 Wide Date	Inc. Above	215	360	425	550	850	1600	3500	7500	—
1802 Narrow Date	Inc. Above	225	375	450	600	875	1650	3500	7500	—
1802 Proof Restrike	Unknown	—	—	—	—	—	—	—	—	145000
1803 Lg. 3	85,634	178	348	428	565	770	1350	3475	7500	—
1803 Restrike	Unknown	—	—	—	—	—	—	—	—	135000
1803 Sm. 3	Inc. Above	188	360	443	593	800	1425	3600	7500	—
1804 (3 Varieties)	15	—	—	—	—	—	525000	—	—	990000*

* PRF-64 $650,000

GOBRECHT TYPE (PATTERNS)
1836-1839

THESE PATTERN COINS DESIGNED BY CHRISTIAN GOBRECHT LED TO THE INTRODUCTION OF THE U.S. LIBERTY SEATED COINAGE ALTHOUGH THESE PATTERNS WERE NEVER INTENDED TO CIRCULATE, SEVERAL EXISTING SPECIMENS SHOW CONSIDERABLE WEAR.

The Gobrecht dollars of 1836-1839 are technically defined as pattern coins because they were designed in preparation for the origination of a new dollar type that Congress hoped would circulate more actively than its predecessors. A reduction of the silver standard in 1837 made this possible.

Gobrecht dollars in circulated grades have declined slightly in the 1990's, while uncirculated specimens have edged upward. Although still at depressed prices, Gobrecht dollars are still well beyond the reach of the average coin buyer.

	MINTAGE	VF-20	EF-40	AU-50	Prf-60	Prf-65
1836 "C. Gobrecht F." below base. Rev: eagle flying amid stars. Plain edge		—	—	—	—	16500	40000
1836 Obverse: "C. Gobrecht F." below base. Rev: eagle flying in plain field. Plain edge	Est. 1,000	—	—	—	—	—

EDMUND'S 1996 U.S. COIN PRICES

SILVER DOLLARS

	MINTAGE	VF-20	EF-40	AU-50	Prf-60	Prf-65
1836 "C. Gobrecht F." on base. Rev: eagle flying left amid stars. Plain edge	—	2800	3750	4500	7250	23500
1836 "C. Gobrecht F." on base. Rev: eagle flying left amid stars. Reeded edge	—	—	—	—	—	—
1836 Obverse: "C. Gobrecht F." on base. Rev: eagle flying in plain field. Plain edge	—	—	—	—	35000	—
1838 Similar obverse, designer's name omitted, stars added around border. Rev: eagle flying left in plain field. Reeded edge	—	6500	7500	—	12500	18000
1838 Similar obverse, designer's name omitted, stars added around border. Rev: eagle flying left in plain field. Plain edge. Restrikes only	Est. 25	—	—	—	—	—
1838 Similar obverse, designer's name omitted, stars added around border. Rev: eagle flying left amid stars. Plain edge. Restrikes only	—	—	—	—	17500	30000
1839 Similar obverse, designer's name omitted, stars added around border. Rev: eagle in plain field. Reeded edge. Also known with plain edge with eagle amid stars.	Est. 300	6500	—	—	15000	20000

LIBERTY SEATED TYPE
1840-1873

The Liberty Seated silver dollar was patterned after the Gobrecht dollar, although the coin's reverse was completely overhauled before its release in 1840. The Liberty Seated dollar saw heavy circulation until its demise in 1873.

Liberty Seated dollars are indeed rare coins. Only a small fraction of the original 6½ million survive to this day. In spite of this restricted supply, a lack of collector passion has kept Liberty Seated dollars priced much lower than comparable rarities.

If you're looking for a coin with practically no adverse potential, then Liberty Seated dollars are a good choice despite their noteworthy appreciation of late in MS-60. As an investment device, Liberty Seated dollars have displayed consistent, if not spectacular growth. On occasions when there has been a softening in the Seated dollar market, prices for this coin merely remain stable, unlike most other series. We can expect similar occurrences in the foreseeable future. If you are an investor with a great deal of money at your disposal, you may want to entertain thoughts about the MS-65 and Proof Seated dollars. Of course, there looms the possibility of a short term fallout since prices are already so much higher than they were a few years ago. As

SILVER DOLLARS

a farsighted investment, however, these coins have very promising potential, as genuine specimens of these grades are almost nonexistent.

During their years of active duty, Seated dollars were extensively used and abused, which explains why so many of the surviving coins are slightly impaired. When choosing Liberty Seated dollars, make the extra effort to locate examples free of rough gouges and nicks or otherwise damaged. This could require persistence on your part, since most dealers are apt to have at best only a small inventory of Seated dollars to choose from. Once you find the problem-free specimen you've been searching for, don't feel uneasy about paying a premium well over the list price; it's an investment you'll someday be happy you made.

**VARIETY ONE
NO MOTTO
ABOVE
EAGLE
1840-1866**

DIAMETER: 38.1mm
WEIGHT: 26.73 Grams
COMPOSITION: .900 Silver, .100 Copper
DESIGNER: Christian Gobrecht
EDGE: Reeded

DATE	MINTAGE	G-4	VG-8	F-12	VF-20	EF-40	AU-50	MS-60	MS-63	MS-65	MS-67	PRF-65
1840	61,005	130	168	208	280	463	713	1375	3750	6000	40000	—
1841	173,000	90	120	170	218	360	588	1575	4875	24000	—	30000
1842	184,618	84	106	158	205	278	513	1043	3175	24000	—	30000
1843	165,100	84	106	158	210	280	518	1700	4775	24000	—	30000
1844	20,000	175	240	295	385	563	975	2300	8000	—	—	60000
1845	24,500	148	213	258	338	475	1025	9000	—	—	—	60000
1846	110,600	84	108	160	218	280	500	1375	3425	24000	—	—
1846 O	59,000	123	168	218	315	580	1700	5250	31500	—	—	—
1847	140,750	84	105	158	208	275	560	1225	2575	15000	—	40000
1848	15,000	250	278	413	563	738	1288	3500	11750	—	—	35000
1849	62,600	110	145	190	250	363	663	905	5250	23000	—	40000
1850	7,500	363	450	575	788	1250	2300	5125	17500	—	—	—
1850 O	40,000	183	265	350	625	1325	3550	9000	37500	—	—	—
1851	1,300	—	—	8000	9500	13500	16500	17500	31000	80000	—	40000
1852	1,100	—	—	6000	7500	11500	14000	18000	32500	70000	—	40000
1853	46,110	140	175	238	363	563	750	1875	5000	—	—	30000
1854	33,140	813	1075	1338	1825	3050	4400	6625	9250	22500	—	25000
1855	26,000	688	913	1163	1675	2700	4575	9500	32500	—	—	25000

EDMUND'S 1996 U.S. COIN PRICES

SILVER DOLLARS

DATE	MINTAGE	G-4	VG-8	F-12	VF-20	EF-40	AU-50	MS-60	MS-63	MS-65	MS-67	PRF-65
1856	63,500	250	338	408	600	975	1575	2875	7050	—	—	25000
1857	94,000	248	335	410	575	913	1475	2450	4950	—	—	25000
1858 Proof Only	Est. 80	—	—	—	3975	5000	5825	6250	9000	—	—	30000
1859	256,500	213	255	345	428	595	1100	2825	4750	15000	—	—
1859 O	360,000	81	99	150	203	255	475	943	2275	15000	—	—
1859 S	20,000	210	275	375	588	1300	2700	7000	47500	—	—	—
1860	218,930	153	198	250	333	488	813	1288	3600	15000	—	—
1860 O	515,000	81	99	150	203	255	473	938	2250	15000	—	—
1861	78,500	318	450	580	788	1100	1650	2475	4900	—	—	13500
1862	12,090	293	413	538	713	963	1450	2650	7150	—	—	13500
1863	27,660	205	258	323	463	650	1138	2225	5000	—	—	13500
1864	31,170	168	205	268	385	593	1088	2425	5200	17500	—	13500
1865	47,000	158	200	258	380	563	1100	2250	5150	—	—	13500
1866 V-1	2	—	—	—	—	—	—	—	—	—	—	—

VARIETY TWO MOTTO ABOVE EAGLE
1866-1873

DIAMETER: 38.1mm
WEIGHT: 26.73 Grams
COMPOSITION: .900 Silver, .100 Copper
DESIGNER: Christian Gobrecht
EDGE: Reeded

DATE	MINTAGE	G-4	VG-8	F-12	VF-20	EF-40	AU-50	MS-60	MS-63	MS-65	MS-67	PRF-65
1866 V-2	49,625	150	200	250	350	550	900	1600	—	28500	—	4000
1867	47,525	155	225	278	388	570	963	2000	5150	28500	—	7000
1868	162,700	135	180	228	335	465	875	2050	5250	—	—	7000
1869	424,300	103	140	208	283	428	813	1950	3600	28500	—	6500
1870	416,000	94	128	160	205	313	553	1500	4250	28500	—	12000
1870 CC	12,462	213	305	380	593	1175	2400	6625	24000	—	—	—
1870 S	Unknown				Stacks, March 1995 EF-40 $462,000							
1871	1,074,760	87	108	158	190	283	525	1038	2425	137000	—	6500
1871 CC	1,376	1600	2225	3200	4625	8250	16750	—	—	—	—	—
1872	1,106,450	83	98	150	190	285	525	1125	2475	28500	—	7000
1872 CC	3,150	825	1250	1825	2450	4300	8250	19000	56250	—	—	—
1872 S	9,000	175	245	393	850	2075	4325	8750	22500	—	—	—
1873	293,600	128	160	200	235	308	563	1188	2500	28500	—	7000
1873 CC	2,300	2725	3925	5625	8075	19500	30000	40000	—	—	—	—
1873 S	700				NONE KNOWN TO EXIST							

SILVER DOLLARS

TRADE DOLLARS
1873-1885

DIAMETER: 38.1mm
WEIGHT: 27.22 Grams
COMPOSITION: .900 Silver,
.100 Copper
DESIGNER: William Barber
EDGE: Reeded

The issuance of regular silver dollars came to a standstill in 1873 with the release of the slightly larger Trade dollar. The plan for the Trade dollar was to make commerce easier for United States businessmen operating in the Far East. For years, American coins were snubbed by Oriental merchants in favor of the Mexican peso, which contained more silver than our silver dollar. To compete in the region, Americans were forced to negotiate for pesos to trade with. Not coincidentally, Mexican dealers assessed extra charges to the Americans during the currency swaps. The heavier Trade dollar was supposed to eliminate the advantages that the peso held over the dollar.

Trade dollars were approved by Congress as legal tender in transactions up to five dollars. When the price of silver dropped a few years after the Trade dollar was introduced, the government revoked its domestic legal tender status, making it in effect the only United States coin ever to be demonetized. Because there were so many Trade dollars circulating about, widespread confusion resulted. To compound matters, the mints kept releasing new Trade dollars upon an already confused nation. Confronted with an angry population, the government in 1878 acted to suspend the production of Trade dollars other than proof sets. Proof examples were struck each year thereafter until 1885. The 1884 and 1885 proofs are among the rarest and most prized of all United States coins.

The quantity of Trade dollars existing today is deceivingly small for the total number minted. Remember, millions of these coins went overseas, but many never returned to the United States. Additionally, after Congress repealed the act authorizing the Trade dollar, over 7.7 million Trade dollars were redeemed in a government sponsored program.

For an investor planning to resell a newly purchased Trade dollar in five years or so at a respectable profit, the best hope lies in the MS-63 to MS-65 conditions, which have lost a lot of ground since 1989. In fact, all grades

EDMUND'S 1996 U.S. COIN PRICES

SILVER DOLLARS — TRADE DOLLARS

have cooled off period in recent years, and now stand poised for positive growth. For long range planners, there is every reason to expect appreciation records similar to those in the past.

DATE	MINTAGE	G-4	VG-8	F-12	VF-20	EF-40	AU-50	MS-60	MS-63	MS-65	PRF-65
1873	397,500	90	105	113	150	213	275	823	1675	13250	10050
1873 CC	124,500	150	175	175	288	443	713	1475	6750	17500	—
1873 S	703,000	130	145	133	160	225	333	1030	3150	11500	—
1874	987,800	80	90	115	150	198	278	718	1650	8500	10050
1874 CC	1,373,200	80	90	98	138	213	363	938	4625	15750	—
1874 S	2,549,000	70	80	84	101	148	238	560	11225	10500	—
1875	218,900	295	300	338	413	595	738	1525	2650	15250	7175
1875 CC	1,573,700	80	90	99	123	200	363	800	1900	16000	—
1875 S	4,487,000	70	80	84	100	140	233	540	1000	6750	—
1875 S/CC	Inc. Above	275	325	313	430	675	1100	1750	5750	15000	—
1876	456,150	70	80	88	104	148	310	543	1050	6875	7125
1876 CC	509,000	110	125	124	178	280	450	1488	9500	15750	—
1876 S	5,227,000	60	70	79	90	120	218	450	1025	7875	—
1877	3,039,710	60	70	80	94	125	220	490	1300	10250	13325
1877 CC	534,000	110	150	180	243	345	550	1225	4000	15000	—
1877 S	9,519,000	60	70	79	90	118	215	443	1025	7250	—
1878 CC	97,000	425	525	650	863	1550	2425	5625	9500	55000	—
1878 Proof Only	900	—	—	—	—	—	—	—	—	—	14775
1878 S	4,162,000	60	70	79	90	118	223	460	1225	6950	—
1879 Proof Only	1,541	—	—	—	850	900	1100	1400	2000	—	6750
1880 Proof Only	1,987	—	—	—	825	875	1050	1300	3250	—	7400
1881 Proof Only	960	—	—	—	900	950	1100	1400	3100	—	7500
1882 Proof Only	1,097	—	—	—	950	1000	1250	1600	2750	—	7850
1883 Proof Only	979	—	—	—	950	1000	1250	1600	2000	—	7000
1884 Proof Only	10	—	—	—	—	—	—	40000	200000	—	400000
1885 Proof Only	5	—	—	—	—	—	—	210000	400000	—	650000

SILVER DOLLARS

MORGAN TYPE
1878-1921

DIAMETER: 38.1mm
WEIGHT: 26.73 Grams
COMPOSITION: .900 Silver
.100 Copper
DESIGNER: George T. Morgan
EDGE: Reeded
PURE SILVER CONTENT: .77344 Tr. Oz.

The passage of the Bland-Allison Act of 1878 restored mintage of the regular silver dollar. The new type of dollar, called the Morgan dollar, was named after its designer, George T. Morgan. The powerful silver mining lobby, concerned over the decreasing value of their commodity, pressured Congress into approving the Bland-Allison Act. As part of the new law, the Treasury Department was required to purchase huge amounts of silver and convert it into dollar coins, in the hope of maintaining the price of silver at high levels. Under this plan, quantities of silver dollars became so large that they far exceeded the commercial need, resulting in millions of unused dollars piling up in bank and Treasury vaults.

The Bland-Allison Act was modified by the Sherman Silver Purchase Act of 1890. The Act mandated a government purchase of 4.5 million ounces of silver each month, to be paid for with Treasury bonds redeemable either in gold or silver. Unexpectedly, most bond holders redeemed their notes in gold, depleting the Treasury's gold reserve and throwing the entire country into a severe financial panic in 1893. The financial panic led to the repeal of the Sherman Act, which greatly slowed the production of silver dollars throughout most of the 1890's. Coinage of the silver dollar was suspended after 1904 when the bullion supply allotted for the dollar pieces became exhausted.

Under the guidelines of the Pittman Act of 1918, over 270 million silver dollars were melted down for export and recoinage into smaller coins. The big melt-down explains why some of the Morgan dollars with reported mintages of over a million pieces are so scarce today. Some of the silver derived from the Pittman Act was used in the production of the 1921 dollars, the final year of the Morgan dollar.

SILVER DOLLARS

Many dates of the Morgan dollars are not exceptionally rare, not even in MS-60 Uncirculated condition. As you'll recall, great numbers of the dollars never reached circulation. However, top grade Morgan dollars in MS-65 or better Uncirculated condition are much tougher to come by. The size and weight of silver dollars, when stored and handled in bags of 1000, left relatively few unscratched. Moreover, in the rush to produce the required quotas, Morgans were often struck in less than top quality form and luster. Morgan dollars having only a few blemishes with sharply detailed features on a bright reflective surface are indeed rare coins.

As investment coins, there is no doubt that Morgan dollars have been a major force in the numismatic market. The total number of investor dollars spent on Morgans over the last twenty years is probably higher than for any other style of coin or denomination. Many early buyers of Morgan dollars realized stunning profits.

Morgan dollars in upper grades can be extremely volatile. The momentous price shifts of the past two decades have been caused by unparalleled promoter and speculator involvement. Morgan dollars are ideal for promoters because of the relatively large quantity of uncirculated specimens available and the coin's high silver content. The beauty and larger size of the coin also make it easier to push. Not surprisingly, key date Morgan dollars have been immune to wild swings, no doubt because of collector influence.

Presently, MS-65 and PR-65, and even superior specimens have tumbled to small fractions of their previous highs. Prices have been consistently soft for some time, suggesting that Morgans no longer enjoy a disproportionate share of the coin commodity headlines, as they once did. This fall from grace pertains to better dates as well as common date issues. The best time to buy is following a price collapse, meaning that now is the prime time to purchase these gems.

If you wanted to purchase only one Morgan dollar, consider the 1893-S. It is the rarest of the business strike Morgans and the critical key date of the set. If a high price tag for a Very Fine example frightens you, then remember this: the 1893-S has been, now is, and always will be a prized acquisition for numismatists and investors alike. Downside risk is something owners of this rarity need not worry about.

In short, the Morgan dollar is an interesting, historically significant series, which is sure to continue to attract investment capital. As an investor you will be able to profit best by staying informed of the latest price movements, and not by following the psychology of the masses. Think for yourself and use every method available to analyze the market, and you should do very, very well with Morgan dollars.

SILVER DOLLARS

DATE	MINTAGE	F-12	VF-20	EF-40	AU-50	MS-60	MS-63	MS-65	MS-67	PRF-65
1878 8 TF	750,000	12	14	18	29	51	73	850	—	5850
1878 7 TF 3rd Rev	Inc. Above	11	13	15	21	38	115	1700	—	—
1878 7 TF Rev	Inc. Above	10	12	13	19	25	54	838	—	7800
1878 7/8 TF	9,759,550	13	17	21	33	64	103	1725	—	—
1878 CC	2,212,000	22	29	33	50	70	100	925	—	—
1878 S	9,744,000	9.40	11	12	15	20	33	238	5500	—
1879	14,807,100	8.90	9.65	11	14	21	39	700	—	4000
1879 CC	756,000	45	103	298	700	1325	2425	13125	—	—
1879 O	2,887,000	9.25	9.75	11	17	47	158	2675	—	—
1879 S 2nd Rev	9,110,000	13	15	17	33	100	265	4725	—	—
1879 S 3rd Rev	Inc. Above	9.50	11	12	14	17	32	135	900	—
1880	12,601,335	8.90	9.50	11	13	19	37	850	—	4000
1880 S	8,900,000	9.15	9.75	11	14	19	32	123	900	—
1880 CC 3rd Rev	Inc. Above	54	65	94	130	168	270	1350	—	—
1880 O	5,305,000	9.00	9.25	12	20	60	350	14500	—	—
1881	9,163,975	8.90	9.75	11	14	21	37	800	—	4000
1881 CC	296,000	98	118	125	135	165	195	380	3400	—
1881 O	5,708,000	9.00	9.65	12	13	18	34	1250	—	—
1881 S	12,760,000	9.40	10	11	13	17	31	115	900	—
1882	11,101,100	9.15	9.65	11	13	18	36	448	13500	4000
1882 CC	1,133,000	30	36	43	49	58	68	240	7500	—
1882 O	6,090,000	8.90	9.65	11	13	18	34	838	—	—
1882 S	9,250,000	9.40	10	12	14	18	36	115	1050	—
1883	12,291,039	8.75	9.50	10	13	20	35	128	2500	4000
1883 CC	1,204,000	29	35	40	44	54	62	188	4400	—
1883 O	8,725,000	8.75	9.40	11	13	16	31	115	—	—
1883 S	6,250,000	11	14	22	103	370	1350	22000	—	—
1884	14,070,875	8.75	9.40	11	12	17	37	250	6950	4000
1884 CC	1,136,000	41	43	45	47	54	63	203	4500	—
1884 O	9,730,000	8.75	9.25	10	12	16	31	115	7550	—
1884 S	3,200,000	11	15	33	255	3750	16500	106000	—	—
1885	17,787,767	8.75	9.25	10	12	15	31	118	2950	4000
1885 CC	228,000	168	173	178	183	190	205	440	5050	—
1885 O	9,185,000	8.75	9.25	10	12	16	31	115	2350	—
1885 S	1,497,000	13	16	22	47	103	163	1450	—	—
1886	19,963,886	8.75	9.40	10	12	15	31	115	1350	4000
1886 O	10,710,000	11	13	17	59	283	2200	30500	—	—
1886 S	750,000	17	24	39	57	120	268	2125	—	—
1887	20,290,710	9.00	9.65	11	12	15	31	115	3800	4000
1887 O	11,550,000	12	13	15	26	41	95	1660	3800	—
1887 S	1,771,000	13	15	17	31	62	150	3225	—	—
1888	19,183,833	8.90	9.65	11	12	15	31	173	11500	4400
1888 O	12,150,000	9.15	10	12	14	17	36	425	—	—
1888 S	657,000	18	24	30	55	123	223	2625	—	—
1889	21,726,811	9.15	9.90	11	12	15	33	368	7000	4000
1889 CC	350,000	233	328	898	2850	6300	12750	79800	—	—

EDMUND'S 1996 U.S. COIN PRICES

SILVER DOLLARS

DATE	MINTAGE	F-12	VF-20	EF-40	AU-50	MS-60	MS-63	MS-65	MS-67	PRF-65
1889 O	11,875,000	9.40	10	15	30	74	208	3875	—	—
1889 S	700,000	20	23	26	49	89	178	988	—	—
1890	16,802,590	9.15	9.75	11	13	17	40	2400	—	4000
1890 CC	2,309,041	24	30	41	82	195	375	3625	—	—
1890 CC Tail Bar	Inc. Above	24	30	41	82	195	375	3625	—	—
1890 O	10,710,000	9.40	10	13	25	53	129	2800	—	—
1890 S	8,230,373	9.65	11	13	20	35	58	775	—	—
1891	8,694,206	9.90	12	14	22	44	143	4175	—	4000
1891 CC	1,618,000	27	34	42	87	133	273	2125	—	—
1891 O	7,954,529	9.65	12	15	31	81	203	5375	—	—
1891 S	5,296,000	9.40	10	13	20	37	74	975	—	—
1892	1,037,245	12	13	17	56	126	250	2300	—	—
1892 CC	1,352,000	41	57	95	188	243	490	3000	—	—
1892 O	2,744,000	11	12	16	44	90	225	4325	—	—
1892 S	1,200,000	16	34	140	2450	13000	34000	50000	—	—
1893	378,792	49	61	93	175	315	730	4250	—	4000
1893 CC	677,000	79	140	430	725	1140	2650	34500	—	—
1893 O	300,000	79	103	173	443	1375	4475	83500	—	—
1893 S	100,000	1070	1350	3350	12500	25000	45500	197000	—	—
1894	110,972	218	250	338	518	1013	2275	10625	—	4100
1894 O	1,723,000	55	34	47	148	638	2750	27000	—	—
1894 S	1,260,000	24	40	82	188	343	750	4275	—	—
1895	12,880	6250	9500	12000	13000	14000	16500	—	—	—
1895 O	450,000	110	138	205	695	8650	20000	96000	—	—
1895 Proof Only	12,880	—	—	—	—	—	—	—	—	31500
1896 O	4,900,000	10	13	18	88	733	5500	62750	—	—
1896 S	5,000,000	20	37	148	358	670	1350	7625	—	—
1897	2,822,731	9.40	10	12	13	17	34	275	7950	4800
1897 O	4,004,000	9.90	11	16	83	453	2975	27750	—	—
1897 S	5,825,000	9.75	11	13	21	34	59	488	4300	—
1898	5,884,735	9.25	9.90	11	12	15	36	200	—	4000
1898 O	4,440,000	12	13	15	16	17	35	120	4050	—
1898 S	4,102,000	12	17	24	58	123	233	1225	—	—
1899	330,846	26	31	39	54	73	98	563	—	5850
1899 O	12,290,000	9.15	9.90	11	13	16	35	118	2850	—
1899 S	2,562,000	13	18	27	56	123	258	1225	—	—
1900	8,880,938	8.65	9.25	10	12	15	32	163	10500	4000
1900 O	12,590,000	8.90	10	12	13	17	32	115	9500	—
1900 O/CC	Inc. Above	23	27	38	89	170	303	1188	—	—
1900 S	3,540,000	13	17	27	45	91	153	1300	—	—
1901	6,962,813	18	28	48	260	1400	9625	117000	—	5850
1901 O	13,320,000	9.15	9.75	11	13	17	33	193	—	—
1901 S	2,284,000	15	25	43	115	243	398	2600	—	—
1902	7,994,777	9.75	11	12	20	36	55	513	5050	4000
1902 O	8,636,000	9.90	11	11	13	15	32	128	—	—

SILVER DOLLARS

DATE	MINTAGE	F-12	VF-20	EF-40	AU-50	MS-60	MS-63	MS-65	MS-67	PRF-65
1902 S	1,530,000	30	43	60	87	153	245	2050	—	—
1903	4,652,755	14	15	16	19	29	42	195	3500	4000
1903 O	4,450,000	113	118	125	130	143	155	300	4500	—
1903 S	1,241,000	23	56	283	838	2375	3825	7100	—	—
1904	2,788,650	10	12	16	30	62	158	2500	—	4000
1904 O	3,720,000	9.40	10	12	13	15	32	118	6500	—
1904 S	2,304,000	17	32	180	500	888	1625	4950	—	—
1921	44,690,000	7.50	7.90	8.40	8.75	10	19	118	—	—
1921 D	20,345,000	7.65	8.00	8.75	10	19	34	313	—	—
1921 S	21,695,000	7.65	8.00	8.75	11	19	35	1250	—	—

PEACE TYPE
1921-1935

DIAMETER: 38.1mm
WEIGHT: 26.73 Grams
COMPOSITION: .900 Silver,
.100 Copper
DESIGNER: Anthony De Francisci
EDGE: Reeded
PURE SILVER CONTENT: .77344 Tr. Oz.

The Peace dollar was introduced in 1921, the same year that production of the Morgan dollar ended. The new dollar was belatedly issued to celebrate the end of the Great War (later renamed World War I) and dedicated to the ideal of lasting worldwide peace. Production of the Peace dollar continued until 1928, when it was suspended because of lack of demand. More Peace dollars were struck in 1934 to help eliminate war-debt accounts, but a law passed later in the year stated that paper Silver Certificates should be backed by "one dollar in silver" rather than "one silver dollar," as in the past. The Silver Act of 1934, as the new law was called, ended any further need for silver dollars. After the 1935 series was released, silver dollars were not struck again until 1971.

As investment pieces, the Peace dollars have been exploited by promoters and speculators almost as much as Morgan dollars. Similar to the strategy advocated for Morgans, buy properly graded MS-65 or better dollars. They can be yours at an 80% "close-out" discount from where they crested in

SILVER DOLLARS

1990. Collectors will delight in learning they can easily replace their circulated slot fillers with MS-60 examples. Unbelievably, these attractive coins have been sloping downward steadily since 1983. Perhaps smaller investors should likewise observe this undervaluation.

DATE	MINTAGE	G-4	VG-8	F-12	VF-20	EF-40	AU-50	MS-60	MS-63	MS-65	MS-67
1921	1,006,473	16	22	26	32	41	79	115	215	1500	10000
1922	51,737,000	6.00	6.50	7.15	7.65	8.00	8.25	10	21	153	9000
1922 D	15,063,000	6.50	7.00	7.65	8.00	8.75	10	17	33	450	—
1922 S	17,475,000	6.50	7.00	7.50	7.90	8.65	10	18	59	1763	—
1923	30,800,000	6.00	6.50	7.15	7.50	8.00	8.25	10	21	155	9000
1923 D	6,811,000	6.50	7.00	7.65	8.00	8.65	14	24	90	1450	—
1923 S	19,020,000	6.50	7.00	7.50	8.00	8.75	10	20	65	4400	—
1924	11,811,000	6.50	7.00	7.40	7.90	8.50	9.25	11	24	158	10500
1924 S	1,728,000	7.00	8.50	9.15	13	16	46	138	388	4700	—
1925	10,198,000	6.50	7.00	7.50	7.90	8.50	9.50	11	23	163	7000
1925 S	1,610,000	6.50	7.50	8.40	9.65	14	25	43	108	7875	—
1926	1,939,000	6.50	8.50	8.65	9.65	11	16	21	36	415	—
1926 D	2,348,700	6.50	7.50	8.65	9.50	13	26	45	98	625	—
1926 S	6,980,000	—	—	7.50	8.00	10	16.50	26	65	925	—
1927	848,000	8.00	12.50	13	16	21	31	46	85	2150	—
1927 D	1,268,900	7.50	11.50	12	14	22	67	115	203	3525	—
1927 S	866,000	9.00	11.50	12	14	20	51	85	190	4550	—
1928	360,649	65	95	95	103	118	135	155	280	2200	—
1928 S	1,632,000	6.50	10	12	13	16	39	74	293	11250	—
1934	954,057	8.00	12.50	13	15	20	32	59	105	1125	—
1934 D	1,569,500	6.50	11.50	13	14	18	36	73	190	1450	—
1934 S	1,011,000	8.00	11.50	14	44	148	428	1125	2475	5525	—
1935	1,576,000	6.50	9.00	9.75	12	16	22	37	64	713	—
1935 S	1,964,000	6.50	9.00	9.75	13	18	60	123	223	950	—

EDMUND'S 1996 U.S. COIN PRICES

EISENHOWER TYPE
SILVER DOLLARS

EISENHOWER TYPE
1971-1978

DIAMETER: 38.1mm
WEIGHT: Silver Clad: 24.50 Grams,
         Copper-Nickel Clad: 22.68 Grams
COMPOSITION:
Silver Issue: Outer Layers- .800 Silver, .200 Copper
         Inner Core- .210 Silver, .790 Copper, .400 Silver Overall
Copper Clad Issue: Outer Layers- .750 Copper, .250 Nickel,
         Pure Copper Inner Core
DESIGNER: Frank Gasparro
EDGE: Reeded
PURE SILVER CONTENT FOR SILVER ISSUE: .31625 Tr. Oz.

NOTE: This type has been divided into two separate listings because different metallic compositions were used concurrently from 1971 to 1974. The Eisenhower dollars of 1976 are listed on page 175 with the other bicentennial coinage.

After 30 years, silver dollar production resumed in 1971 with the Eisenhower, or "Ike" dollar. "Metallic" dollar is a more accurate description of an Eisenhower coin since all Eisenhower dollars struck for circulation were composed of the familiar copper-nickel combination used since 1965.

The Eisenhower dollar, last released in 1978, was one of the shortest series of American coins. For such a brief time span, however, the Ike dollar series has plenty of varieties to study and collect. In all, there are 32 distinct coins compressed into only eight years of production! Many of the varieties came about because of composition changes.

One of the varieties you'll run into when you study the "Ike" is the "Blue Box" Ike. This refers to the 40% silver Uncirculated Ikes sold directly by the Mint to collectors, and packaged in blue boxes. The dates for the Blue Box Ikes are 1971-S, 1972-S, 1973-S, 1974-S, and 1776-1976-S. In a similar fashion, "Brown Box" Ikes are Proof coins mailed in brown boxes, also containing 40% silver. Brown Box Ikes are dated 1971-S, 1972-S, 1973-S, 1974-S, and 1976-S. All other Eisenhower dollars were minted in the copper-nickel composition.

All Ike dollars made in 1975 and 1976 carry the dual date 1776-1976, in observance of our bicentennial celebration, meaning of course, there are no dollars dated 1975. Dollars struck in 1975 can easily be distinguished from those produced in 1976, despite the fact they bear the identical dual date. Numismatists therefore classify 1776-1976 dollars as Type I and Type II.

SILVER DOLLARS — EISENHOWER TYPE

The Type I dollars have a low relief design and bold flat lettering on the reverse. The Type II coins have a sharp design and thinner, more contoured lettering on the reverse. Taking into account the two designs, the metallic diversity, and mint marks, there are eight different varieties of 1776-1976 dollars to collect.

Eisenhower dollars are good long term investments, particularly if purchased at today's prices. Their values have plunged recently, most notably the MS-65 Uncirculated and Proof Ikes, now selling for only about one-third their 1989 record highs. Overall, the cost of assembling a complete set of quality Ikes is extremely low.

As you assemble your collection of Ikes, try to locate MS-67 specimens. The bidding for these pieces is not fierce, so you ought to be able to purchase them at reasonable prices. Be prepared to do some searching, as many notable dealers say locating true MS-67 Eisenhower dollars is more difficult than finding MS-67 Morgan dollars, especially with the regular clad Ikes. It could be a real challenge!

.400 SILVER CLAD COMPOSITION 1971-1974

DATE	MINTAGE	MS-65	PRF-65
1971 S	6,868,530	39	—
1971 S Proof	4,265,234	—	4.00
1972 S	2,193,056	15	—
1972 S Proof	1,811,631	—	4.25
1973 S	1,883,140	—	—
1973 S Proof	1,013,646	—	19
1974 S	1,900,000	13	—
1974 S Proof	1,306,579	—	5.75

COPPER-NICKEL CLAD COMPOSITION 1971-1978

DATE	MINTAGE	MS-65	Prf-65
1971	47,799,000	13	—
1971 D	68,587,424	7.50	—
1972	75,890,000	3.25	—
1972 D	92,548,511	6.75	—
1973	2,000,056	20	—
1973 D	2,000,000	33	—
1973 S	2,769,624	—	4.85
1974	27,366,000	8.00	—
1974 D	35,466,000	7.00	—
1974 S	2,617,350	—	4.60

See pages 174-175 for 1976 bicentennial silver dollars

EISENHOWER/SUSAN B. ANTHONY TYPE *SILVER DOLLARS*

DATE	MINTAGE	MS-65	Prf-65
1977	12,596,000	—	—
1977 D	32,938,006	—	—
1977 S	3,251,152	—	—
1978	25,702,000	—	—
1978 D	33,012,890	—	—
1978 S	3,127,788	—	—

SUSAN B. ANTHONY TYPE
1979-1981

DIAMETER: 26.5mm
WEIGHT: 8.1 Grams
COMPOSITION: .750 Copper
              .250 Nickel Clad Copper
DESIGNER: Frank Gasparro
EDGE: Reeded

The ill-fated Susan B. Anthony dollar was minted from 1979 to 1981. Production was halted following objections from many groups representing various special interests. It seems as if the Anthony dollar satisfied hardly anyone.

Not only were the Anthony dollars not accepted as a medium for exchange, most have little potential as investment items. Hundreds of millions sit idle in Treasury vaults, never released for circulation. The day these common coins become attractive investments will probably be a day well beyond our lifetime. But let's use our imagination for a moment. It is entirely possible our government could act on an edict to destroy all Anthony dollars currently in storage, which in effect would transform all privately held Anthonys into scarce coins. Those MS-67 Anthonys purchased in 1996 for next to nothing, all of a sudden will become highly prized collectibles. Who is to say that a scenario like this couldn't unfold?

DATE	MINTAGE	MS-65	PRF-65
1979 S Type 1	109,576,000	2.70	4.00
1979 D	288,015,744	2.50	—
1979 P	360,222,000	2.50	—
1979 S	109,576,000	—	—
1979 S Type 2	Inc. Above	—	52
1980 D	41,628,708	2.50	—
1980 P	27,610,000	—	—
1980 S	20,422,000	2.50	4.60
1981 D	3,250,000	8.25	—
1981 P	3,000,000	2.75	—
1981 S	3,492,000	—	—
1981 S Type 1	4,063,083	8.25	6.00
1981 S Type 2	Inc. Above	—	65

EDMUND'S 1996 U.S. COIN PRICES

BICENTENNIAL COINAGE

BICENTENNIAL COINAGE DATED 1776-1976

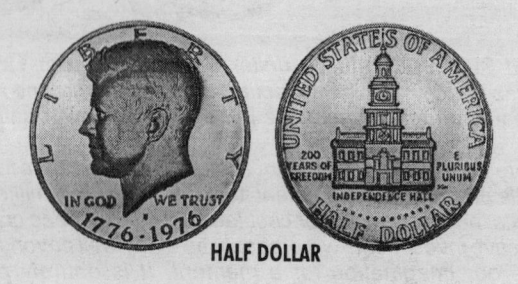

DOLLAR

HALF DOLLAR

QUARTER DOLLAR

BICENTENNIAL COINAGE

DATE	MINTAGE	MS-65	PRF-65
1976 D Dollar Type 1	21,048,710	2.50	—
1976 D Dollar Type 2	82,179,564	1.75	—
1976 D Half Dollar	287,565,248	1.00	—
1976 D Quarter Dollar	860,118,839	0.50	—
1976 Dollar Type 1	4,019,000	4.00	—
1976 Dollar Type 2	113,318,000	2.00	—
1976 Half Dollar	234,308,000	1.00	—
1976 Quarter Dollar	809,784,016	0.50	—
1976 S Dollar Silver Clad	3,295,714	—	—
1976 S Dollar Silver Clad	3,295,714	—	14.50
1976 S Dollar Silver Clad	4,239,722	—	—
1976 S Dollar Silver Clad	4,239,722	13.50	—
1976 S Dollar Type 1 Proof	2,845,450	—	15
1976 S Dollar Type 2 Proof	4,149,730	—	15
1976 S Half Dollar Proof	7,059,099	—	4.00
1976 S Half Dollar Silver Clad	4,239,722	6.25	—
1976 S Half Dollar Silver Clad Proof	3,295,714	—	7.50
1976 S Quarter Dollar Proof		—	2.50
1976 S Quarter Dollar Silver Clad	4,239,722	3.50	—
1976 S Quarter Dollar Silver Clad Proof	3,295,714	—	5.00

BICENTENNIAL COIN SETS (3-PIECES)

DATE	MINTAGE	MS-65	Prf-65
1976 Silver Clad Bicentennial Proof Set		—	12
1976 Silver Clad Bicentennial Uncirculated Set		7.50	—

GOLD COINS

UNITED STATES GOLD COINS

Almost since the beginning of recorded time, gold has been the world's most sought after metal. Historically, gold coins carried the highest face value of any nation's coinage system, and the United States is no exception. A brief chronology of American gold coinage and some general comments concerning gold coins as investment devices follow.

The first United States gold coins were issued for circulation in 1795. They were the $5 and $10 coins, as specified by the law of April 2, 1792. Eventually, a total of six gold denominations saw service in America's channels of commerce. These denominations were $1, $2½, $3, $5, $10 and $20. The government considered striking $4 and $50 denominations for regular circulation also, but those visions never got off the ground. Before these plans were finally scrubbed, however, several hundred $4 gold patterns were struck, as well as a few $50 gold specimens. These prizes are each valued at tens of thousands of dollars on today's market.

Numismatists still make use of the names originally given to the gold issues. The basic gold coin unit was the $10 piece, called the "eagle." Thus the $2½ coins were called the "quarter eagles," the $5 coins were the "half eagles," and the $20 pieces became known as "double eagles." There were no special names given to the $1 and $3 gold issues.

Despite the troubles gold coins had in circulating during the early 19th century (because of the face value to metal value imbalances), the production of gold coins was necessary and so it continued. In the absence of a stable paper currency system, gold coins were the primary medium used to conduct very large business transactions, particularly with foreign governments. The need for gold coins decreased after 1861, with the advent of a standardized paper money system backed by the United States government. However, in response to a growing nation, production of gold coins actually increased following the implementation of the paper money network.

Coinage of the gold denominations went on until 1933, when President Franklin Roosevelt, in an attempt to lift the nation out of the Great Depression, made it illegal to own gold bullion. Collectors were allowed to keep their gold coins, but the vast majority of all existing American gold coins stored in Treasury and bank vaults were melted down. Once the gold had been secured, Uncle Sam pushed the price of gold bullion from $20.67 an ounce to $35 an ounce, realizing a tidy profit in the process. The price of gold was then controlled by the government to varying degrees until January 1, 1975, when all gold ownership and price regulations were terminated.

GOLD COINS

The Gold Order of 1933, coupled with the heavy meltings of the early 1800's, leaves collectors and investors of today with but a very small fraction of the original number of gold coins to scramble for. Indeed, between 1795 and 1933, the United States struck a face value of 4.25 billion dollars in gold coinage, with only less than an estimated 300 million dollars surviving today.

As an investor of American gold coins, you have two factors working in your favor: bullion value and numismatic value. The bullion factor acts as a shield against the erosion of the United States dollar and will simultaneously benefit from any price increases in gold bullion. The price movements of well-worn, common date gold coins rely mainly upon the direction of the metals market.

Gold coins have numismatic value because of their inclusion in date set or type set collections. Naturally, demand and rarity go hand-in-hand in determining specific values. It is the numismatic value that provides a price floor for gold coins when bullion prices collapse. The numismatic factor is also responsible for price jumps of gold coins during periods of sluggish activity on the metals market. In fact, the best performances are caused by collector interest, and not so much the bullion factor, although both methods of appreciation have done extremely well in the past.

The gold coin market bounced back nicely since the bullion shake-out in early 1980, despite the fact that gold prices have been languishing. The purchase of gold coins in any denomination should consist of high grade issues, or coins of great interest to collectors. By remembering these simple facts, there is very little chance of picking a loser. In addition to owning an historically important artifact, you'll have a lot of fun in the pursuit!

Since there is so much to learn about American gold, we recommend further research to help you make wise investments in gold coinage. A good learning tool for any prospective buyer is a book entitled United States Gold Coins: An Illustrated History, by Q. David Bowers. Several chapters of the book are devoted to each gold denomination. Information is given concerning availability of individual issues and other pertinent details. You can check out this book from the American Numismatic Association Library in Colorado, or perhaps your local library may have it. At any rate, whether you are a collector, an investor, or the intellectual sort, American gold coinage is a topic worthy of extensive study.

GOLD COINS

GOLD DOLLARS 1849-1889

The smallest gold coin, the $1 piece, was one of the last gold denominations to be introduced. Immediately, the gold dollar became more important than the silver dollar of its time. Because the relative value of gold declined due to the large influx of the metal discovered during the California Gold Rush, large quantities of gold dollars remained in circulation.

There were three types of gold dollars produced. Type I, or the Liberty Head dollars, were minted from 1849 to 1854. In 1854 the gold dollar was redesigned larger in diameter (but thinner), and the woman on the obverse side donned a feathered headdress. Her head was also reduced in size, compared to the Type I head. The Small Indian Head dollars, or Type II dollars, ran only until 1856. The Type III dollar, also known as the large Indian Head dollar, was distinguished from Type II dollars by a slight enlargement of the figure's head size.

By the mid-1860's, the price of gold began to rise, resulting in the disappearance of many of the gold dollars. Smaller numbers were minted thereafter. When legislation required the massive production of silver dollars starting in 1878, the gold dollar series toiled in virtual anonymity until Congress ordered its cancellation following the release of the 1889 issues.

Nearly all of the upper grade gold dollars, Almost Uncirculated or better, advanced sharply in the late 1980's and first part of the 1990's, but have leveled off for now. With this in mind, these high grade dollars still represent solid investments, especially if considered as long term holdings. The higher the grade that you purchase, the more pleased you'll be. For most dates and mint marks in lower circulated grades, gold dollars are priced at levels well below those of the past. This is a tremendous time to obtain the most significant numismatic gold dollars. These unbelievably rare coins are being offered at affordable prices.

GOLD DOLLARS

GOLD COINS

TYPE 1 - LIBERTY HEAD
1849-1854

DIAMETER: 13mm
WEIGHT: 1.672 Grams
COMPOSITION: .900 Gold, .100 Copper
DESIGNER: James B. Longacre
EDGE: Reeded
PURE GOLD CONTENT: .04837 Tr. Oz.

DATE	MINTAGE	VF-20	EF-40	AU-50	MS-60	MS-63	MS-65
1849 Open Wreath	688,567	128	165	183	448	1800	6900
1849 Closed Wreath	Inc. Above	128	163	175	430	1500	6550
1849 C Closed Wreath	11,634	488	988	2350	6350	22500	—
1849 C Open Wreath	Inc. Above	225000	—	—	—	—	—
1849 D	21,588	425	838	1300	4150	9250	41500
1849 O	215,000	165	210	395	900	3000	18000
1850	481,953	135	165	175	363	1850	8750
1850 C	6,966	630	1113	2325	8600	—	—
1850 D	8,382	583	1188	2325	8625	21000	—
1850 O	14,000	275	385	788	2875	6100	30000
1851	3,317,671	125	163	173	335	1475	5350
1851 C	41,267	445	713	1100	2450	5750	39000
1851 D	9,882	443	838	1600	4525	9500	43500
1851 O	290,000	170	210	263	695	2650	16500
1852	2,045,351	140	165	180	375	1475	5450
1852 C	9,434	445	875	1550	4100	9750	43500
1852 D	6,360	638	1313	2075	6850	—	—
1852 O	140,000	168	215	365	1325	4400	29000
1853	4,076,051	140	165	180	375	1450	5300
1853 C	11,515	513	1050	1825	6175	13750	—
1853 D	6,583	645	1313	2575	8000	30000	70000
1853 O	290,000	160	198	253	588	2700	14000
1854	736,709	140	165	180	375	1475	7000
1854 D	2,935	858	1875	5650	17250	—	—
1854 S	14,632	333	450	788	2075	6750	30000

EDMUND'S 1996 U.S. COIN PRICES

GOLD COINS

GOLD DOLLARS

TYPE 2 - INDIAN HEAD SMALL HEAD
1854-1856

DIAMETER: 15mm
WEIGHT: 1.672 Grams
COMPOSITION: .900 Gold, .100 Copper
DESIGNER: James B. Longacre
EDGE: Reeded
PURE GOLD CONTENT: .04837 Tr. Oz.

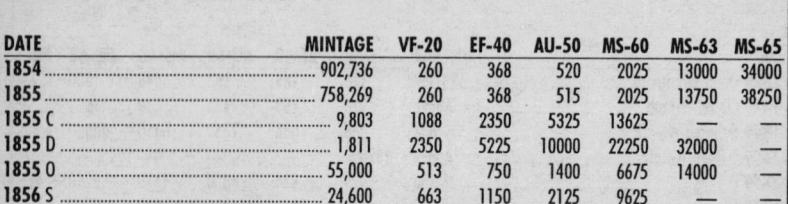

DATE	MINTAGE	VF-20	EF-40	AU-50	MS-60	MS-63	MS-65
1854	902,736	260	368	520	2025	13000	34000
1855	758,269	260	368	515	2025	13750	38250
1855 C	9,803	1088	2350	5325	13625	—	—
1855 D	1,811	2350	5225	10000	22250	32000	—
1855 O	55,000	513	750	1400	6675	14000	—
1856 S	24,600	663	1150	2125	9625	—	—

TYPE 3 - INDIAN HEAD LARGE HEAD
1856-1889

DIAMETER: 15mm
WEIGHT: 1.672 Grams
COMPOSITION: .900 Gold, .100 Copper
DESIGNER: James B. Longacre
EDGE: Reeded
PURE GOLD CONTENT: .04837 Tr. Oz.

The 1861-D is probably the most famous of all $1 gold pieces. No one knows how many were made, but the number is assuredly very small. The 1861-D dollars were struck by the Confederacy following the takeover of the Dahlonega Mint by southern forces in April 1861. It is believed that a small quantity of gold on hand at the time of the seizure was used to produce the coins. The well-to-do investor of the modern world will pay considerably more for this historical rarity today than a few years ago, but this is nothing compared to the dizzying height we will see in the future. The 1861-D will

EDMUND'S 1996 U.S. COIN PRICES

GOLD DOLLARS — GOLD COINS

continue to go higher in response to demands placed upon it by both collectors and investors. If you have thousands of dollars to spend on a $1 gold, give this beauty some serious thought...if you can find one for sale, that is.

DATE	MINTAGE	VF-20	EF-40	AU-50	MS-60	MS-63	MS-65	PRF-65
1856 Upright 5	1,762,936	145	175	313	630	1175	3600	—
1856 Slant 5	Inc. Above	130	155	178	348	1100	2600	—
1856 D	1,460	3825	6500	10500	27500	—	—	—
1857	774,789	130	155	178	348	1100	2550	—
1857 C	13,280	550	1250	3425	11500	—	—	—
1857 D	3,533	850	1775	3400	11500	—	—	—
1857 S	10,000	488	713	1675	6900	22000	—	—
1858	117,995	130	168	188	353	1125	4100	19000
1858 D	3,477	763	1425	2475	9000	26500	—	—
1858 S	10,000	345	563	1600	5475	—	—	—
1859	168,244	138	163	190	378	1100	3900	12000
1859 C	5,235	460	1475	3175	13750	35000	125000	—
1859 D	4,952	825	1350	2675	9500	25500	—	—
1859 S	15,000	280	538	1825	6300	18000	—	—
1860	36,668	140	173	195	425	1600	4650	12000
1860 D	1,566	2575	5775	8100	27500	—	—	—
1860 S	13,000	288	388	825	3125	6500	19000	—
1861	527,499	130	158	183	340	1150	3800	18000
1861 D	Unknown	6275	10750	18000	34250	60000	225000	—
1862	1,361,390	120	150	173	293	1125	3350	12000
1863	6,250	438	888	1900	4325	8000	19500	12000
1864	5,950	343	425	663	1450	2250	7500	12000
1865	3,725	380	530	738	1550	2750	9500	12000
1866	7,130	348	438	600	1188	2050	6700	12000
1867	5,250	410	500	675	1300	2100	7000	12000
1868	10,525	273	345	533	1175	1850	6950	12000
1869	5,925	343	465	675	1338	2200	7250	12000
1870	6,335	263	350	498	963	1800	5200	12000
1870 S	3,000	438	688	1225	3025	8250	32500	—
1871	3,930	263	355	478	775	1650	4500	18000
1872	3,530	283	388	520	950	2600	6750	18000
1873 Closed 3	125,125	400	763	1150	2625	4000	17500	18000
1873 Open 3	Inc. Above	120	150	170	295	1125	3150	—
1874	198,820	120	153	173	293	1100	2500	19000
1875	420	2325	3725	5200	7925	9500	27500	45000
1876	3,245	240	313	475	945	1250	3950	12000
1877	3,920	178	295	458	868	1200	3800	24000
1878	3,020	203	313	448	935	1225	3900	12000
1879	3,030	180	258	338	738	1175	3550	12000
1880	1,636	148	178	203	365	1100	2375	12000
1881	7,707	148	178	203	365	1100	2400	12000

GOLD COINS
GOLD DOLLARS

DATE	MINTAGE	VF-20	EF-40	AU-50	MS-60	MS-63	MS-65	PRF-65
1882	5,125	158	185	210	403	1125	2450	12000
1883	11,007	150	178	203	365	1100	2375	12000
1884	6,236	148	173	200	375	1100	2425	12000
1885	12,261	148	178	203	373	1100	2400	12000
1886	6,016	150	178	208	390	1125	3150	12000
1887	8,543	150	178	203	365	1000	2375	12000
1888	16,580	150	178	203	365	1000	2350	12000
1889	30,729	150	178	203	323	1000	2325	12000

QUARTER EAGLES 1796-1929

($2.50 GOLD PIECES)

Although mintage of quarter eagles was authorized by the law of April 2, 1792, they did not appear until 1796. The quarter eagle denomination was carried by five different designs until 1929: Liberty Cap, Classic Head, Coronet or Liberty Head, Indian Head and Turban Head.

Take special notice of what has happened with the common date quarter eagles of the Coronet and Indian Head series. Since the middle of 1990, many MS-60 coins of this vintage have doubled in price. How much longer we'll see upward price movements here is anyone's guess, but it's safe to say that most of the appreciation for now has probably already occurred. MS-63's also saw sharp increases during this time, though not as much, and not for most Coronet quarter eagles minted in Philadelphia. If you're interested in obtaining MS-63 quarter eagles, these Philadelphia products could be your most cost effective purchase. Once again, however, if you're looking at the long term situation, you should do very well by owning quarter eagles in clean MS-60 or MS-63 condition.

GOLD COINS

QUARTER EAGLES

LIBERTY CAP TYPE
1796-1807

DIAMETER: 20mm
WEIGHT: 4.37 Grams
COMPOSITION: .9167 Gold,
.0833 Copper
DESIGNER: Robert Scot
EDGE: Reeded

**VARIETY ONE
NO STARS ON
OBVERSE - 1796**

**VARIETY TWO
STARS ON OBVERSE
1796-1807**

The first type was the Liberty Cap design, minted for eight years between 1796 and 1807. Strangely, the face value designation was not a part of the coin's features.

The track record for the premier quarter eagle type is a good one. Liberty Cap quarter eagles are among the most consistent advancers of all United States coins, and there is no reason to expect this to change. Even in their lowest conditions, unfortunately, Liberty Cap quarter eagles are limited primarily to wealthy buyers.

DATE	MINTAGE	F-12	VF-20	EF-40	AU-50	MS-60
1796 No Stars	963	10000	20750	31250	61250	132500
1796 Stars	432	8125	11250	18250	41500	100000
1797	427	7875	9750	13250	20000	86750
1798	1,094	3100	4475	7000	14500	28500
1802	3,035	2925	4000	5250	7900	16750
1804 13 Star Reverse	3,327	12750	18500	32250	85000	—
1804 14 Star Reverse	Inc. Above	3075	4125	5650	7950	18250
1805	1,781	2925	4150	5550	7950	20000
1806/4	1,616	3025	4100	5225	11150	20500
1806/5	Inc. Above	5250	10000	1250	20000	—
1807	6,812	2825	3875	4925	9175	16500

EDMUND'S 1996 U.S. COIN PRICES

QUARTER EAGLES
GOLD COINS

The Turban Head type made its debut in 1808, and was minted sporadically until 1834. These coins were minted only in very small numbers because the increasing value of gold prevented them from staying in circulation. Because the 1808 issue had a slightly larger diameter than the other Turban Head quarter eagles, it is considered a type all by itself. Because of a very low mintage and unrelenting pressure from type set collectors, the 1808 is an excellent investment for either short term or long term growth. If you want to consider other Turban Head quarter eagles, you'll be happy to know they also have excellent potential. Be advised, for here too, you'll need a bundle of money to get started.

CAPPED BUST TO LEFT
1808

DIAMETER: 20mm
WEIGHT: 4.37 Grams
COMPOSITION: .9167 Gold, .0833 Copper
DESIGNER: John Reich
EDGE: Reeded

DATE	MINTAGE	F-12	VF-20	EF-40	AU-50	MS-60
1808	2,710	8250	12750	17625	23000	41250

GOLD COINS

QUARTER EAGLES

CAPPED HEAD TO LEFT
1821-1834

DIAMETER: 1821-1827 18.5mm
1829-1834 18.2mm
WEIGHT: 4.37 Grams
COMPOSITION: .9167 Gold, .0833 Copper
DESIGNER: John Reich
EDGE: Reeded

VARIETY ONE - LARGE DIAMETER
1821-1827

DATE	MINTAGE	F-12	VF-20	EF-40	AU-50	MS-60	MS-63
1821	6,448	3250	3713	5025	7125	15000	36000
1824	2,600	3200	3700	4600	5750	12500	2500
1825	4,434	3150	3725	4950	5700	12250	21000
1826/5	760	3750	5100	6625	9750	24250	—
1827	2,800	3850	4325	5900	8000	15500	36500

VARIETY TWO - SMALL DIAMETER
1829-1834

DATE	MINTAGE	F-12	VF-20	EF-40	AU-50	MS-60	MS-63
1829	3,403	2850	3500	4388	5400	8750	15500
1830	4,540	2950	3550	4400	5425	8750	15750
1831	4,520	3000	3563	4425	5450	8875	16000
1832	4,400	2950	3350	4025	4938	7625	13625
1833	4,160	3200	3700	4625	5575	9500	22500
1834	4,000	8125	9625	22250	33250	—	—

QUARTER EAGLES

GOLD COINS

CLASSIC HEAD TYPE
1834-1839

DIAMETER: 18.2mm
WEIGHT: 4.18 Grams
COMPOSITION: .8992 Gold, .1008 Copper
DESIGNER: William Kneass
EDGE: Reeded

The Classic Head type was released in 1834. These quarter eagles were reduced in size and weight to take the profit out of exportation and meltdowns. They were minted in much larger quantities than their predecessors. With the exception of the 1838-C, the Classic Head quarter eagles have been rather quiet over the last few years, indicating that we're bound to see some upward price movement. As far as the aforementioned 1838-C is concerned, here is a piece destined to continue its impressive climb, just as it has done for the better part of four decades.

DATE	MINTAGE	F-12	VF-20	EF-40	AU-50	MS-60	MS-63
1834	112,234	200	288	483	888	2400	5000
1835	131,402	200	270	418	688	1875	8500
1836	547,986	200	265	408	618	1663	5250
1837	45,080	200	270	468	705	2800	10000
1838	47,030	200	270	458	850	2575	8000
1838 C	7,880	575	1075	2600	6100	27250	57000
1839	27,021	210	278	563	1400	5125	13000
1839 C	18,140	435	713	2000	4300	19300	55000
1839 D	13,674	485	1025	2450	5625	36375	—
1839 O	17,781	350	475	1038	2175	6250	19000

EDMUND'S 1996 U.S. COIN PRICES

GOLD COINS

QUARTER EAGLES

CORONET OR LIBERTY HEAD TYPE
1840-1907

DIAMETER: 18mm
WEIGHT: 4.18 Grams
COMPOSITION: .900 Gold, .100 Copper
DESIGNER: Christian Gobrecht
EDGE: Reeded
PURE GOLD CONTENT: .12094 Tr. Oz.

In 1840, the quarter eagle was redesigned slightly to match the style of the half eagle and eagle. The new type was called the Coronet quarter eagle. The Coronet quarter eagle was minted every year up to and including 1907, making it one of the longest series of United States coins, along with the Coronet half eagle and eagle.

One of the most valuable Coronet quarter eagles is the 1848 CAL. specimen. These coins were minted from a special shipment of gold sent from California to the east coast following the fabulous gold strike. The letters "CAL." were counterstamped on the reverse above the eagle by mint officials to show that they were coined out of gold originating from the California gold fields. Only 1,389 of these quarter eagles were produced, and it is a real sleeper with an interesting historical aspect, yet it hasn't appreciated as much as it should have in almost 15 years. This artifact of the Old West cannot be ignored much longer by collectors and investors. Be careful when you buy the 1848 CAL. quarter eagle, as there are many forgeries of this rarity.

Higher grade gems, such as MS-63 and proofs, have suffered serious setbacks over the last several years, now selling at only 30% of their once lofty heights. Still, you'll need a minimum of $1500 to take advantage of this offer.

For those with fewer funds to part with, the Coronet quarter eagles present numerous opportunities as well. You'll discover a surprising number of dates priced barely above bullion levels despite mintages of under 10,000. Those prices are in the same ballpark as the common date quarter eagles. The injustice becomes more acute when you consider specific examples. For instance, the 1869 issue, with an original mintage of 4,345, is valued in Fine condition only a little above the 1853 quarter eagle, having an original mintage of 1,404,668. Even though these mintage figures can be misleading because of the huge meltdowns, it is inconceivable that the 1853 is almost as rare as the 1869, as their values would suggest. Take advantage of the low prices for these very rare coins. If nothing else, you'll benefit from bullion increases, but you'll probably also reap extra profits as these coins attract more numismatic attention in the upcoming years.

QUARTER EAGLES — GOLD COINS

DATE	MINTAGE	F-12	VF-20	EF-40	AU-50	MS-60	MS-63	PRF-65
1840	18,859	160	298	738	2913	6550	—	—
1840 C	12,822	355	600	1550	4800	16000	—	—
1840 D	3,532	750	2025	5925	16000	—	—	—
1840 O	33,580	190	290	1013	2275	8000	—	—
1841	Unknown	—	60000	70000	125000	—	—	—
1841 C	10,281	280	525	1200	3300	19750	—	—
1841 D	4,164	550	1288	2925	8625	21750	50000	—
1842	2,823	330	825	3050	6250	14500	—	—
1842 C	6,729	575	1188	3325	6500	18500	—	—
1842 D	4,643	650	1450	2950	12000	16000	—	—
1842 O	19,800	225	400	1363	2875	13500	—	—
1843	100,546	145	193	240	388	1325	5600	—
1843 C Sm. Date	26,064	1100	2350	5450	10000	24000	—	—
1843 C Lg. Date	Inc. Above	600	788	1300	3925	8000	—	—
1843 D	36,209	415	613	1075	2375	8000	—	—
1843 O Sm. Date	368,002	155	220	303	425	1500	5050	—
1843 O Lg. Date	Inc. Above	225	338	475	2025	5125	28500	—
1844	6,784	225	225	938	2375	8000	—	—
1844 C	11,622	390	725	1625	7150	16000	—	—
1844 D	17,332	365	613	1150	2375	7250	31000	—
1845	91,051	150	253	308	513	1625	5600	—
1845 D	19,460	375	688	1488	2850	10625	—	—
1845 O	4,000	550	1300	2450	6000	14375	—	—
1846	21,598	215	383	738	1950	6875	—	—
1846 C	4,808	575	975	2300	6750	18500	46500	—
1846 D	19,303	445	713	1175	2475	9500	—	—
1846 O	66,000	170	270	513	1450	5425	—	—
1847	29,814	140	255	420	1038	4650	11000	—
1847 C	23,226	420	605	1050	2050	7225	25000	—
1847 D	15,784	430	625	1125	2525	9375	25000	—
1847 O	124,000	150	270	450	1200	3650	—	—
1848	7,497	300	575	1050	2850	7225	—	—
1848 C	16,788	400	713	1375	2925	12125	—	—
1848 CAL	1,389	7000	8500	15000	21000	33750	72500	—
1848 D	13,771	425	613	1213	12800	8000	—	—
1849	23,294	145	383	575	1275	3350	—	—
1849 C	10,220	410	650	1700	5125	21375	—	—
1849 D	10,945	430	705	1350	2975	13875	—	—
1850	252,923	135	180	205	303	1200	4650	—
1850 C	9,148	325	675	1588	3425	15750	—	—
1850 D	12,148	375	700	1300	2850	14500	—	—
1850 O	84,000	160	293	563	1375	4925	14000	—
1851	1,372,748	135	135	170	193	335	1750	—
1851 C	14,923	350	688	1600	3950	14000	—	—
1851 D	11,264	400	675	1225	2950	13250	—	—
1851 O	148,000	150	213	338	1088	5150	13750	—

GOLD COINS — QUARTER EAGLES

DATE	MINTAGE	F-12	VF-20	EF-40	AU-50	MS-60	MS-63	PRF-65
1852	1,159,681	135	143	175	210	340	1700	—
1852 C	9,772	400	650	1425	3625	18500	—	—
1852 D	4,078	485	950	2600	5900	17750	—	—
1852 O	140,000	145	218	300	950	4025	—	—
1853	1,404,668	135	135	185	228	430	1600	—
1853 D	3,178	550	1325	2625	4900	17375	—	—
1854	596,258	135	165	185	228	425	1825	—
1854 C	7,295	365	738	1650	4850	17000	—	—
1854 D	1,760	2000	2975	5500	10750	18000	—	—
1854 O	153,000	150	225	275	563	1788	5250	—
1854 S	246	32500	48750	65000	95000	—	—	—
1855	235,480	135	168	190	245	515	2150	—
1855 C	3,677	620	1325	2925	5775	26000	—	—
1855 D	1,123	1900	3825	7750	15000	23000	—	—
1856	384,240	125	138	170	190	315	1950	32000
1856 C	7,913	490	875	2200	5100	17250	—	—
1856 D	874	3950	6500	11250	20500	42500	—	—
1856 O	21,100	175	338	745	2050	7250	—	—
1856 S	71,120	150	228	425	1125	6625	12500	—
1857	214,130	135	165	193	228	1835	2500	—
1857 D	2,364	500	1250	2500	4000	12125	—	—
1857 O	34,000	155	215	363	1650	5775	14000	—
1857 S	69,200	150	253	450	1325	5250	16000	—
1858	47,377	135	203	270	425	1850	5150	20000
1858 C	9,056	340	600	1250	2675	9875	—	—
1859	39,444	135	200	285	610	1325	5150	20000
1859 D	2,244	550	1300	2625	5850	25500	—	—
1859 S	14,200	225	413	1225	3450	7625	16500	—
1860	22,675	135	203	278	538	1225	4400	20000
1860 C	7,469	375	800	2050	5950	24250	60000	—
1860 S	35,600	195	275	775	1850	5175	15000	—
1861	1,283,878	135	135	170	193	305	1300	20000
1861 S	24,000	210	413	1450	3925	5500	—	—
1862	98,543	140	210	278	550	1575	4900	20000
1862 S	8,000	485	950	2325	5350	17750	—	—
1863 Proof Only	30	—	—	—	—	19000	38000	80000
1863 S	10,800	400	570	1850	4125	12800	—	—
1864	2,874	2750	5450	12750	28250	42000	—	20000
1865	1,545	2200	4288	9300	21000	32000	—	37500
1865 S	23,376	180	255	778	1825	5125	—	—
1866	3,110	650	1275	4800	9250	18250	—	20000
1866 S	38,960	195	313	1038	2725	9075	25500	—
1867	3,250	200	373	758	1588	4750	7500	20000
1867 S	28,000	190	265	788	2175	5000	—	—
1868	3,625	160	253	423	820	3125	7750	20000
1868 S	34,000	160	220	563	1350	5375	14500	—

EDMUND'S 1996 U.S. COIN PRICES

QUARTER EAGLES — GOLD COINS

DATE	MINTAGE	F-12	VF-20	EF-40	AU-50	MS-60	MS-63	PRF-65
1869	4,345	165	218	438	775	4300	8500	20000
1869 S	29,500	—	—	—	—	—	—	—
1869 S	29,500	175	243	583	1163	5025	15000	—
1870	4,555	155	228	450	843	3625	8000	20000
1870 S	16,000	160	243	393	1125	5350	—	—
1871	5,350	160	228	350	770	2375	5500	20000
1871 S	22,000	155	230	345	733	2750	5900	—
1872	3,030	250	393	788	1888	7000	13000	20000
1872 S	18,000	165	280	495	1313	4775	14000	—
1873 Closed 3	178,025	145	208	248	378	1125	1650	20000
1873 Open 3	Inc. Above	135	173	1208	220	340	1375	—
1873 S	27,000	170	243	525	1150	3250	6750	—
1874	3,940	180	250	433	868	3150	7500	20000
1875	420	2500	3550	5075	8625	16000	—	35000
1875 S	11,600	145	225	400	775	4750	13750	—
1876	4,221	170	310	713	1350	5700	12000	20000
1876 S	5,000	145	245	695	1488	5750	14250	—
1877	1,652	305	418	733	1363	3050	7500	48000
1877 S	35,400	140	168	188	235	763	6450	—
1878	286,260	135	148	158	195	370	1050	18000
1878 S	178,000	135	148	160	205	405	3100	—
1879	88,990	135	148	158	183	303	1250	18000
1879 S	43,500	140	160	193	938	2400	5800	—
1880	2,996	155	238	320	550	1375	3900	20000
1881	691	725	1425	3825	6375	13000	—	20000
1882	4,067	180	223	278	370	1000	3000	18000
1883	2,002	180	235	450	900	2525	5500	20000
1884	2,023	180	228	393	550	1850	3400	32000
1885	887	400	775	1575	2700	6500	8500	32000
1886	4,088	165	210	283	475	1400	3300	18000
1887	6,282	165	190	223	438	1125	2950	18000
1888	16,098	165	185	210	278	500	1100	18000
1889	17,648	165	185	223	248	443	1175	18000
1890	8,813	165	185	238	263	525	1225	18000
1891	11,040	165	185	220	243	438	1150	18000
1892	2,545	165	200	238	413	938	2400	18000
1893	30,106	145	155	193	233	323	1050	18000
1894	4,122	155	165	235	363	743	2000	15250
1895	6,199	135	145	195	250	438	1100	18000
1896	19,202	135	145	158	178	285	900	18000
1897	29,904	135	148	88	183	273	900	18000
1898	24,165	135	145	158	178	268	925	18000
1899	27,350	135	140	850	175	253	623	18000
1900	67,205	135	145	158	178	268	875	18000
1901	91,322	135	145	158	178	268	850	18000
1902	133,733	135	145	158	178	268	875	16000

GOLD COINS — QUARTER EAGLES

DATE	MINTAGE	F-12	VF-20	EF-40	AU-50	MS-60	MS-63	PRF-65
1903	201,257	135	145	158	178	268	900	16000
1904	160,960	135	145	158	178	268	875	16000
1905	217,944	135	145	158	178	268	875	16000
1906	176,490	135	145	158	178	268	850	16000
1907	336,448	135	145	158	178	268	850	16000

INDIAN HEAD TYPE
1908-1929

DIAMETER: 18mm
WEIGHT: 4.18 Grams
COMPOSITION: .900 Gold, .100 Copper
DESIGNER: Bela Lyon Pratt
EDGE: Reeded
PURE GOLD CONTENT: .12094 Tr. Oz.

The final quarter eagle, the Indian Head type, was minted from 1908 to 1929, with a ten year lapse between the 1915 and 1925. The values of all the Indian Head quarter eagles are remarkably similar, with the one notable exception being the 1911-D. The 1911-D has had a checkered history, as some of the past appreciation has been very flat or negative. This is surprising for the "key" coin in a series. In grades Fine to MS-60, this item reached its popularity zenith in 1981, but today carries a much smaller price tag. In light of these facts, you ought to do well with this quarter eagle as a long term investment.

DATE	MINTAGE	EF-40	AU-50	MS-60	MS-63	MS-65	PRF-65
1908	565,057	158	170	235	935	3600	14000
1909	441,899	158	170	253	978	3675	19000
1910	492,682	158	170	240	1005	6200	14400
1911	704,191	158	170	240	935	5575	14400
1911 D	55,680	950	1375	2650	6950	40500	—
1912	616,197	160	173	245	1030	7350	15000
1913	722,165	155	170	243	945	5075	14000
1914	240,117	163	193	465	2375	14125	15500
1914 D	448,000	158	173	318	1238	21500	—
1915	606,100	155	170	233	980	4525	15000
1925 D	578,000	153	168	228	875	3425	—
1926	446,000	153	168	228	875	3425	—
1927	388,000	153	168	228	875	3675	—
1928	416,000	153	168	228	888	3625	—
1929	532,000	153	168	228	900	4475	—

EDMUND'S 1996 U.S. COIN PRICES

THREE DOLLAR GOLD PIECES 1854-1889

The $3 gold piece, introduced in 1854, was one of the most unpopular coins of all time. Scholars today guess that the $3 denomination was minted because a sheet of 100 postage stamps, a frequently purchased item, cost three dollars to buy. The three cent charge for a single stamp was the primary reason for the origination of the 3 cent trime.

Because of its unacceptability to the public, $3 gold coins were produced in tiny quantities only. During its 36 year lifespan from 1854 to 1889, only about half a million pieces were struck in all the mints combined. A very small number of $3 gold coins remain today.

For much of the 1980's, led by the MS-65 coins, the $3 gold series experienced strong advances. Prices have plummeted since then. These coins are poised for an active market in a few years, or less; after all, coins this rare will not go unnoticed forever. Spend your investment dollars on the highest grade possible, being certain that the coin has been professionally graded.

DIAMETER: 20.5mm
WEIGHT: 5.015 Grams
COMPOSITION: .900 Gold, .100 Copper
DESIGNER: James B. Longacre
EDGE: Reeded
PURE GOLD CONTENT: .14512 Tr. Oz.

DATE	MINTAGE	VF-20	EF-40	AU-50	MS-60	MS-63	MS-65	PRF-65
1854	138,618	588	788	1875	5025	5000	17000	35000
1854 D	1,120	6625	12000	21000	70000	—	—	—
1854 O	24,000	663	1100	2475	16000	—	—	8200
1855	50,555	528	628	748	2275	5400	19750	—
1855 S	6,600	1000	2100	5500	16375	—	—	—
1856	26,010	555	675	1013	2400	6200	26500	—
1856 S	34,500	730	1525	2025	7750	2250	—	—
1857	20,891	558	670	1025	2900	8500	33500	35000
1857 S	14,000	918	2025	3925	13500	—	—	—
1858	2,133	793	1425	2300	5625	15500	—	35000
1859	15,638	545	638	753	2000	15500	—	35000
1860	7,155	688	758	1075	2600	6250	20750	35000
1860 S	7,000	780	2425	5100	12500	—	—	—
1861	6,072	718	950	1800	3250	8600	26000	35000

GOLD COINS

THREE DOLLARS

DATE	MINTAGE	VF-20	EF-40	AU-50	MS-60	MS-63	MS-65	PRF-65
1862	5,785	718	950	1813	3600	8400	27750	35000
1863	5,039	725	963	1975	3625	8600	22750	35000
1864	2,680	730	988	1988	3650	9250	27000	35000
1865	1,165	988	2050	5125	12750	20000	42500	35000
1866	4,030	735	1213	1950	3675	8550	26750	35000
1867	2,650	753	1050	1963	3625	9000	26250	35000
1868	4,875	723	1000	1925	3500	8350	26500	35000
1869	2,525	715	1050	1700	3650	9150	30000	35000
1870	3,535	738	1075	2050	4050	10000	38500	35000
1870 S	Unique	—	1500000	—	—	—	—	—
1871	1,330	795	1138	2175	3625	8750	29000	35000
1872	2,030	755	1138	1975	3425	8750	29000	35000
1873 Closed 3	Unknown	3675	5375	8000	23500	—	—	—
1873 Open 3 - Proof Only	25	—	—	10750	20500	30000	—	80000
1874	41,820	538	703	1018	2375	4850	13000	35000
1875 Proof Only	20	—	—	—	60000	80000	—	183000
1876 Proof Only	45	—	—	—	28000	—	73750
1877	1,488	1013	2825	5125	8600	31500	—	35000
1878	82,324	513	613	728	1675	4750	12750	30000
1879	3,030	713	1113	1875	3075	5250	18500	30000
1880	1,036	808	1375	2300	3400	5550	19000	30000
1881	554	1325	2250	3875	5750	11000	38500	32000
1882	1,576	845	1413	2275	3475	5600	19750	30000
1883	989	850	1400	2400	3800	5800	22500	32000
1884	1,106	975	1750	2650	3525	5750	23000	45000
1885	910	938	1575	2438	3575	5850	23500	32000
1886	1,142	900	1513	2600	3850	6000	24000	30000
1887	6,160	700	963	1625	2675	5350	15000	30000
1888	5,291	700	963	1625	2675	5350	15000	30000
1889	2,429	700	963	1625	2675	5350	15000	30000

FOUR DOLLAR GOLD (STELLA)

THE STELLAS ARE ACTUALLY PATTERN COINS THAT, BECAUSE OF THEIR UNIQUE DENOMINATION, HAVE BEEN COLLECTED ALONG WITH THE REGULAR SERIES.

DATE	MINTAGE	VF-20	EF-40	AU-50	PRF-65
1879 Flowing Hair	415	—	—	—	70000
1879 Coiled Hair	10	—	—	—	400000
1879 Impaired Proof	—	10000	13000	33000	—
1880 Flowing Hair	15	—	—	—	162500
1880 Coiled Hair	10	—	—	—	400000

GOLD COINS

HALF EAGLES 1795-1929
($5.00 GOLD PIECES)

In 1795, the $5 gold piece, or half eagle, became the first U.S. gold coin struck. It is the only denomination of United States coinage to be produced in as many as seven mints. The history of type changes for the half eagles closely parallels that of the quarter eagles, with weight specifications always being double those of the smaller coin.

Low grade half eagles are relatively common and advance or decline in unison with the gold bullion market. This makes these particular eagles a strong hedge against inflation, and a slight numismatic premium as well.

Gold half eagles in uncirculated grades, even common date examples, have shown consistent appreciation over time, with a few slips here and there. Fortunately for 1996 buyers, the most recent reversal has taken place over the last five years, indicating a clear "buy" signal. This downward trend will eventually correct itself as investors and speculators rediscover the allure of high grade gold half eagles.

For investors bitten by the numismatic bug, pre-1839 half eagles, and rare dates issued in 1839 and beyond, are proven winners, although expensive. Half eagles meeting these criteria, in problem-free condition, should always be in demand by collectors from now until the end of the world, regardless of whether they are uncirculated or not. Many experts argue that there is far greater potential here than with gem quality common date material.

HALF EAGLES

GOLD COINS

LIBERTY CAP TYPE
SMALL EAGLE REVERSE
1795-1798

DIAMETER: 25mm
WEIGHT: 8.75 Grams
COMPOSITION: .9167 Gold,
.0833 Copper
DESIGNER: Robert Scot
EDGE: Reeded

DATE	MINTAGE	F-12	VF-20	EF-40	AU-50	MS-60	MS-63
1795 /6	6,196	6000	8500	13250	27500	60000	—
1795 Sm. Eagle	8,707	5500	7000	8125	12375	22625	31500
1797 15 Stars	3,609	8000	13500	18000	27500	45000	—
1797 16 Stars	Inc. Above	7250	9000	15750	36750	53750	122500
1798 Sm. Eagle	6	—	30000	51750	—	—	—

LIBERTY CAP TYPE
HERALDIC EAGLE REVERSE
1795-1807

DIAMETER: 25mm
WEIGHT: 8.75 Grams
COMPOSITION: .9167 Gold,
.0833 Copper
DESIGNER: Robert Scot
EDGE: Reeded

DATE	MINTAGE	F-12	VF-20	EF-40	AU-50	MS-60	MS-63
1795 Heraldic Eagle	Inc. w/1798	6575	8500	16000	34000	90000	—
1797 /5	Inc. w/1798	5500	7500	11050	43000	60000	—
1797 16 Stars	Inc. w/1798	—	—	—	60000	—	—
1798 Sm. 8	24,867	1750	2200	3100	9000	—	—
1798 Lg. 8, 13 Star Rev.	Inc. Above	1450	2100	3100	5700	13000	—
1798 Lg. 8, 14 Star Rev.	Inc. Above	1850	2550	6250	27500	—	—
1799	7,451	1450	1725	3175	7000	13250	37500
1800	37,628	1238	1600	2250	3150	6025	15500
1802 /01	53,176	1225	1588	2150	4525	5625	13250
1803 /02	33,508	1225	1588	2150	3000	5800	13000

EDMUND'S 1996 U.S. COIN PRICES

GOLD COINS — HALF EAGLES

DATE	MINTAGE	F-12	VF-20	EF-40	AU-50	MS-60	MS-63
1804 Sm. 8	30,475	1275	1618	2163	3025	5875	17000
1804 Lg. 8	Inc. Above	1288	1625	2275	4875	6500	18500
1805	33,183	1250	1613	2150	3000	5825	13500
1806 Pointed 6	64,093	1350	1688	2388	3800	8375	29000
1806 Round 6	Inc. Above	1225	1575	2138	2850	5800	12900
1807	32,488	1250	1588	2175	3000	5825	13250

CAPPED BUST TO LEFT
1807-1812

DIAMETER: 25mm
WEIGHT: 8.75 Grams
COMPOSITION: .9167 Gold, .0833 Copper
DESIGNER: John Reich
EDGE: Reeded

DATE	MINTAGE	F-12	VF-20	EF-40	AU-50	MS-60	MS-63
1807	51,605	1250	1650	2150	2900	6000	12750
1808	55,578	1313	1663	2238	2875	5800	12750
1808/07	Inc. Above	1288	1638	2225	2950	5825	12450
1809	33,875	1275	1550	2200	2800	5750	12500
1810 Sm. Date, Sm 5	100,287	9500	10250	22750	45000	—	—
1810 Lg. Date, Lg 5	Inc. Above	1313	1525	2150	2975	5800	12750
1810 Lg. Date, Sm 5	Inc. Above	3875	4875	7750	16000	24000	—
1810 Sm. Date, Lg 5	Inc. Above	1550	1875	2450	3200	6175	16000
1811 Sm. 5	99,581	1288	1513	2138	2800	5475	12500
1811 Lg. 5	Inc. Above	1263	1500	2163	3150	6325	29000
1812	58,087	1138	1463	2125	2825	5875	12250

HALF EAGLES   **GOLD COINS**

CAPPED HEAD TO LEFT
1813-1834

DIAMETER: 1813-1829 25mm,
                    1829-1834 22.5mm
WEIGHT: 8.75 Grams
COMPOSITION: .9167 Gold,
                       .0833 Copper
DESIGNER: John Reich
EDGE: Reeded

VARIETY ONE - LARGE DIAMETER
1813-1829

DATE	MINTAGE	F-12	VF-20	EF-40	AU-50	MS-60	MS-63
1813	95,428	1400	1563	2263	3050	6300	13500
1814	14,454	1688	2125	3325	3800	10250	26000
1815	635	—	—	42500	63750	145000	—
1818	45,588	1625	2063	2775	3900	6125	23500
1819	51,723	—	—	32500	55000	—	—
1820 Curved Base, 2 Sm. Letters	263,806	1638	2025	4550	8000	16000	—
1820 Curved Base 2, Lg. Letters	Inc. Above	1650	2038	4575	8000	40000	—
1820 Square Base 2	Inc. Above	1625	2013	3025	5850	9050	18500
1821	29,060	2250	3775	7200	17500	22500	50000
1822	17,796	—	687500	1000000	—	—	—
1823	14,485	1713	2038	3625	6750	13750	42000
1824	17,340	2225	3575	8650	15000	30500	47500
1825 /21	29,060	3375	4875	6125	8250	24000	47000
1825 /24	Inc. Above	Bowers & Merena 1989			$148,500		
1826	18,069	2825	5750	7075	13000	24000	—
1827	24,913	—	—	—	35000	61250	—
1828 /7	28,029	—	—	30000	27500	72500	—
1828	Inc. Above	—	—	30000	—	—	—
1829 Lg. Date	57,442	Superior1985 MS-65		$104,500			

EDMUND'S 1996 U.S. COIN PRICES

GOLD COINS

HALF EAGLES

VARIETY TWO - SMALL DIAMETER
1829-1834

DATE	MINTAGE	F-12	VF-20	EF-40	AU-50	MS-60	MS-63
1829 Sm. Date	Inc. Above	—	—	80000	225000	—	—
1830 Sm. 5D	126,351	3500	5025	6500	8400	15250	43000
1830 Lg. 5D	Inc. Above	3650	5200	7025	9250	17000	47500
1831	140,594	3550	5175	6550	8400	16375	44000
1832 Curved Base 2, 12 Stars	157,487	—	100000	—	—	—	—
1832 Square Base 2, 13 Stars	Inc. Above	5000	6250	8575	10500	17875	48500
1833	193,630	3475	5025	6325	8250	15125	32500
1834 Plain 4	50,141	3500	5050	6350	9750	16750	47500
1834 Crosslet 4	Inc. Above	4125	5875	8125	14000	28250	—

CLASSIC HEAD TYPE
1834-1838

DIAMETER: 22.5mm
WEIGHT: 8.36 Grams
COMPOSITION: .8992 Gold, .1008 Copper
DESIGNER: William Kneass
EDGE: Reeded

DATE	MINTAGE	EF-40	AU-50	MS-60	MS-63	MS-65
1834 Plain 4	657,460	500	850	3000	7000	90000
1834 Crosslet 4	Inc. Above	2400	5250	15000	42500	—
1835	371,534	500	900	3000	8500	62000
1836	553,147	500	900	3000	8500	62000
1837	207,121	525	925	3500	11500	62000
1838	286,588	500	900	3250	12500	62000
1838 C	17,719	4250	9500	20000	37500	—
1838 D	20,583	3500	7000	15000	30000	—

HALF EAGLES   *GOLD COINS*

CORONET OR LIBERTY HEAD TYPE
1839-1908

VARIETY ONE
NO MOTTO ABOVE EAGLE
1839-1866

DIAMETER: 21.6mm
WEIGHT: 8.359 Grams
COMPOSITION: .900 Gold, .100 Copper
DESIGNER: Christian Gobrecht
EDGE: Reeded
PURE GOLD CONTENT: .24187 Tr. Oz.

DATE	MINTAGE	F-12	VF-20	EF-40	AU-50	MS-60	MS-63
1839 C	17,205	488	1013	2325	7000	14250	87500
1839 D	18,939	433	875	2075	6150	14625	—
1840	137,382	190	218	363	1550	4100	9750
1840 C	18,992	418	763	2325	9500	22000	—
1840 D	22,896	420	738	1475	5250	15250	—
1840 O	40,120	218	375	863	2150	7125	—
1841	15,833	223	395	1100	2300	6750	12500
1841 C	21,467	340	725	1438	3450	17500	—
1841 D	30,495	355	663	1425	3850	13000	80000
1841 O	50		Only 2 Known				
1842 Sm. Letters	27,578	158	325	1200	4500	10000	—
1842 Lg. Letters	Inc. Above	375	763	2250	5850	11500	—
1842 C Sm. Date	28,184	1900	4000	17125	57500	140000	—
1842 C Lg. Date	Inc. Above	370	763	1600	3500	21000	47500
1842 D Sm. Date	59,608	438	713	1275	3250	15000	—
1842 D Lg. Date	Inc. Above	1200	2300	6250	14500	31500	—
1842 O	16,400	363	900	4700	12750	24000	42500
1843	611,205	148	168	1223	325	2100	10000
1843 C	44,201	375	680	1350	5500	17500	47500
1843 D	98,452	370	3555	975	1950	7500	31000
1843 O Sm. Letters	19,075	345	638	3150	4500	11000	—
1843 O Lg. Letters	82,000	190	293	1050	2800	15750	37500
1844	340,330	153	178	238	315	1975	8000
1844 C	23,631	408	938	3150	8750	22750	—
1844 D	88,982	438	618	1175	2750	12500	41500
1844 O	364,600	180	213	450	975	4725	15500

EDMUND'S 1996 U.S. COIN PRICES

GOLD COINS
HALF EAGLES

DATE	MINTAGE	F-12	VF-20	EF-40	AU-50	MS-60	MS-63
1845	417,099	153	175	220	320	2400	9750
1845 D	90,629	448	775	1550	1950	62625	31000
1845 O	41,000	228	375	938	3500	12625	31500
1846	395,942	148	175	225	390	2575	10250
1846 C	12,995	458	975	2725	6850	23250	87500
1846 D	80,294	423	600	1300	3800	9000	38000
1846 O	58,000	218	363	1225	4400	12375	25000
1847	915,981	148	168	208	370	1450	7500
1847 C	84,151	413	615	1363	3400	17750	37500
1847 D	64,405	433	563	1225	2400	8625	—
1847 O	12,000	538	2275	8625	15000	29000	—
1848	260,775	153	183	240	475	2200	9000
1848 C	64,472	438	675	1350	2250	17750	75000
1848 D	47,465	420	613	1413	3350	14000	—
1849	133,070	148	180	270	675	2800	—
1849 C	64,823	380	550	1050	2250	14750	—
1849 D	39,036	388	678	1325	3000	15000	—
1850	64,491	205	320	775	1350	5100	9750
1850 C	63,591	370	575	1038	7650	16000	41500
1850 D	43,984	425	600	925	2825	25000	18000
1851	377,505	153	170	250	335	2500	9250
1851 C	49,176	388	630	1125	3400	16500	80000
1851 D	62,710	375	600	1375	3000	13750	42000
1851 O	41,000	303	625	1475	4750	15500	—
1852	573,901	148	165	198	305	1325	6750
1852 C	72,574	375	625	1100	2300	11000	24000
1852 D	92,584	378	600	1075	2200	11500	—
1853	305,770	153	175	205	315	1825	7250
1853 C	65,571	375	563	975	1975	12000	39000
1853 D	89,678	378	555	938	1950	7250	32000
1854	160,675	163	208	390	575	2450	—
1854 C	39,283	418	700	1400	3300	17250	—
1854 D	56,413	370	558	1088	2050	9375	—
1854 O	46,000	245	300	450	1550	7650	—
1854 S	268	Bower's & Ruddy - Oct. 1982, AU-55				$170,000	
1855	117,098	158	185	258	330	2150	9150
1855 C	39,788	390	738	1650	3450	16000	47500
1855 D	22,432	418	713	1488	2800	16750	42500
1855 O	11,100	365	800	2775	7500	18750	—
1855 S	61,000	218	380	1175	7250	—	—
1856	197,990	163	238	275	315	2725	10650
1856 C	28,457	388	663	1375	8000	22500	—
1856 D	19,786	408	700	1400	3200	25000	—

EDMUND'S 1996 U.S. COIN PRICES

HALF EAGLES — GOLD COINS

DATE	MINTAGE	F-12	VF-20	EF-40	AU-50	MS-60	MS-63
1856 O	10,000	400	775	2188	5250	19000	—
1856 S	105,100	195	293	788	1800	—	—
1857	98,188	158	185	230	1675	1750	8750
1857 C	31,360	335	613	1250	2850	10250	39000
1857 D	17,046	358	625	1325	2950	13500	—
1857 O	13,000	328	763	1800	5000	—	—
1857 S	87,000	210	295	713	1700	7750	—
1858	15,136	208	258	663	1100	4500	10550
1858 C	38,856	385	750	1175	2950	15250	—
1858 D	15,362	363	675	1125	2250	14000	—
1858 S	18,600	413	763	2875	7000	—	—
1859	16,814	210	268	560	1150	5625	—
1859 C	31,847	345	650	1500	3700	16500	62500
1859 D	10,366	420	763	1725	2800	14125	42500
1859 S	13,220	525	1450	4900	7600	—	—
1860	19,825	200	275	538	1050	5125	13250
1860 C	14,813	388	875	1975	5000	14500	—
1860 D	14,635	365	863	1800	2800	15250	51000
1860 S	21,200	500	1100	2375	1850	18500	—
1861	688,150	148	165	193	315	1275	6750
1861 C	6,879	725	1700	3700	8750	31250	115000
1861 D	1,597	2625	4150	6875	18500	5000	—
1861 S	18,000	488	1100	4300	9800	—	—
1862	4,465	453	800	2250	5500	—	—
1862 S	9,500	1350	3875	9000	19000	—	—
1863	2,472	475	1163	3600	8500	—	—
1863 S	17,000	425	1300	4500	13500	—	—
1864	4,220	380	638	1888	4000	13500	—
1864 S	3,888	2300	7000	18000	45000	—	—
1865	1,295	550	1250	3075	9500	22500	—
1865 S	27,612	475	1338	3450	8250	25000	—
1866 S	34,920	—	4500	5975	100625	—	—

GOLD COINS

HALF EAGLES

VARIETY TWO - MOTTO ABOVE EAGLE
1866-1908

DIAMETER: 21.6mm
WEIGHT: 3.359 Grams
COMPOSITION: .900 Gold, .100 Copper
DESIGNER: Christian Gobrecht
EDGE: Reeded
PURE GOLD CONTENT: .24187 Tr. Oz.

DATE	MINTAGE	F-12	VF-20	EF-40	AU-50	MS-60	MS-63	MS-65	PRF-65
1866 S	9,000	—	—	—	—	—	—	—	—
1867	6,920	—	—	4838	4100	—	—	—	35000
1867 S	29,000	—	—	4225	12125	—	—	—	—
1868	5,725	—	—	1388	4175	10500	—	—	35000
1868 S	52,000	—	—	2000	5850	—	—	—	—
1869	1,785	—	—	1900	4700	—	—	—	35000
1869 S	31,000	—	—	2100	9375	—	—	—	—
1870	4,035	—	—	1888	4400	—	—	—	35000
1870 CC	7,675	—	—	10500	25000	—	—	—	—
1870 S	17,000	—	—	3250	12250	—	—	—	—
1871	3,230	—	—	1850	5550	—	—	—	35000
1871 CC	20,770	—	—	3150	15000	—	—	—	—
1871 S	25,000	—	—	1575	5325	20750	—	—	—
1872	1,690	—	—	1500	4275	13625	28500	—	35000
1872 CC	16,980	—	—	3825	15750	—	—	—	—
1872 S	36,400	—	—	1700	5675	19500	—	—	—
1873 CC	7,416	—	—	8500	21750	—	—	—	—
1873 Closed 3	49,305	—	—	220	563	1975	11500	—	35000
1873 Open 3	63,200	—	—	218	316	1588	950	5500	—
1873 S	31,000	—	—	2075	7500	20000	—	—	—
1874	3,508	—	—	1650	4325	—	—	—	35000
1874 CC	21,198	—	—	2100	9250	20250	—	—	—
1874 S	16,000	—	—	3325	9375	—	—	—	—
1875	220	—	—	48500	80250	—	—	—	—
1875 CC	11,828	—	—	5175	14250	33500	—	—	—
1875 S	9,000	—	—	3050	10250	27500	—	42500	—
1876	1,477	—	—	2175	4850	14000	27500	46000	35000
1876 CC	6,887	—	—	5275	10625	—	—	—	—
1876 S	4,000	—	—	5125	12625	—	—	—	—
1877	1,152	—	—	1900	4175	12000	—	—	35000
1877 CC	8,680	—	—	3450	8250	—	—	—	—
1877 S	26,700	—	—	900	3050	—	—	—	—
1878	131,740	—	—	190	240	700	2950	—	35000
1878 CC	9,054	—	—	7875	18250	—	—	—	—

EDMUND'S 1996 U.S. COIN PRICES

HALF EAGLES
GOLD COINS

DATE	MINTAGE	F-12	VF-20	EF-40	AU-50	MS-60	MS-63	MS-65	PRF-65
1878 S	144,700	—	—	225	430	1200	5250	—	—
1879	301,950	—	—	168	218	450	2350	—	20000
1879 CC	17,281	—	—	1450	2975	—	—	—	—
1879 S	426,200	—	—	223	273	925	3600	—	—
1880	3,166,436	—	—	158	178	243	1350	3200	20000
1880 CC	51,017	—	—	775	1725	8750	—	—	—
1880 S	1,348,900	—	—	158	178	233	1150	—	—
1881 /80	5,708,802	—	—	668	1475	3500	6500	—	—
1881	Inc. Above	—	—	158	178	223	3975	7000	20000
1881 CC	13,886	—	—	1550	5000	13000	—	—	—
1881 S	969,000	—	—	158	178	238	1300	—	—
1882	2,514,568	—	—	168	188	240	3988	7000	20000
1882 CC	82,817	—	—	558	1200	5875	—	—	—
1882 S	969,000	—	—	158	178	235	1150	—	—
1883	233,461	—	—	168	195	550	4200	7000	20000
1883 CC	12,958	—	—	850	3325	14250	—	—	—
1883 S	83,200	—	—	213	283	975	4100	—	—
1884	191,078	—	—	175	240	1075	3350	17000	20000
1884 CC	16,402	—	—	888	3500	—	—	—	—
1884 S	177,000	—	—	238	273	563	2300	—	—
1885	601,506	—	—	158	173	225	1050	—	20000
1885 S	1,211,500	—	—	168	185	223	3988	7000	—
1886	388,432	—	—	175	205	330	1600	—	20000
1887 Proof Only	87	—	—	—	—	—	—	—	150000
1887 S	1,912,000	—	—	168	185	230	1100	—	—
1888	18,296	—	—	225	313	1425	4500	—	20000
1888 S	293,900	—	—	253	583	2300	—	—	—
1889	7,565	—	—	538	1038	1100	5000	—	20000
1890	4,328	—	—	488	1250	3700	—	—	20000
1890 CC	53,800	—	—	368	525	1163	5500	—	—
1891	61,413	—	—	213	238	663	4650	7500	20000
1891 CC	208,000	—	—	338	438	750	3350	—	—
1892	753,572	—	—	158	175	220	975	5750	20000
1892 CC	82,968	—	—	460	625	1700	7300	—	—
1892 O	10,000	—	—	1000	1725	5100	—	—	—
1892 S	298,400	—	—	203	278	1750	3950	—	—
1893	1,528,197	—	—	168	183	223	2463	4000	20000
1893 CC	60,000	—	—	375	613	1775	7250	—	—
1893 O	110,000	—	—	273	375	1863	6100	—	—
1893 S	224,000	—	—	195	280	463	4450	7500	—
1894	957,955	—	—	168	183	260	2500	6250	20000
1894 O	16,600	—	—	305	408	1825	5500	—	—
1894 S	55,900	—	—	338	775	3325	8625	7500	—
1895	1,345,936	—	—	158	168	210	2475	4000	20000

EDMUND'S 1996 U.S. COIN PRICES

GOLD COINS — HALF EAGLES

DATE	MINTAGE	F-12	VF-20	EF-40	AU-50	MS-60	MS-63	MS-65	PRF-65
1895 S	112,000	—	—	328	700	4250	26000	26000	—
1896	59,063	—	—	180	213	350	4875	7500	20000
1896 S	155,400	—	—	280	538	1925	—	—	—
1897	867,883	—	—	158	168	210	2488	4600	20000
1897 S	354,000	—	—	255	463	1600	8500	—	—
1898	633,495	—	—	158	168	215	2500	4600	20000
1898 S	1,397,400	—	—	160	193	300	2600	4600	—
1899	1,710,729	—	—	158	168	213	2463	3875	20000
1899 S	1,545,000	—	—	160	173	235	2525	4600	—
1900	1,405,730	—	—	158	168	210	2450	3500	20000
1900 S	329,000	—	—	195	275	613	3575	5000	—
1901	616,040	—	—	158	168	210	2488	4600	12500
1901 S 1/0	3,648,000	—	—	210	265	360	1290	4600	—
1901 S	Inc. Above	—	—	158	168	210	2450	4600	—
1902	172,562	—	—	158	173	218	2500	4600	12500
1902 S	939,000	—	—	158	168	210	2488	4600	—
1903	227,024	—	—	158	173	223	2500	4600	15000
1903 S	1,855,000	—	—	158	168	210	2488	4600	—
1904	392,136	—	—	158	168	210	2475	4600	12500
1904 S	97,000	—	—	205	275	950	7375	11000	—
1905	302,308	—	—	158	173	220	4100	7200	12500
1905 S	880,700	—	—	173	243	800	3425	4600	—
1906	348,820	—	—	158	168	215	2513	4600	12500
1906 D	320,000	—	—	158	168	213	2475	4600	—
1906 S	598,000	—	—	160	180	270	1325	4600	—
1907	626,192	—	—	158	168	210	2450	4600	20000
1907 D	888,000	—	—	158	168	210	2488	4600	—
1908	421,874	—	—	158	168	213	2450	4600	—

EDMUND'S 1996 U.S. COIN PRICES

HALF EAGLES
GOLD COINS

INDIAN HEAD TYPE
1908-1929

DIAMETER: 21.6mm
WEIGHT: 8.359 Grams
COMPOSITION: .900 Gold, .100 Copper
DESIGNER: Bela Lyon Pratt
EDGE: Reeded
PURE GOLD CONTENT: .24187 Tr. Oz.

DATE	MINTAGE	EF-40	AU-50	MS-60	MS-63	MS-65	PRF-65
1908	578,012	223	233	335	2100	12750	22000
1908 D	148,000	223	233	333	2050	18625	—
1908 S	82,000	468	558	1425	3275	14250	—
1909	627,138	223	233	345	2125	13750	26500
1909 D	3,423,560	223	233	333	2200	17250	—
1909 O	34,200	900	1625	7575	25750	117500	—
1909 S	297,200	230	308	1213	6375	34000	—
1910	604,250	223	233	340	2200	16875	23000
1910 D	193,600	225	245	430	2275	36750	—
1910 S	770,200	240	303	1300	7850	41000	—
1911	915,139	223	233	333	2075	15750	21500
1911 D	72,500	530	725	3375	16125	68500	—
1911 S	1,416,000	235	255	548	3013	42000	—
1912	790,144	223	235	333	2075	16625	21500
1912 S	392,000	235	263	1750	12750	66000	—
1913	916,099	223	238	333	2050	17500	25000
1913 S	408,000	275	358	1530	15950	66000	—
1914	247,125	223	238	345	2250	19250	21500
1914 D	247,000	225	240	433	2425	32000	—
1914 S	263,000	240	308	1675	14350	47000	—
1915	588,075	223	238	330	2050	14250	33000
1915 S	164,000	300	463	2125	14250	66000	—
1916 S	240,000	230	258	638	2825	21750	—
1929	662,000	3500	4250	5250	6275	34250	—

GOLD COINS

EAGLES 1795-1933

($10.00 GOLD PIECES)

The $10 gold piece, or eagle, was the largest denomination authorized by the original coinage act. Many of the early specimens have file marks, created by mint employees to adjust the weight to meet legal specifications.

There are not as many types of $10 gold coins as seen with some of the smaller gold coins. The basic types (with slight variations within each type) are the Liberty Cap, the Coronet, and the Indian Head types. The Indian Head eagle type bears a different depiction from the Indian Head quarter eagle and the Indian Head half eagle. Designed by perhaps America's finest sculptor of the time, Augustus Saint Gaudens, the Indian Head eagle is one of the most highly acclaimed artistic coins in the world.

LIBERTY CAP TYPE SMALL EAGLE REVERSE 1795-1797

DIAMETER: 33mm
WEIGHT: 17.50 Grams
COMPOSITION: .9167 Gold, .0833 Copper
DESIGNER: Robert Scot
EDGE: Reeded

DATE	MINTAGE	F-12	VF-20	EF-40	AU-50	MS-60
1795 13 Leaves	5,583	5825	7875	6038	15500	38750
1795 9 Leaves	Inc. Above	16500	29500	44250	82500	165000
1796	4,146	6175	8575	13125	31500	49500
1797 Sm. Eagle	3,615	6750	5763	29250	42500	—

EAGLES

GOLD COINS

LIBERTY CAP TYPE HERALDIC EAGLE REVERSE
1797-1804

DIAMETER: 33mm
WEIGHT: 17.50 Grams
COMPOSITION: .9167 Gold, .0833 Copper
DESIGNER: Robert Scot
EDGE: Reeded

DATE	MINTAGE	F-12	VF-20	EF-40	AU-50	MS-60
1797 Lg. Eagle	10,940	2525	3500	5125	11250	20000
1798 /7 9 Stars Left, 4 Right	900	5250	9500	18750	45000	80000
1798 /7 Stars Left, 6 Right	842	15000	27250	46250	77500	180000
1799	37,449	2325	2825	4200	5200	9800
1800	5,999	2500	3400	4950	5850	13875
1801	44,344	2350	2850	3975	5250	9875
1803	15,017	2525	2850	4250	5800	12000
1804	3,757	3700	4200	7250	10500	27500

CORONET OR LIBERTY HEAD TYPE
1838-1907

VARIETY ONE
NO MOTTO ABOVE EAGLE
1838-1866

DIAMETER: 27mm
WEIGHT: 16.718 Grams
COMPOSITION: .900 Gold, .100 Copper
DESIGNER: Christian Gobrecht
EDGE: Reeded
PURE GOLD CONTENT: .48375 Tr. Oz.

DATE	MINTAGE	F-12	VF-20	EF-40	AU-50	MS-60	MS-63	MS-65
1838	7,200	550	900	2750	5000	26000	—	—
1839 Lg. Letters	25,801	450	800	1700	3000	16000	—	—
1839 Sm. Letters	12,447	775	1675	3875	—	—	—	—
1840	47,338	350	398	688	1650	13500	—	—
1841	63,131	348	380	618	1800	12000	—	—
1841 O	2,500	975	2125	6125	20000	—	—	—

EDMUND'S 1996 U.S. COIN PRICES

GOLD COINS — EAGLES

DATE	MINTAGE	F-12	VF-20	EF-40	AU-50	MS-60	MS-63	MS-65
1842 O	27,400	275	325	713	3600	16750	—	—
1842 Sm. Date	81,507	333	388	625	2150	7500	27500	—
1842 Lg. Date	Inc. Above	338	388	675	2400	11250	27500	—
1843	75,462	338	383	650	2850	7500	—	—
1843 O	175,162	335	378	538	4650	7500	—	—
1844	6,361	500	1350	3425	9250	—	—	—
1844 O	118,700	378	393	550	1750	20000	11000	—
1845	26,153	390	675	1550	3250	21000	—	—
1845 O	47,500	390	513	800	3250	16000	—	—
1846	20,095	488	838	2225	6000	—	—	—
1846 O	81,780	328	550	1225	7250	—	—	—
1847	862,258	250	280	323	550	5075	22500	—
1847 O	571,500	268	315	433	750	5100	17000	—
1848	145,484	293	345	433	750	5350	23500	—
1848 O	38,850	368	543	1288	5750	—	—	140000
1849	653,618	255	288	333	600	4150	12000	—
1849 O	23,900	443	800	2825	5950	—	—	—
1850	291,451	255	288	355	650	4250	16000	—
1850 O	57,500	330	400	775	5550	—	—	—
1851	176,328	285	308	450	1000	7900	—	—
1851 O	263,000	273	288	443	1200	10500	—	—
1852	263,106	300	358	438	595	4400	1500	—
1852 O	18,000	385	495	1475	595	5300	15000	—
1853	201,253	255	290	315	615	4150	12500	—
1853 O	51,000	328	370	525	1400	—	—	—
1854	54,250	330	368	568	1150	—	—	—
1854 O Lg. Date	52,500	358	463	1150	3250	11000	—	—
1854 O Sm. Date	Inc. Above	255	388	1150	2350	—	—	—
1854 S	123,826	320	363	575	1200	14000	—	—
1855	121,701	258	290	338	635	4500	40000	—
1855 O	18,000	340	588	1875	5400	—	—	—
1855 S	9,000	800	1650	3500	6500	—	—	—
1856	60,490	293	318	355	635	5125	15500	—
1856 O	14,500	408	788	2750	5100	—	—	—
1856 S	68,000	298	345	588	1350	9375	—	—
1857	16,606	318	453	1125	4500	—	—	—
1857 O	5,500	650	625	2875	5500	26000	—	—
1857 S	26,000	355	460	888	2250	7750	—	—
1858	15,136	2500	4875	10750	19000	—	—	—
1858 O	20,000	308	365	825	1450	13000	—	—
1858 S	11,800	825	2075	5650	9250	—	—	—
1859	16,093	315	383	913	2400	—	—	—
1859 O	2,300	1463	3875	8750	18500	—	—	—
1859 S	7,000	1075	2375	6325	23000	—	—	—
1860	15,105	303	398	888	2100	9625	—	—
1860 O	11,100	388	638	1725	3450	17750	37500	—

EAGLES — GOLD COINS

DATE	MINTAGE	F-12	VF-20	EF-40	AU-50	MS-60	MS-63	MS-65
1860 S	5,000	1250	3100	7275	21500	—	—	—
1861	113,233	273	323	365	600	6000	18500	—
1861 S	15,500	650	1825	4300	9750	—	—	—
1862	10,995	310	538	1250	2850	—	—	—
1862 S	12,500	675	1900	4625	12000	—	—	—
1863	1,248	2000	3650	10500	22500	51250	130000	—
1863 S	10,000	700	1763	5275	11750	—	—	—
1864	3,580	763	1800	4200	9250	20000	—	—
1864 S	2,500	2750	5150	11750	—	—	—	—
1865	4,005	725	2075	4700	8750	—	—	—
1865 S	16,700	1850	6250	20500	—	—	—	—
1865 S Inverted 186	Inc. Above	1200	2475	7000	16000	—	—	—

VARIETY TWO
MOTTO ABOVE EAGLE
1866-1907

DIAMETER: 27mm
WEIGHT: 16.718 Grams
COMPOSITION: .900 Gold, .100 Copper
DESIGNER: Christian Gobrecht
EDGE: Reeded
PURE GOLD CONTENT: .48375 Tr. Oz.

DATE	MINTAGE	F-12	VF-20	EF-40	AU-50	MS-60	MS-63	MS-65	PRF-65
1866	3,780	—	—	2700	6750	—	—	—	60000
1866 S	11,500	—	—	4350	12500	—	—	—	—
1867	3,140	—	—	4050	9000	—	—	—	60000
1867 S	9,000	—	—	7875	15625	—	—	—	—
1868	10,655	—	—	1425	4650	16250	—	—	60000
1868 S	13,500	—	—	4150	13950	—	—	—	—
1869	1,855	—	—	4225	10200	—	115000	—	65000
1869 S	6,430	—	—	4300	10750	27500	—	—	—
1870	4,025	—	—	1275	4325	—	—	—	60000
1870 CC	5,908	—	—	23250	32500	—	—	—	—
1870 S	8,000	—	—	5325	10800	—	—	—	—
1871	1,820	—	—	4000	6750	10000	—	—	60000
1871 CC	8,085	—	—	5625	14500	38500	—	—	—
1871 S	16,500	—	—	3975	7875	—	—	—	—
1872	1,650	—	—	6250	15250	27000	125000	—	60000

EDMUND'S 1996 U.S. COIN PRICES

GOLD COINS — EAGLES

DATE	MINTAGE	F-12	VF-20	EF-40	AU-50	MS-60	MS-63	MS-65	PRF-65
1872 CC	4,600	—	—	10000	23250	—	—	—	—
1872 S	17,300	—	—	2025	6250	—	—	—	—
1873 CC	4,543	—	—	13000	27000	—	—	—	—
1873 Closed 3	49,305	—	—	14000	28000	—	—	—	60000
1873 S	12,000	—	—	3525	7625	—	—	—	—
1874	53,160	—	—	315	443	1850	9000	—	60000
1874 CC	16,767	—	—	3950	9925	—	—	—	—
1874 S	10,000	—	—	4750	11375	—	—	—	—
1875	120			Akers Avg. 1990 Proof	$115,000				
1875 CC	7,715	—	—	13875	30000	—	—	—	—
1876	732	—	—	10000	19250	—	—	—	50000
1876 CC	4,696	—	—	10750	20750	—	—	—	—
1876 S	5,000	—	—	3850	9625	—	—	—	—
1877	817	—	—	7125	14250	—	—	—	40000
1877 CC	3,332	—	—	6250	12000	—	—	—	—
1877 S	17,000	—	—	1575	5150	—	—	—	—
1878	73,800	—	—	320	395	1925	5800	—	50000
1878 CC	3,244	—	—	10125	23250	—	—	—	—
1878 S	26,100	—	—	1438	6550	—	—	—	—
1879	384,770	—	—	283	348	825	6000	—	40000
1879 CC	1,762	—	—	14000	29250	—	—	—	—
1879 O	1,500	—	—	6350	13500	—	—	—	—
1879 S	224,000	—	—	308	353	1600	—	—	—
1880	1,644,876	—	—	265	280	388	4650	—	40000
1880 CC	11,190	—	—	863	2275	12750	—	—	—
1880 O	9,200	—	—	813	1950	8425	—	—	—
1880 S	506,250	—	—	288	325	550	—	—	—
1881	3,877,260	—	—	268	288	333	1550	—	40000
1881 CC	24,015	—	—	550	1175	7350	—	—	—
1881 O	8,350	—	—	863	2150	7875	—	—	—
1881 S	970,000	—	—	268	290	368	—	6500	—
1882	2,324,480	—	—	268	285	323	1450	6500	40000
1882 CC	6,764	—	—	1500	4550	10000	—	—	—
1882 O	10,820	—	—	763	1875	5000	—	—	—
1882 S	132,000	—	—	280	308	863	5750	13500	—
1883	208,740	—	—	273	305	403	5725	6500	40000
1883 CC	12,000	—	—	800	2625	8375	—	—	—
1883 O	800	—	—	8875	17250	37500	—	—	—
1883 S	38,000	—	—	363	438	1275	—	13500	—
1884	76,905	—	—	273	338	1375	4450	13500	8600
1884 CC	9,925	—	—	1225	3450	9875	—	—	—
1884 S	124,250	—	—	280	365	1038	—	6500	—
1885	253,527	—	—	328	293	593	5400	6500	40000
1885 S	228,000	—	—	273	318	498	6075	6500	—
1886	236,160	—	—	283	350	783	2750	6500	40000
1886 S	826,000	—	—	270	278	338	1550	6500	—

EAGLES — GOLD COINS

DATE	MINTAGE	F-12	VF-20	EF-40	AU-50	MS-60	MS-63	MS-65	PRF-65
1887	53,680	—	—	275	403	1350	50000	—	40000
1887 S	817,000	—	—	273	288	373	3150	6500	—
1888	132,996	—	—	295	345	1163	—	50000	40000
1888 O	21,335	—	—	275	335	763	7500	—	—
1888 S	648,700	—	—	270	290	415	4900	6500	—
1889	4,485	—	—	515	950	3650	—	—	20000
1889 S	425,400	—	—	270	283	348	1900	6500	—
1890	58,043	—	—	293	378	1575	9250	13500	40000
1890 CC	17,500	—	—	463	675	1925	15000	—	—
1891	91,868	—	—	275	290	395	2200	13500	40000
1891 CC	103,732	—	—	375	520	900	4950	—	—
1892	797,552	—	—	268	280	320	1350	6500	40000
1892 CC	40,000	—	—	488	795	6000	—	—	—
1892 O	28,688	—	—	285	308	525	—	—	—
1892 S	115,500	—	—	288	318	565	8000	13500	—
1893	1,840,895	—	—	268	283	330	1050	3500	40000
1893 CC	14,000	—	—	638	1438	2700	—	—	—
1893 O	17,000	—	—	290	343	675	5500	—	—
1893 S	141,350	—	—	293	323	700	—	13500	—
1894	2,470,778	—	—	270	283	333	1050	3500	40000
1894 O	107,500	—	—	285	363	1650	5750	13500	—
1894 S	25,000	—	—	430	1050	4375	—	13500	—
1895	567,826	—	—	265	278	315	1350	6500	40000
1895 O	98,000	—	—	290	323	638	3000	13500	—
1895 S	49,000	—	—	383	1038	3825	—	40000	—
1896	76,348	—	—	275	288	328	1950	6500	40000
1896 S	123,750	—	—	338	800	5625	—	—	—
1897	1,000,159	—	—	268	280	313	1250	5000	—
1897 O	42,500	—	—	298	365	738	2200	13000	—
1897 S	234,750	—	—	315	435	1400	4500	6500	—
1898	812,197	—	—	265	278	310	1300	11250	40000
1898 S	473,600	—	—	278	295	375	1900	3500	—
1899	1,262,305	—	—	265	278	313	1050	3750	40000
1899 O	37,047	—	—	300	348	850	4000	13500	—
1899 S	841,000	—	—	330	303	408	1750	6500	—
1900	293,960	—	—	268	280	313	3788	6500	40000
1900 S	81,000	—	—	313	425	1325	4100	12500	—
1901	1,718,825	—	—	265	278	308	2250	3750	40000
1901 O	72,041	—	—	295	328	540	1675	13500	—
1901 S	2,812,750	—	—	265	278	310	975	4250	—
1902	82,513	—	—	270	285	350	1500	12500	40000
1902 S	469,500	—	—	268	280	325	3775	5200	—
1903	125,926	—	—	273	288	333	1300	6500	40000
1903 O	112,771	—	—	278	323	488	2650	6500	—
1903 S	538,000	—	—	280	313	383	1050	5250	—
1904	162,038	—	—	268	280	318	1250	4250	40000

GOLD COINS — EAGLES

DATE	MINTAGE	F-12	VF-20	EF-40	AU-50	MS-60	MS-63	MS-65	PRF-65
1904 O	108,950	—	—	288	325	513	1850	8250	—
1905	201,078	—	—	270	283	300	1200	6500	40000
1905 S	369,250	—	—	310	383	2925	—	6500	—
1906	165,497	—	—	270	283	320	1400	6500	40000
1906 D	981,000	—	—	265	278	315	1150	6500	—
1906 O	86,895	—	—	295	350	688	2200	13500	—
1906 S	457,000	—	—	285	313	658	3900	6500	—
1907	1,203,973	—	—	265	278	310	1025	3500	40000
1907 D	1,030,000	—	—	273	288	345	1150	3500	—
1907 S	210,500	—	—	295	380	883	3050	6500	—

INDIAN HEAD TYPE
1907-1933

VARIETY ONE
NO MOTTO ON REVERSE
1907-1908

DIAMETER: 27mm
WEIGHT: 16.718 Grams
COMPOSITION: .900 Gold, .100 Copper
DESIGNER: Augustus Saint-Gaudens
EDGE: 46 Raised Stars
PURE GOLD CONTENT: .48375 Tr. Oz.

DATE	MINTAGE	EF-40	AU-50	MS-60	MS-63	MS-65	PRF-65
1907 Periods	239,406	443	453	493	1800	5850	—
1907 Plain Edge	Unique	—	—	—	—	—	—
1907 Rolld Edge, Periods	500	—	—	21500	34000	50000	—
1907 Wire Edge, Periods	42	4500	5850	7400	11250	37250	—
1908 D No Motto	210,000	450	500	748	5150	36750	—
1908 No Motto	33,500	530	588	765	2475	12125	37500

EAGLES

GOLD COINS

VARIETY TWO
MOTTO ON REVERSE
1908-1933

DIAMETER: 27mm
WEIGHT: 16.718 Grams
COMPOSITION: .900 Gold, .100 Copper
DESIGNER: Augustus Saint-Gaudens
EDGE: 1908-1911-46 Raised Stars
　　　　1912-1933-48 Raised Stars
PURE GOLD CONTENT: .48375 Tr. Oz.

DATE	MINTAGE	EF-40	AU-50	MS-60	MS-63	MS-65	PRF-65
1908	341,486	440	460	480	1300	5375	27500
1908 D	836,500	453	483	725	3275	22750	—
1908 S	59,850	535	638	2113	5625	27500	—
1909	184,863	445	460	493	1513	8375	39000
1909 D	121,540	453	485	825	5000	42250	—
1909 S	292,350	455	498	770	2450	14750	—
1910	318,704	440	458	483	1238	6050	35000
1910 D	2,356,640	438	455	480	1225	4975	—
1910 S	811,000	465	495	975	4250	46500	—
1911	505,595	435	453	478	1213	4825	35000
1911 D	30,100	575	1025	4450	21500	88750	—
1911 S	51,000	478	613	1125	3075	10200	—
1912	405,083	438	458	478	1288	5950	33500
1912 S	300,000	453	518	940	2450	43000	—
1913	442,071	435	453	478	1238	4975	36000
1913 S	66,000	613	865	4525	30000	162000	—
1914	151,050	438	455	490	1363	7925	35000
1914 D	343,500	435	453	490	1388	8200	—
1914 S	208,000	443	478	705	3450	40250	—
1915	351,075	438	458	483	1258	4775	42000
1915 S	59,000	508	713	2500	9650	69000	—
1916 S	138,500	470	490	755	3350	13375	—
1920 S	126,500	6750	7750	14500	32750	115000	—
1926	1,014,000	435	453	470	1063	4500	—
1930 S	96,000	5000	6375	7525	9125	38000	—
1932	4,463,000	435	453	470	1050	4300	—
1933	312,500	—	—	52250	80000	495000	—

EDMUND'S 1996 U.S. COIN PRICES

GOLD COINS — DOUBLE EAGLES

DOUBLE EAGLES 1849-1933

($20.00 GOLD PIECES)

The largest regular denomination ever issued by the United States was the $20 gold piece. The first double eagles released for circulation came in 1850. A single double eagle specimen was struck in 1849 and today resides in the Smithsonian Institute in Washington, D.C.

The double eagles quickly became the preferred denomination for international transactions and bank deposit holdings. Thus, larger quantities of double eagles were minted than any other gold denominations.

The Coronet double eagles, often called the Liberty Head double eagles, were produced continuously from 1850 to 1907. The same year the Coronet double eagle series came to an end, the Saint-Gaudens type was released. Although designed by the same sculptor, these coins were completely different in appearance than the Indian Head eagles. The Saint-Gaudens double eagle was praised as a marvelous work of art just as much if not more than the Indian Head eagle.

Production of the double eagle ceased in 1933. There were over 400,000 double eagles struck in the final year, but none were ever placed in circulation. It is assumed that the Gold Order sent all of the 1933 examples to the melting pot. Should anyone ever offer up for sale a 1933 double eagle, he/she might get in trouble with Uncle Sam, for ownership of such a piece is declared illegal.

Traditionally, the double eagles are the most sought after gold coins by speculators. Double eagles are favored because there is a relatively large supply of them, and they each contain nearly one ounce of gold. In addition, even the common dates carry some numismatic value.

Double eagles appear to be terrific investments on today's market. For the most part, MS-65 prices are attractive for buyers in comparison to a few years ago. Currently, the cost of acquiring an uncirculated double eagle is about as low as it can get, down almost 80%. You can bet that when the market heats up, millions of speculators will push for choice eagles, driving prices higher and higher. Buy now before the herd comes thundering along!

DOUBLE EAGLES **GOLD COINS**

CORONET OR LIBERTY HEAD TYPE
1849-1907

**VARIETY ONE
NO MOTTO,
TWENTY D.**
1849-1866

DIAMETER: 34mm
WEIGHT: 33.436 Grams
COMPOSITION: .900 Gold, .100 Copper
DESIGNER: James B. Longacre
EDGE: Reeded
PURE GOLD CONTENT: .96750 Tr. Oz.

DATE	MINTAGE	EF-40	AU-50	MS-60	MS-63	MS-65
1849	One Specimen U.S. Mint					
1850	1,170,261	650	1050	3425	43000	—
1850 O	141,000	1100	3300	7500	—	—
1851	2,087,155	570	698	2225	—	—
1851 O	315,000	788	1550	13125	45500	—
1852	2,053,026	570	750	2250	14000	—
1852 O	190,000	775	1925	13500	34000	—
1853	1,261,326	590	850	5500	17000	—
1853 O	71,000	1050	3275	12750	—	—
1854	757,899	610	900	5750	—	—
1854 O	3,250	31000	58750	220000	250000	—
1854 S	141,468	628	943	3850	17500	28000
1855	364,666	825	4975	16150	40000	22000
1855 O	8,000	10000	15500	—	—	—
1855 S	879,675	938	4858	7000	—	—
1856	329,878	580	950	6375	38500	—
1856 O	2,250	29750	60000	—	175000	—
1856 S	1,189,750	578	775	5050	18000	—
1857	439,375	568	758	4325	26500	—
1857 O	30,000	1725	4375	—	—	—
1857 S	970,500	598	838	4850	11000	—
1858 O	35,250	1750	6000	8000	—	—
1858 S	846,710	1975	5500	8000	—	—
1859	13,597	608	900	7625	22000	—
1859 O	9,100	6500	14500	25000	—	—
1859 S	636,445	628	925	5175	—	—
1860	577,670	590	758	5225	16000	—
1860 O	6,600	5875	13500	—	—	—

EDMUND'S 1996 U.S. COIN PRICES

GOLD COINS

DOUBLE EAGLES

DATE	MINTAGE	EF-40	AU-50	MS-60	MS-63	MS-65
1860 S	544,950	628	1238	6025	24500	—
1861	2,976,453	558	693	2325	6500	—
1861 A.C. Paquet Reverse	Inc. Above	—	—	—	—	—
1861 O	17,741	3625	6825	—	—	—
1861 S	768,000	633	1275	6750	29000	—
1861 S A.C. Paquet Reverse	Inc. Above	—	19500	—	—	—
1862	92,133	1500	3225	12375	35000	—
1862 S	854,173	718	1750	9250	—	—
1863	142,790	825	1650	11375	35500	—
1863 S	966,570	625	1400	5750	20000	—
1864	204,285	688	1700	8750	—	—
1864 S	793,660	—	2350	7825	—	—
1865	351,200	613	975	6225	21500	—
1865 S	1,042,500	623	1275	7000	22750	—
1866 S	842,250	3400	9625	—	—	—

VARIETY TWO
MOTTO ABOVE EAGLE
TWENTY D.
1866-1876

DIAMETER: 34mm
WEIGHT: 33.436 Grams
COMPOSITION: .900 Gold, .100 Copper
DESIGNER: James B. Longacre
EDGE: Reeded
PURE GOLD CONTENT: .96750 Tr. Oz

DATE	MINTAGE	EF-40	AU-50	MS-60	MS-63	MS-65	PRF-65
1866	698,775	633	1225	6625	37000	—	—
1866 S	842,250	800	2600	14000	—	—	—
1867	251,065	510	718	1400	19000	—	—
1867 S	920,750	738	1613	13125	—	—	—
1868	98,600	913	2150	7125	29000	—	—
1868 S	837,500	688	1625	11125	—	—	—
1869	175,155	850	2825	11750	44000	200000	—
1869 S	686,750	593	1325	4750	24500	—	—
1870	155,185	850	2063	4250	—	—	—
1870 CC	3,789	67500	80000	125000	—	—	—
1870 S	982,000	568	800	5175	23500	—	—
1871	80,150	1463	3975	3350	15000	—	—
1871 CC	17,387	4400	9625	33000	—	—	—
1871 S	928,000	543	760	4625	17500	—	—

DOUBLE EAGLES — GOLD COINS

DATE	MINTAGE	EF-40	AU-50	MS-60	MS-63	MS-65	PRF-65
1872	251,880	513	678	2950	17000	—	75000
1872 CC	26,900	1650	5225	18750	—	—	—
1872 S	780,000	515	650	2125	—	—	—
1873	22,140	1500	4350	18500	—	—	—
1873 Closed 3	1,709,825	715	1275	8875	—	—	—
1873 Open 3	Inc. Above	490	533	620	5000	—	—
1873 S	1,040,600	523	603	1900	16500	—	—
1874	366,800	523	733	1500	16500	—	—
1874 CC	115,085	733	1813	9750	—	—	—
1874 S	1,214,000	505	648	1675	16250	—	—
1875	295,740	515	575	830	5750	—	110000
1875 CC	111,151	650	850	2250	15500	—	—
1875 S	1,230,000	505	580	895	15000	90000	—
1876	583,905	500	535	803	5250	—	45000
1876 CC	138,441	690	1013	6125	39000	—	—
1876 S	1,597,000	510	568	888	13750	—	—

VARIETY THREE TWENTY DOLLARS SPELLED OUT
1877-1907

DIAMETER: 34mm
WEIGHT: 33.436 Grams
COMPOSITION: .900 Gold, .100 Copper
DESIGNER: James B. Longacre
EDGE: Reeded
PURE GOLD CONTENT: .96750 Tr. Oz.

DATE	MINTAGE	EF-40	AU-50	MS-60	MS-63	MS-65	PRF-65
1877	397,670	505	535	713	615	2600	—
1877 CC	42,565	850	1650	13000	46500	—	—
1877 S	1,735,000	498	570	825	2700	—	—
1878	543,645	503	553	713	5000	—	—
1878 CC	13,180	1775	4375	17000	—	—	—
1878 S	1,739,000	508	568	1175	10000	—	—
1879	207,630	518	590	1238	6750	—	—
1879 CC	10,708	1975	5425	20250	—	—	—
1879 O	2,325	4300	12250	35000	—	—	—
1879 S	1,223,800	508	568	1475	10000	—	—
1880	51,456	538	800	3250	13500	—	—
1880 S	836,000	545	683	1400	6000	—	—
1881	2,260	7375	14750	45000	—	—	—

EDMUND'S 1996 U.S. COIN PRICES

GOLD COINS
DOUBLE EAGLES

DATE	MINTAGE	EF-40	AU-50	MS-60	MS-63	MS-65	PRF-65
1881 S	727,000	528	650	800	5750	—	—
1882	630	16000	30000	50000	—	—	—
1882 CC	39,140	725	1163	5650	20500	—	—
1882 S	1,125,000	503	535	835	17500	—	—
1883	92	—	—	—	—	—	185000
1883 CC	59,962	655	1050	4800	19500	—	—
1883 S	1,189,000	498	528	670	2900	—	—
1884	71	—	—	—	65000	—	—
1884 CC	81,139	725	913	2675	10750	—	—
1884 S	916,000	493	528	608	2800	—	—
1885	828	6875	14175	39250	—	—	100000
1885 CC	9,450	1875	3650	10750	30000	—	—
1885 S	683,500	505	540	630	2750	—	—
1886	1,106	11750	21875	36000	67500	—	60000
1887	121	—	—	—	—	—	150000
1887 S	283,000	513	550	810	2600	—	—
1888	226,266	518	548	950	5000	—	—
1888 S	859,600	508	525	630	2000	—	—
1889	44,111	603	660	938	4850	—	—
1889 CC	30,945	713	1045	3525	15500	—	—
1889 S	774,700	513	538	643	2750	—	—
1890	75,995	590	623	838	2550	—	50000
1890 CC	91,209	688	913	3550	15750	—	—
1890 S	802,750	515	540	1003	3250	—	—
1891	1,442	4125	7875	27000	—	—	—
1891 CC	5,000	2700	4950	14375	—	—	—
1891 S	1,228,125	493	510	588	1750	—	—
1892	4,523	1575	2675	6500	19000	—	—
1892 CC	27,265	800	1375	4550	17000	—	—
1892 S	930,150	498	520	610	1600	—	—
1893	344,339	493	525	628	2250	—	—
1893 CC	18,402	850	1175	2500	8000	—	—
1893 S	996,175	495	515	590	1700	—	—
1894	1,368,990	493	493	585	1425	—	50000
1894 S	1,048,550	498	523	598	1350	—	—
1895	1,114,656	475	500	535	703	—	—
1895 S	1,143,500	498	515	588	4125	7200	—
1896	792,663	493	513	575	875	—	40000
1896 S	1,403,925	498	515	615	1600	—	—
1897	1,383,261	493	510	575	800	—	—
1897 S	1,470,250	493	515	583	875	—	—
1898	170,470	500	523	763	5500	—	—
1898 S	2,575,175	485	503	570	3975	7000	—
1899	1,669,384	485	503	572	760	7000	—
1899 S	2,010,300	490	513	590	1450	—	35000
1900	1,874,584	485	503	570	760	7100	—

EDMUND'S 1996 U.S. COIN PRICES

DOUBLE EAGLES GOLD COINS

DATE	MINTAGE	EF-40	AU-50	MS-60	MS-63	MS-65	PRF-65
1900 S	2,459,500	485	513	600	1500	7200	—
1901	111,526	485	505	585	775	7000	—
1901 S	1,596,000	498	518	588	1900	—	—
1902	31,254	553	688	1050	3250	7200	—
1902 S	1,753,625	500	515	598	1700	—	—
1903	287,428	485	503	570	760	7000	35000
1903 S	954,000	498	515	583	875	7200	—
1904	6,256,797	483	500	568	740	4000	—
1904 S	5,134,175	485	503	573	760	7000	—
1905	59,011	548	598	1425	18000	—	—
1905 S	1,813,000	505	523	598	1600	—	—
1906	69,690	580	713	925	2000	7000	17500
1906 D	620,250	493	513	628	1575	—	—
1906 S	2,065,750	490	508	575	1550	—	—
1907	1,451,864	485	503	570	775	7200	—
1907 D	842,250	490	510	575	825	7000	—
1907 S	2,165,800	485	505	578	1100	—	—

SAINT-GAUDENS TYPE
1907-1933

**VARIETY ONE
HIGH RELIEF
ROMAN NUMERAL
DATE
1907**

DIAMETER: 34mm
WEIGHT: 33.436 Grams
COMPOSITION: .900 Gold, .100 copper
DESIGNER: Augustus Saint-Gaudens
EDGE: E PLURIBUS UNUM with stars dividing the words
PURE GOLD CONTENT: .96750 Tr. Oz.

DATE	MINTAGE	VF-20	EF-40	AU-50	MS-60	MS-63	MS-65	PRF-65
1907 High Relief, Flat Rim	Inc. Above	—	3975	4650	6950	11500	25750	—
1907 High Relief, Wire Rim	11,250	—	3725	4375	6900	11250	25000	—
1907 Lettered edge, Relief, Lettered Edge	PROOF ONLY	—	—	—	—	—	—	1500000
1907 Plain edge, Ex Relief, Plain Edge	Unique	—	—	—	—	—	375000	—

EDMUND'S 1996 U.S. COIN PRICES

GOLD COINS — DOUBLE EAGLES

VARIETY TWO
ARABIC NUMERALS
NO MOTTO
1907-1908

DIAMETER: 34mm
WEIGHT: 33.436 Grams
COMPOSITION: .900 Gold,
.100 Copper
DESIGNER: Augustus Saint-Gaudens
EDGE: E PLURIBUS UNUM With Stars Dividing The Words
PURE GOLD CONTENT: .96750 Tr. Oz.

DATE	MINTAGE	VF-20	EF-40	AU-50	MS-60	MS-63	MS-65
1907 Lg. Letters on Edge	Unique	—	—	—	—	—	—
1907 Sm. Letters on Edge	361,667	495	515	540	600	870	3100
1908 D	663,750	—	500	520	590	725	14500
1908 S	22,000	—	800	1350	4000	11500	50000
1908	4,271,551	—	545	675	1200	5500	47500

VARIETY THREE
MOTTO ADDED
BELOW EAGLE
1908-1933

DIAMETER: 34mm
WEIGHT: 33.436 Grams
COMPOSITION: .900 Gold,
.100 Copper
DESIGNER: Augustus Saint-Gaudens
EDGE: E PLURIBUS UNUM With Stars Dividing the Words
PURE GOLD CONTENT: .96750 Tr. Oz.

DATE	MINTAGE	VF-20	EF-40	AU-50	MS-60	MS-63	MS-65	PRF-65
1908 D	349,500	—	500	560	590	690	3100	—
1908	156,359	—	500	560	600	975	13250	41000
1909	Inc. Above	—	490	685	700	3600	47500	35000
1909/8	161,282	—	545	675	1200	5500	47500	—
1909 D	52,500	—	583	700	1338	2725	34250	—
1909 S	2,774,925	—	495	533	590	723	4575	—
1910	482,167	—	495	533	583	765	6150	50000

DOUBLE EAGLES — GOLD COINS

DATE	MINTAGE	VF-20	EF-40	AU-50	MS-60	MS-63	MS-65	PRF-65
1910 D	429,000	—	495	533	583	660	2525	—
1910 S	2,128,250	—	495	538	593	845	10000	—
1911	197,350	—	500	560	595	1175	11000	50000
1911 D	846,500	—	498	533	575	653	1595	—
1911 S	775,750	—	500	543	590	733	3988	—
1912	149,824	—	503	570	710	1550	12750	36000
1913	168,838	—	498	558	735	2000	18875	36000
1913 D	393,500	—	495	530	588	748	3775	—
1913 S	34,000	—	528	688	1230	3525	52250	—
1914	95,320	—	515	558	675	1250	12000	36000
1914 D	453,000	—	498	535	585	655	2550	—
1914 S	1,498,000	—	495	530	588	675	1900	—
1915	152,050	—	503	555	633	1288	10675	42000
1915 S	567,500	—	500	535	588	653	1738	—
1916 S	796,000	—	498	535	593	660	1663	—
1920	228,250	—	500	538	620	1115	22750	—
1920 S	558,000	—	6175	8100	20250	46500	90000	—
1921	528,500	—	9300	14750	32250	63000	187500	—
1922	1,375,500	—	495	530	578	645	3825	—
1922 S	2,658,000	—	538	613	770	1575	34250	—
1923	566,000	—	495	528	570	688	5525	—
1923 D	1,702,250	—	495	528	575	663	1313	—
1924	4,323,500	—	495	528	573	653	1275	—
1924 D	3,049,500	—	1000	1275	1825	5225	49000	—
1924 S	2,927,500	—	800	1013	1925	4925	49250	—
1925	2,831,750	—	495	528	570	633	1238	—
1925 D	2,938,500	—	1100	1238	2225	5700	53250	—
1925 S	3,776,500	—	925	1450	4650	20250	66250	—
1926	816,750	—	495	528	583	650	1363	—
1926 D	481,000	—	1800	2500	6100	21125	91250	—
1926 S	2,041,500	—	888	1150	1800	2825	35250	—
1927	2,946,750	—	495	528	565	633	1238	—
1927 D	180,000	—	—	150000	260000	225000	550000	—
1927 S	3,107,000	—	3625	6000	12500	24000	97500	—
1928	8,816,000	—	495	528	565	633	1238	—
1929	1,779,750	—	5000	6675	10500	14000	47500	—
1930 S	74,000	—	7500	5675	17125	29250	91000	—
1931	2,938,250	—	8500	11250	14250	21250	52000	—
1931 D	106,500	—	7500	10000	13000	18000	57500	—
1932	1,101,750	—	9500	10000	13250	16125	34900	—
1933 None Circulate	445,500	—	—	—	—	—	—	—

EDMUND'S 1996 U.S. COIN PRICES

MINT SETS

MINT SETS 1947 TO DATE

Mint sets consist of one uncirculated business strike coin from each mint of every denomination minted during a given year. Official mint sets are assembled and packaged by the Treasury's Bureau of the Mint, and are sold directly from the government to collectors and dealers.

The United States first began offering mint sets in 1947. Mint assembled sets through 1958 contained two examples of each coin from the various mints. Beginning in 1959, only one specimen of each coin struck for the year was included in the sets.

No official government mint sets were produced in 1950, 1982, and 1983, although many sets were assembled by private means. During the years 1965-1967, the government issued what were called "Special Mint Sets." At a time when silver coins were rapidly disappearing from circulation, Treasury officials decided to adopt measures that would discourage collecting to alleviate the coin shortage. The Special Mint Sets contained only five coins (as compared to at least ten in all the previous years), but were sold at almost double the cost of a 1964 Mint set. The 1965 sets were sealed in pliofilm packets and contained low quality specimens. In 1966 and 1967 the coins were encased in plastic holders and possessed a proof-like appearance. The Mint renewed the nominal Mint set program in 1968.

Mint sets are good long term investments, primarily because of the potential for the Uncirculated coins contained within the sets. In the years ahead, Uncirculated examples existing today will be worth many times more than their present values. Of course, Mint sets containing choice examples will be worth more than those that don't.

Some dealers believe the Special Mint Sets are severely underpriced because they are such oddities. If you're looking at inexpensive mint sets with a "wild card" factor, then these sets may fit the bill.

By virtue of being a "set," Mint sets have some promise by themselves. No set older than 1959 was produced in quantities greater than 55,000, and many of those were broken up. Compare that with the two million or more sold each year recently, and the promise becomes more evident. Moreover, because Mint sets are sealed at the Mint, grading concerns are not paramount, because buyers feel assured they're getting what they paid for...uncirculated coins. This factor could provide some upward impetus for Mint sets. When buying Mint sets, don't totally abandon caution, however, for it is possible that someone could have cleverly substituted lesser specimens for some of the coins.

The figures listed in the "mintage" column on the next page do not actually indicate a separate actual mintage for these coins, but actually the number of sets packaged by the Treasury Department for the specified year.

MINT SETS

This listing applies to United States Government packaged mint sets. These sets consist of two coins of each denomination for each mint from 1947 to 1958 and one coin of each denomination and mint from 1959 to date. Mint sets were not produced in 1950, from 1965 to 1967, or from 1982 to 1983. The "mintage" listed does not actually indicate a separate actual mintage for these coins, and is actually the number of sets packaged by the Treasury Department for the specified year.

DATE	MINTAGE	VALUE	DATE	MINTAGE	VALUE
1947	Est. 5,000	540	1972	2,750,000	3.00
1948	Est. 6,000	210	1973	1,767,691	7.35
1949	Est. 5,200	412	1974	1,975,981	5.80
1951	8,654	360	1975	1,921,488	5.40
1952	11,499	265	1976	1,892,513	11
1953	15,538	212	1977	2,006,869	5.25
1954	25,599	95	1978	2,162,609	5.25
1955	49,656	61	1979	2,526,000	5.15
1956	45,475	55	1980	2,813,118	6.00
1957	32,324	90	1981	2,908,145	7.85
1958	50,315	83	1984	1,832,857	3.65
1959	187,000	14	1985	1,710,571	3.90
1960	260,485	13	1986	1,153,536	13
1961	223,704	13	1987	2,890,758	5.60
1962	385,285	9.00	1988	1,646,204	3.25
1963	606,622	9.00	1989	1,987,915	2.50
1964	978,157	8.50	1990		4.35
1968	2,105,128	3.60	1991		12
1969	1,306,723	3.90	1992		14
1970	2,150,000	11	1993		8.75
1971	2,193,396	3.25	1994		9.60
			1995		9.75

NOTE: The Eisenhower Dollars were not included in the 1971 and 1972 Mint Sets.
The 1979 S Susan B. Anthony Dollar is not included in the 1979 Mint Set.

SPECIAL MINT SETS 1965-1967

These sets were sold to collectors during the suspension of proof coinage from 1965 to 1967. These coins possess a proof-like surface and are of better quality than regular circulation strikes. However, the 1965 special mint sets are of lower quality than the 1966 and 1967 sets.

DATE	MINTAGE	VALUE
1965	2,360,000	4.00
1966	2,261,583	4.40
1967	1,863,344	6.50

EDMUND'S 1996 U.S. COIN PRICES

PROOF SETS

PROOF SETS 1936 TO DATE

Proof sets are composed of examples of each Proof coin produced during a single year. They are sealed together and shipped directly from the Mint to private citizens. The values for Proof sets are listed, beginning with the 1936 edition.

The United States Mint began striking Proof coins in the 1820's and has annually offered Proof sets and individual Proofs to the public since 1858 with several lapses, including the periods between 1916 to 1936, and 1942 to 1950. There were no Proof sets per se offered from 1965-1967, but the Special Mint Sets of those years were proclaimed by the government to be adequate substitutes for the Proof sets. Prior to 1968, all regular Proof coins were struck at the Philadelphia Mint, but since then they have been produced at the San Francisco facility. The most notable exception to this was the striking of 20 proof 1938 O half dollars to commemorate the opening of the New Orleans Branch Mint. There are a few other branch mint proof coins of various types and all are very rare.

In the past, the Proof sets of the 1930's, 1940's and 1950's increased profoundly during several intervals. Presently, their movement has stagnated or even retreated. For those who have been holding out for more bargain prices, now is an opportune time to acquire such a set.

Many of the Proof sets of the 1960's, 1970's and 1980's can now be purchased at prices below their original costs. The price movement can only be upward, although this will probably not occur immediately. As long term investments, these sets are attractive. Many of these more recent sets have been dismantled to furnish collectors with singles so they can include the Proof-only San Francisco coins in their collections. This will also contribute to their potential upward price movement.

Proof sets do not increase in value solely on the basis of the Proof coins themselves. Proof sets have been a highly visible segment of the coin market to collectors and investors, being advertised every year by the Mint. The sets are housed in attractive, compact display holders, and are popular even with the casual coin collector. 1995 was no exception, as the Mint reported strong sales of Proof sets. As millions of new collectors enter the hobby in the future, Proof sets are certainly destined for even greater things to come.

PROOF SETS

The listing below contains the popular modern era proof coinage from 1936 to date. Proof coinage was suspended by the Mint between 1943-1949 and 1965-1967. Proof sets from 1936 to 1972 contain the cent through half dollar. Starting in 1973, the dollar coin was included.

DATE	MINTAGE	VALUE	DATE	MINTAGE	VALUE
1936	3,837	3675	1976 S 3 pcs		11.75
1937	5,542	2400	1977 S	3,251,152	4.30
1938	8,045	1000	1978 S	3,127,788	5.30
1939	8,795	977	1979 S	3,677,175	6.60
1940	11,246	745	1979 S Type II	Inc. Above	64
1941	15,287	600	1980 S	3,554,806	4.90
1942 Both Nickels	21,120	700	1981 S	4,063,083	6.55
1942 One Nickel	Inc. Above	590	1981 S Type II		188
1950	51,386	415	1982 S	3,857,479	3.80
1951	57,500	285	1983 S	3,138,765	5.30
1952	81,980	157	1984 S	2,748,430	9.25
1953	128,800	130	1984 S Prestige		23
1954	233,300	75	1985 S	3,362,821	5.50
1955 Box Pack	378,200	60	1986 S	2,411,180	23
1955 Flat Pack	Inc. Above	53	1986 S Prestige		28
1956	669,384	27	1987 S	3,792,233	4.55
1957	1,247,952	13	1987 S Prestige		18
1958	875,652	18	1988 S	3,031,287	8.75
1959	1,149,291	15	1988 S Prestige		20
1960 Lg. Date 1¢	1,691,602	12	1989 S	3,009,107	6.50
1960 Sm. Date 1¢	Inc. Above	25	1989 S Prestige		24
1961	3,028,244	8.00	1990 S		15
1962	3,218,019	8.00	1990 S No S Cent		1450
1963	3,075,645	8.00	1990 S Prestige		23
1964	3,950,752	8.00	1991 S		24
1968 S	3,041,509	4.80	1991 S Prestige		55
1968 S No Mintmark 10¢	Inc. Above	7950	1992 S		21
1969 S	2,934,631	4.75	1992 S Silver		21
1970 S Lg. Date 1¢	2,632,810	9.50	1992 S Prestige		53
1970 S Sm. Date 1¢	Inc. Above	66	1993 S		21
1970 S No Mintmark 10¢	Est. 2,200	440	1993 S Silver		29
1971 S	3,224,138	3.00	1993 Prem Silver		26
1971 S No Mintmark 5¢	Est. 1,655	735	1994 S		17
1972 S	3,267,667	3.70	1994 S Prestige		50
1973 S	2,769,624	5.80	1994 S Silver		22
1974 S	2,617,350	5.85	1994 Prem Silver		34
1975 S	2,909,369	6.80	1995 S		15
1976 S	4,149,730	7.00	1995 S Prestige		67

EDMUND'S 1996 U.S. COIN PRICES

U.S. COMMEMORATIVE COINS

UNITED STATES COMMEMORATIVE COINS

Commemorative coins are issued by the United States government to honor historical events or persons. They are sold to the general public at prices well above the face values of the coins themselves. Sometimes the money raised from these sales is used to fund a monument or to support some public cause. Commemoratives offer variety, beauty, and history, qualities which have endeared them to collectors.

The first American commemorative coin made its debut in 1892. It was the Columbian half dollar, issued to mark the 400th anniversary of Columbus' discovery of the New World. Up to 1954 many commemoratives were released, observing a wide variety of subjects. No commemoratives were produced between 1954 and 1982. In 1982, the George Washington half dollar ushered in an era of modern commemoratives.

Few of the older commemorative coins were struck in great numbers. In fact, many of them have mintages under 30,000. Since they were never intended as spending money, commemoratives have survived in Uncirculated condition in far higher proportions than regular issues. Occasionally, a collector will encounter slightly worn commemoratives, especially for those types struck before the Great Depression. During those tough economic times, some people did not have the luxury of keeping souvenir coins. The federal government added to the supply of circulated commemoratives by releasing unsold examples into circulation at face value.

Of the remaining stock of older Uncirculated commemoratives, very few have survived to this day in MS-65 condition or better. Some of the lower grade Uncirculated coins have been cleaned or dipped to resemble nicer specimens, so be alert for this sort of thing.

While it is true that the older commemoratives have been consistently popular with collectors, based solely on their intrinsic merits, their wild price fluctuations could make you think otherwise. These pricing irregularities reflect the heavy influence of promoters. These commemoratives are ideal targets for promoters because they have attractive designs, interesting topics, a large collector base to support the market, a high percentage of Uncirculated examples, and are affordable to most buyers. Since many of the older commemorative types have low mintages, a large dealer or group of dealers can corner a fair share of the available supply of a particular commemorative type (which acts to push prices higher by itself), and effectively promote the coin and sell out later at much higher prices. This has happened in the past and undoubtedly

U.S. COMMEMORATIVE COINS

will take place again. Don't let this sort of activity prevent you from purchasing commemoratives for the sake of investing. If you play your cards right, you can actually use the promoter influence to your advantage. The age-old adage "buy low, sell high" should be your guiding principle.

At the present time, the cost of obtaining an older commemorative is generally down from what it was in 1989 by a considerable margin. This holds true for all grades. Inevitably, the spotlight will shine brightly upon them again, and when this happens, watch for the older commemoratives to post impressive gains. If you've been putting off buying that commemorative you've always dreamed about, check into it soon. The chances are good that you'll never see a better opportunity than now.

As far as long range planners are concerned, every older commemorative issue in collectible grades will be a winner. Excellent long term growth is part of their nature. Thus, today's investors are virtually assured of future profits if only they have patience.

The reinstatement of commemorative coinage in 1982 was met with applause, but at present many individuals involved with the coin industry are unhappy with the program. One complaint is that too many commemoratives are being issued, with no expectation that the situation will improve. For example, several dozen varieties of Olympic coins observing the 1996 Atlanta games are being planned! Another distasteful characteristic for many is the political pressure by special interests to have their topic immortalized (not to mention extra revenue brought in by the coin sales). This is the sort of thing that doomed the first commemorative era. And lastly, there has been appreciation on only a very few of the modern commemoratives. In fact, most of them can be had for far less than their original costs.

On the positive side, some of the newer commemoratives are truly beautiful coins that can be yours today at true bargains. That may not be the case in another ten years or so. Either way, you have very little to lose by acquiring some commemoratives.

Buying commemoratives can be downright fun. Take a look at the different subject matters that commemoratives depict. Consult some of the books listed in the Suggested Reading List to gain historical perspective for commemorative coin collecting. People with a general appreciation of American history could spend many enjoyable years putting together a collection of commemoratives.

COMMEMORATIVES
QUARTER/SILVER DOLLAR

COMMEMORATIVE QUARTER DOLLAR

DATE	MINTAGE	AU-50	MS-60	MS-63	MS-65
1893 Isabella, Columbian Exposition	24,214	220	325	530	2025

COMMEMORATIVE SILVER DOLLAR

DATE	MINTAGE	AU-50	MS-60	MS-63	MS-65
1900 Lafayette	36,026	308	525	1375	8175

EDMUND'S 1996 U.S. COIN PRICES

HALF DOLLARS — COMMEMORATIVES

COMMEMORATIVE HALF DOLLARS

DATE	MINTAGE	AU-50	MS-60	MS-63	MS-65
1921 Alabama 2X2	6,000	140	320	625	2900
1921 Alabama	53,038	75	230	530	3000

DATE	MINTAGE	AU-50	MS-60	MS-63	MS-65
1936 Albany	17,671	190	200	215	460

DATE	MINTAGE	AU-50	MS-60	MS-63	MS-65
1937 Antietam	18,028	330	390	440	590

EDMUND'S 1996 U.S. COIN PRICES

COMMEMORATIVES

HALF DOLLARS

DATE	MINTAGE	AU-50	MS-60	MS-63	MS-65
1935 Arkansas PDS Set	5,505	—	215	245	1000
1936 Arkansas PDS Set	9,660	—	215	245	1125
1937 Arkansas PDS Set	5,505	—	235	290	1425
1938 Arkansas PDS Set	3,155	—	300	390	2290
1939 Arkansas PDS Set	2,104	—	800	925	2975
Arkansas, Type Coin	—	68	80	91	340

DATE	MINTAGE	AU-50	MS-60	MS-63	MS-65
1936 S.F. - Oakland Bay Bridge	71,424	90	100	120	330

232 EDMUND'S 1996 U.S. COIN PRICES

HALF DOLLARS COMMEMORATIVES

DATE	MINTAGE	AU-50	MS-60	MS-63	MS-65
1934 Daniel Boone	10,007	71	77	87	135
1935 Boone PDS Set	5,005	—	260	300	450
1935 Boone PDS Set W/1934 on Rev.	2,003	—	550	860	1900
1936 Boone PDS Set	5,005	—	255	285	470
1937 Boone PDS Set	2,506	—	515	650	1150
1938 Boone PDS Set	2,100	—	725	880	1875
Boone, Type Coin	—	70	70	75	120

DATE	MINTAGE	AU-50	MS-60	MS-63	MS-65
1936 Bridgeport	25,015	90	96	105	295

DATE	MINTAGE	AU-50	MS-60	MS-63	MS-65
1925 S California Jubilee	86,594	87	110	190	700

EDMUND'S 1996 U.S. COIN PRICES

COMMEMORATIVES

HALF DOLLARS

DATE	MINTAGE	AU-50	MS-60	MS-63	MS-65
1936 Cincinnati, PDS Set	5,005	—	710	820	2200
1936 Cincinnati, Type Coin	—	210	230	255	550

DATE	MINTAGE	AU-50	MS-60	MS-63	MS-65
1936 Cleveland-Great Lakes	50,030	53	60	67	220

DATE	MINTAGE	AU-50	MS-60	MS-63	MS-65
1936 Columbia, PDS Set	9,007	—	543	605	765
1936 Columbia, Type Coin	—	155	165	180	220

HALF DOLLARS — COMMEMORATIVES

DATE	MINTAGE	AU-50	MS-60	MS-63	MS-65
1892 Columbian Exposition	950,000	13	36	92	850
1893 Columbian Exposition	1,550,405	11	37	85	900

DATE	MINTAGE	AU-50	MS-60	MS-63	MS-65
1935 Connecticut	25,018	155	170	210	675

DATE	MINTAGE	AU-50	MS-60	MS-63	MS-65
1936 Delaware	20,993	155	173	205	635

EDMUND'S 1996 U.S. COIN PRICES

COMMEMORATIVES

HALF DOLLARS

DATE	MINTAGE	AU-50	MS-60	MS-63	MS-65
1936 Elgin, Illinois	20,015	155	167	180	280

DATE	MINTAGE	AU-50	MS-60	MS-63	MS-65
1936 Gettysburg	26,928	185	210	255	600

DATE	MINTAGE	AU-50	MS-60	MS-63	MS-65
1922 Grant, With Star	4,256	510	910	1775	7125
1922 Grant	67,405	65	88	185	800

HALF DOLLARS — COMMEMORATIVES

DATE	MINTAGE	AU-50	MS-60	MS-63	MS-65
1928 Hawaiian	10,008	825	1090	1800	4475

DATE	MINTAGE	AU-50	MS-60	MS-63	MS-65
1935 Hudson	10,008	380	440	505	1475

DATE	MINTAGE	AU-50	MS-60	MS-63	MS-65
1924 Huguenot-Walloon	142,080	74	85	105	635

COMMEMORATIVES — HALF DOLLARS

DATE	MINTAGE	AU-50	MS-60	MS-63	MS-65
1918 Illinois - Lincoln	100,058	70	81	103	560

DATE	MINTAGE	AU-50	MS-60	MS-63	MS-65
1946 Iowa	100,057	62	69	77	107

DATE	MINTAGE	AU-50	MS-60	MS-63	MS-65
1925 Lexington - Concord	162,013	65	75	97	825

HALF DOLLARS — COMMEMORATIVES

DATE	MINTAGE	AU-50	MS-60	MS-63	MS-65
1936 Long Island	81,826	60	68	75	400

DATE	MINTAGE	AU-50	MS-60	MS-63	MS-65
1936 Lynchburg	20,013	147	167	180	330

DATE	MINTAGE	AU-50	MS-60	MS-63	MS-65
1920 Maine	50,028	65	87	168	640

EDMUND'S 1996 U.S. COIN PRICES

COMMEMORATIVES — HALF DOLLARS

DATE	MINTAGE	AU-50	MS-60	MS-63	MS-65
1934 Maryland	25,015	100	120	140	335

DATE	MINTAGE	AU-50	MS-60	MS-63	MS-65
1921 Missouri-2x4	5,000	285	400	780	5775
1921 Missouri	15,428	210	335	685	5650

DATE	MINTAGE	AU-50	MS-60	MS-63	MS-65
1923 S Monroe Doctrine	274,077	34	42	110	2200

EDMUND'S 1996 U.S. COIN PRICES

HALF DOLLARS — COMMEMORATIVES

DATE	MINTAGE	AU-50	MS-60	MS-63	MS-65
1938 New Rochelle	15,266	220	235	340	420

DATE	MINTAGE	AU-50	MS-60	MS-63	MS-65
1936 Norfolk	16,936	350	370	400	450

COMMEMORATIVES — HALF DOLLARS

DATE	MINTAGE	AU-50	MS-60	MS-63	MS-65
1926 Oregon Trail	47,955	80	92	115	215
1926 S Oregon Trail	83,055	90	98	115	220
1928 Oregon Trail	6,028	130	160	175	280
1933 D Oregon Trail	5,008	230	260	335	455
1934 D Oregon Trail	7,006	130	140	175	325
1936 Oregon Trail	10,006	100	110	150	225
1936 S Oregon Trail	5,006	130	150	190	300
1937 D Oregon Trail	12,008	100	120	145	220
1938 Oregon Trail, PDS Set	6,005	—	535	665	925
1939 Oregon Trail, PDS Set	3,004	—	1135	1350	2200
Oregon Trail, Type Coin	—	80	85	110	155

DATE	MINTAGE	AU-50	MS-60	MS-63	MS-65
1915 S Panama-Pacific Exposition	27,134	205	320	710	2375

HALF DOLLARS — COMMEMORATIVES

DATE	MINTAGE	AU-50	MS-60	MS-63	MS-65
1920 Pilgrim	152,112	63	69	85	480
1921 Pilgrim	20,053	88	110	175	850

DATE	MINTAGE	AU-50	MS-60	MS-63	MS-65
1936 Rhode Island, PDS Set	15,010	—	225	255	1125
1936 Rhode Island, Type Coin	—	65	74	83	280

DATE	MINTAGE	AU-50	MS-60	MS-63	MS-65
1937 Roanoke	29,030	163	180	190	230

EDMUND'S 1996 U.S. COIN PRICES

COMMEMORATIVES — HALF DOLLARS

DATE	MINTAGE	AU-50	MS-60	MS-63	MS-65
1936 Robinson - Arkansas	25,265	66	80	95	360

DATE	MINTAGE	AU-50	MS-60	MS-63	MS-65
1935 S San Diego	70,132	57	65	74	100
1936 D San Diego	30,092	61	66	75	105

DATE	MINTAGE	AU-50	MS-60	MS-63	MS-65
1926 Sesquicentennial	141,120	63	75	165	5125

244   EDMUND'S 1996 U.S. COIN PRICES

HALF DOLLARS — COMMEMORATIVES

DATE	MINTAGE	AU-50	MS-60	MS-63	MS-65
1935 Spanish Trail	10,008	620	740	790	1025

DATE	MINTAGE	AU-50	MS-60	MS-63	MS-65
1925 Stone Mountain	1,314,709	31	38	49	203

DATE	MINTAGE	AU-50	MS-60	MS-63	MS-65
1934 Texas	61,463	83	90	95	145
1935 Texas-PDS Set	9,994	—	260	292	495
1936 Texas-PDS Set	8,911	—	265	297	820
1937 Texas-PDS Set	6,571	—	270	315	430
1938 Texas-PDS Set	3,775	—	650	895	1150
Texas, Type Coin	—	77	80	90	120

EDMUND'S 1996 U.S. COIN PRICES

COMMEMORATIVES — HALF DOLLARS

DATE	MINTAGE	AU-50	MS-60	MS-63	MS-65
1925 Fort Vancouver	14,994	220	270	410	1225

DATE	MINTAGE	AU-50	MS-60	MS-63	MS-65
1927 Vermont	28,142	130	165	200	895

DATE	MINTAGE	AU-50	MS-60	MS-63	MS-65
1946 B.T. Washington - PDS Set	200,113	—	39	52	153
1947 B.T. Washington - PDS Set	100,017	—	60	77	290
1948 B.T. Washington - PDS Set	8,005	—	83	110	180
1949 B.T. Washington - PDS Set	6,004	—	177	207	293
1950 B.T. Washington - PDS Set	6,004	—	80	110	173
1951 B.T. Washington - PDS Set	7,004	—	89	140	195
B.T. Washington, Type Coin	(3,091,205 Total for Type)	10	11	12	30

HALF DOLLARS — COMMEMORATIVES

DATE	MINTAGE	AU-50	MS-60	MS-63	MS-65
1951 Washington - Carver PDS Set	10,004	—	77	101	390
1952 Washington - Carver PDS Set	8,006	12	75	120	350
1953 Washington - Carver PDS Set	8,003	—	72	109	525
1954 Washington - Carver PDS Set	12,006	—	67	93	465
Washington - Carver, Type Coin	(2,422,392 Total for Type)	10	11	16	45

DATE	MINTAGE	AU-50	MS-60	MS-63	MS-65
1936 Wisconsin	25,015	150	163	180	210

DATE	MINTAGE	AU-50	MS-60	MS-63	MS-65
1936 York County	25,015	143	153	168	193

EDMUND'S 1996 U.S. COIN PRICES

COMMEMORATIVES — GOLD COINS

COMMEMORATIVE GOLD COINS

GOLD DOLLARS

DATE	MINTAGE	AU-50	MS-60	MS-63	MS-65
1903 Louisiana Purchase-Jefferson	17,500	345	410	850	2400
1903 Louisiana Purchase-McKinley	17,500	320	380	900	2400

DATE	MINTAGE	AU-50	MS-60	MS-63	MS-65
1904 Lewis and Clark Exposition	10,025	525	900	2100	5500
1905 Lewis and Clark Exposition	10,041	515	900	2725	15000

DATE	MINTAGE	AU-50	MS-60	MS-63	MS-65
1915 S Panama-Pacific Exposition	15,000	215	350	725	2500
1916 McKinley Memorial	9,977	290	385	700	2350
1917 McKinley Memorial	10,000	375	460	1200	3200

DATE	MINTAGE	AU-50	MS-60	MS-63	MS-65
1922 Grant Memorial with Star	5,016	1300	1400	1950	2600
1922 Grant Memorial	5,000	1000	1200	1700	2800

GOLD COINS **COMMEMORATIVES**

QUARTER EAGLES ($2.50 Gold Pieces)

DATE	MINTAGE	AU-50	MS-60	MS-63	MS-65
1915 S Panama - Pacific Exposition	6,749	1100	1650	2700	4400

DATE	MINTAGE	AU-50	MS-60	MS-63	MS-65
1926 Philadelphia Sesquicentennial	46,019	70	78	175	5300

FIFTY DOLLARS GOLD

DATE	MINTAGE	AU-50	MS-60	MS-63	MS-65
1915 S Panama - Pacific Exposition - Round	483	20500	26500	45000	115000
1915 S Panama - Pacific Exposition - Octagonal	645	18000	22500	37500	95000

EDMUND'S 1996 U.S. COIN PRICES

COMMEMORATIVES 1982 GEORGE WASHNGTON 250TH

1982 GEORGE WASHINGTON 250TH ANNIVERSARY
HALF DOLLAR

DATE	MINTAGE	MS-65	Prf-65
1982 D Geo. Washington-250th Anniversary	2,210,502	—	4.60
1982 S Geo. Washington-250th Anniversary	4,894,044	—	4.65

1984 OLYMPIC GAMES, LOS ANGELES

SILVER DOLLARS

DATE	MINTAGE	MS-65	Prf-65
1983 P	294,543	9.50	—
1983 D	174,014	13	—
1983 S	174,014	12	11
1983 S PROOF	1,577,025	—	10

DATE	MINTAGE	MS-65	Prf-65
1984 P	217,954	16	—
1984 D	116,675	28	—
1984 S	116,675	30	—
1984 S PROOF	1,801,210	—	14

EAGLE

DATE	MINTAGE	MS-65	Prf-65
1984 W	75,886	250	—
1984 W PROOF	381,085	—	250
1984 P	33,309	—	260
1984 D	34,533	—	250
1984 S	48,551	—	230

COMMEMORATIVES

1986 STATUE OF LIBERTY

1986 STATUE OF LIBERTY CENTENNIAL

HALF DOLLAR

DATE	MINTAGE	MS-65	Prf-65
1986 D	928,008	5.00	—
1986 S	6,925,627	—	7.00

SILVER DOLLAR

DATE	MINTAGE	MS-65	Prf-65
1986 P	723,635	10.00	—
1986 S	6,414,638	—	11.00

HALF EAGLE

DATE	MINTAGE	MS-65	Prf-65
1986 W	95,248	135	—
1986 W PROOF	404,013	—	135

1987 CONSTITUTION BICENTENNIAL

SILVER DOLLAR

DATE	MINTAGE	MS-65	Prf-65
1987 P	451,629	10	—
1987 S	2,747,116	—	10

HALF EAGLE

DATE	MINTAGE	MS-65	Prf-65
1987 W	214,225	135	—
1987 W Proof	651,659	—	135

COMMEMORATIVES
1988 OLYMPIAD

1988 OLYMPIAD

SILVER DOLLAR

DATE	MINTAGE	MS-65	Prf-65
1988 D	191,368	15	—
1988 S	1,359,366	—	11

HALF EAGLE

DATE	MINTAGE	MS-65	Prf-65
1988 W	62,913	130	—
1988 W PROOF	281,465	—	130

254   EDMUND'S 1996 U.S. COIN PRICES

1989 BICENTENNIAL OF CONGRESS

HALF DOLLAR

DATE	MINTAGE	MS-65	Prf-65
1989 D	163,753	13	—
1989 S	767,897	—	7.00

SILVER DOLLAR

DATE	MINTAGE	MS-65	Prf-65
1989 D	135,203	24	—
1989 S	762,198	—	16

HALF EAGLE

DATE	MINTAGE	MS-65	Prf-65
1989 W	46,899	140	—
1989 W Proof	164,690	—	140

EDMUND'S 1996 U.S. COIN PRICES

COMMEMORATIVES — 1990 EISENHOWER CENTENNIAL

1990 EISENHOWER CENTENNIAL
SILVER DOLLAR

DATE	MINTAGE	MS-65	Prf-65
1990 W	241,669	16	—
1990 P	1,144,461	—	12

1991 MOUNT RUSHMORE

HALF DOLLAR

DATE	MINTAGE	MS-65	Prf-65
1991 D	172,754	16	—
1991 S	753,257	—	14

SILVER DOLLAR

DATE	MINTAGE	MS-65	Prf-65
1991 P	133,139	33	—
1991 S	738,419	—	30

HALF EAGLE

DATE	MINTAGE	MS-65	Prf-65
1991 W	31,959	145	—
1991 W PROOF	111,991	—	145

COMMEMORATIVES 1991 KOREAN WAR/U.S.O. FIFTIETH

1991 KOREAN WAR

SILVER DOLLAR

DATE	MINTAGE	MS-65	Prf-65
1991 D	213,049	17	—
1991 P	618,488	—	15

1991 U.S.O. FIFTIETH ANNIVERSARY

SILVER DOLLAR

DATE	MINTAGE	MS-65	Prf-65
1991 D	124,958	29	—
1991 S	321,275	—	19

1992 OLYMPIC GAMES

HALF DOLLAR

DATE	MINTAGE	MS-65	Prf-65
1992 P	161,619	7.00	—
1992 S	519,699	—	9.50

SILVER DOLLAR

DATE	MINTAGE	MS-65	Prf-65
1992 D	187,562	31	—
1992 S	504,544	—	34

HALF EAGLE

DATE	MINTAGE	MS-65	Prf-65
1992 W	27,732	145	145
1992 W PROOF	77,313	140	140

COMMEMORATIVES *1992 COLUMBUS QUINCENTENARY*

1992 COLUMBUS QUINCENTENARY

HALF DOLLAR

DATE	MINTAGE	MS-65	Prf-65
1992 D	135,718	12	—
1992 S	390,255	—	12

SILVER DOLLAR

DATE	MINTAGE	MS-65	Prf-65
1992 D	106,962	30	—
1992 S	385,290	—	28

HALF EAGLE

DATE	MINTAGE	MS-65	Prf-65
1992 W	24,331	145	—
1992 W PROOF	79,734	—	195

1992 WHITE HOUSE 200TH ANNIVERSARY
SILVER DOLLAR

DATE	MINTAGE	MS-65	Prf-65
1992 D	123,803	48	—
1992 W	375,849	—	45

COMMEMORATIVES
1993 JAMES MADISON

1993 JAMES MADISON / BILL OF RIGHTS

HALF DOLLAR

DATE	MINTAGE	MS-65	Prf-65
1993 W	173,224	12	—
1993 S	559,758	—	12

SILVER DOLLAR

DATE	MINTAGE	MS-65	Prf-65
1993 D	92,415	23	—
1993 S	515,038	—	20

HALF EAGLE

DATE	MINTAGE	MS-65	Prf-65
1993 W	22,897	200	—
1993 W Proof	79,422	—	145

1991-1995 WORLD WAR II 50TH ANNIVERSARY

HALF DOLLAR

DATE	MINTAGE	MS-65	Prf-65
1991-1995 P	192,968	13	—
1991-1995 P Proof	290,343	—	13

SILVER DOLLAR

DATE	MINTAGE	MS-65	Prf-65
1991-1995 D	94,700	29	—
1991-1995 W	322,422	—	28

HALF EAGLE

DATE	MINTAGE	MS-65	Prf-65
1991-1995 W	23,089	225	—
1991-1995 W ProofF	65,461	—	225

Note: These coins were struck and released in 1993.

COMMEMORATIVES
1993 JEFFERSON/1994 P.O.W.

1993 THOMAS JEFFERSON
SILVER DOLLAR

DATE	MINTAGE	MS-65	Prf-65
1993 P	—	45	—
1993 S	—	—	43

1994 PRISONER OF WAR
SILVER DOLLAR

DATE	MINTAGE	MS-65	Prf-65
1994 W	—	36	—
1994 P	—	—	35

EDMUND'S 1996 U.S. COIN PRICES

1994 VIETNAM/WOMEN IN MILITARY COMMEMORATIVES

1994 VIETNAM VETERANS MEMORIAL

SILVER DOLLAR

DATE	MINTAGE	MS-65	Prf-65
1994 W	—	36	—
1994 P	—	—	37

1994 WOMEN IN MILITARY SERVICE

SILVER DOLLAR

DATE	MINTAGE	MS-65	Prf-65
1994 W	—	39	—
1994 P	—	—	37

EDMUND'S 1996 U.S. COIN PRICES

COMMEMORATIVES
1994 WORLD CUP SOCCER

1994 WORLD CUP SOCCER

HALF DOLLAR

DATE	MINTAGE	MS-65	Prf-65
1994 D	—	12	—
1994 P	—	—	11

SILVER DOLLAR

DATE	MINTAGE	MS-65	Prf-65
1994 D	—	27	—
1994 S	—	—	29

HALF EAGLE

DATE	MINTAGE	MS-65	Prf-65
1994 W	—	165	—
1994 W PROOF	—	—	165

1994 U.S. CAPITOL BICENTENNIAL

SILVER DOLLAR

DATE	MINTAGE	MS-65	Prf-65
1994 D	—	35	—
1994 S	—	—	41

COMMEMORATIVES
1995 CIVIL WAR BATTLEFIELDS

1995 CIVIL WAR BATTLEFIELDS

CLAD HALF DOLLAR

DATE	MINTAGE	MS-65	Prf-65
1995 D	—	13	—
1995 S	—	—	13

SILVER DOLLAR

DATE	MINTAGE	MS-65	Prf-65
1995 P	—	34	—
1995 S	—	—	35

GOLD HALF EAGLE

DATE	MINTAGE	MS-65	Prf-65
1995 W	—	185	205

1995 SPECIAL OLYMPICS WORLD GAMES
SILVER DOLLAR

DATE	MINTAGE	MS-65	Prf-65
1994 W	—	35	—
1994 P	—	—	34

COMMEMORATIVES *1995-1996 XXVI OLYMPIAD*

1995-1995 XXVI OLYMPIAD, ATLANTA

ATLANTA STADIUM GOLD HALF EAGLE

DATE	MINTAGE	MS-65	Prf-65
1995 W	—	—	—

BASEBALL CLAD HALF DOLLAR

DATE	MINTAGE	MS-65	Prf-65
1995 D	—	13	—
1995 S	—	—	14

BASKETBALL CLAD HALF DOLLAR

DATE	MINTAGE	MS-65	Prf-65
1995 D	—	13	—
1995 S	—	—	14

EDMUND'S 1996 U.S. COIN PRICES

1995-1996 XXVI OLYMPIAD — **COMMEMORATIVES**

CYCLING SILVER DOLLAR

DATE	MINTAGE	MS-65	Prf-65
1995 D	—	35	—
1995 P	—	—	37

FLAGBEARER GOLD HALF EAGLE

DATE	MINTAGE	MS-65	Prf-65
1996 W	—	249	259

GYMNASTICS SILVER DOLLAR

DATE	MINTAGE	MS-65	Prf-65
1995 D	—	35	—
1995 P	—	—	37

EDMUND'S 1996 U.S. COIN PRICES

COMMEMORATIVES
1995-1996 XXVI OLYMPIAD

HIGH JUMP SILVER DOLLAR

DATE	MINTAGE	MS-65	Prf-65
1996 D	—	32	—
1996 P	—	—	35

OLYMPIC FLAME BRAZIER GOLD HALF EAGLE

DATE	MINTAGE	MS-65	Prf-65
1996 W	—	249	259

PARALYMPIC, BLIND RUNNER SILVER DOLLAR

DATE	MINTAGE	MS-65	Prf-65
1995 D	—	35	—
1995 P	—	—	37

1995-1996 XXVI OLYMPIAD **COMMEMORATIVES**

PARALYMPIC, WHEELCHAIR ATHLETE SILVER DOLLAR

DATE	MINTAGE	MS-65	Prf-65
1996 D	—	32	—
1996 P	—	—	35

ROWING SILVER DOLLAR

DATE	MINTAGE	MS-65	Prf-65
1996 D	—	32	—
1996 P	—	—	35

EDMUND'S 1996 U.S. COIN PRICES

COMMEMORATIVES
1995-1996 XXVI OLYMPIAD

SOCCER CLAD HALF DOLLAR

DATE	MINTAGE	MS-65	Prf-65
1996 D	—	12	—
1996 S	—	—	13

SWIMMING CLAD HALF DOLLAR

DATE	MINTAGE	MS-65	Prf-65
1996 D	—	12	—
1996 S	—	—	13

EDMUND'S 1996 U.S. COIN PRICES

1995-1996 XXVI OLYMPIAD — COMMEMORATIVES

TENNIS SILVER DOLLAR

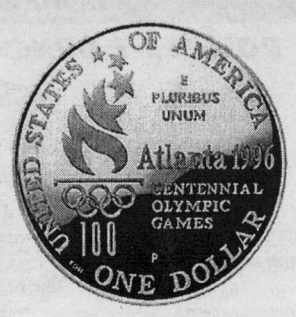

DATE	MINTAGE	MS-65	Prf-65
1996 D	—	32	—
1996 P	—	—	35

TORCH RUNNER GOLD HALF EAGLE

DATE	MINTAGE	MS-65	Prf-65
1995 W	—	—	—

TRACK AND FIELD SILVER DOLLAR

DATE	MINTAGE	MS-65	Prf-65
1995 D	—	35	—
1995 P	—	—	37

EDMUND'S 1996 U.S. COIN PRICES

BULLION COINS — AMERICAN EAGLES

AMERICAN EAGLES
FIFTY DOLLARS-1 OUNCE

DIAMETER: 32.7mm
WEIGHT: 33.931 Grams
COMPOSITION: .9167 Gold,
.03 Silver,
.0533 Copper
DESIGNER: Augustus Saint-Gaudens (Obverse)
Miley Busiek (Reverse)
EDGE: Reeded
PURE GOLD CONTENT: 1.000 Tr. Oz.

DATE	MINTAGE	MS-65	Prf-65
1986	1,362,650	402	—
1986 W	446,290	—	463
1987	1,045,500	404	—
1987 W	147,498	—	450
1988	465,500	404	—
1988 W	87,133	—	462
1989	415,790	404	—
1989 W	54,570	—	463
1990	373,210	404	—
1990 W	62,401	—	475
1991	243,100	412	—
1991 W	50,411	—	480
1992	275,000	410	—
1992 W	44,835	—	515
1993	—	410	—
1993 W	—	—	528
1994	—	407	—
1994 W	—	—	564
1995	—	405	—
1995 W	—	—	625

AMERICAN EAGLES — BULLION COINS

TWENTY-FIVE DOLLARS— 1/2 OUNCE

DIAMETER: 27mm
WEIGHT: 16.966 Grams
COMPOSITION: .9167 Gold,
.03 Silver,
.0533 Copper
DESIGNER: Augustus Saint-Gaudens (Obverse)
Miley Busiek (Reverse)
EDGE: Reeded
PURE GOLD CONTENT: .50 Tr. Oz.

DATE	MINTAGE	MS-65	Prf-65
1986	599,566	216	—
1987	131,255	221	—
1987 P	143,398	—	230
1988	45,000	248	—
1988 P	76,528	—	238
1989	44,829	265	—
1989 P	44,798	—	258
1990	31,000	508	—
1990 P	51,636	—	260
1991	24,100	365	—
1991 P	53,125	—	270
1992	54,404	245	—
1992 P	40,982	—	252
1993	—	219	—
1993 P	—	—	268
1994	—	216	—
1994 P	—	—	297
1995	—	210	—
1995 P	—	—	275

BULLION COINS — AMERICAN EAGLES

TEN DOLLARS— 1/4 OUNCE

DIAMETER: 22mm
WEIGHT: 8.483 Grams
COMPOSITION: .9167 Gold,
.03 Silver,
.0533 Copper
DESIGNER: Augustus Saint-Gaudens (Obverse)
Miley Busiek (Reverse)
EDGE: Reeded
PURE GOLD CONTENT: .25 Tr. Oz.

DATE	MINTAGE	MS-65	Prf-65
1986	726,031	112	—
1987	269,255	115	—
1988	49,000	120	—
1988 P	98,028	—	124
1989	81,789	125	—
1989 P	54,170	—	130
1990	41,000	133	—
1990 P	62,674	—	134
1991	36,100	135	—
1991 P	50,840	—	134
1992	59,546	115	—
1992 P	46,290	—	140
1993	—	112	—
1993 P	—	—	160
1994	—	111	—
1994 P	—	—	170
1995	—	112	—
1995 P	—	—	160

AMERICAN EAGLES — BULLION COINS

FIVE DOLLARS—1/10 OUNCE

DIAMETER: 16.5mm
WEIGHT: 3.393 Grams
COMPOSITION: .9167 Gold,
.03 Silver,
.0533 Copper
DESIGNER: Augustus Saint-Gaudens (Obverse)
Miley Busiek (Reverse)
EDGE: Reeded
PURE GOLD CONTENT: .10 Tr. Oz.

DATE	MINTAGE	MS-65	Prf-65
1986	912,609	50	—
1987	580,266	51	—
1988	159,500	67	—
1988 P	143,881	—	60
1989	264,790	59	—
1989 P	84,647	—	58
1990	210,210	52	—
1990 P	99,349	—	60
1991	165,200	52	—
1991 P	70,334	—	60
1992	209,300	51	—
1992 P	64,902	—	65
1993	—	50	—
1993 P	—	—	83
1994	209,300	50	—
1994 P	64,902	—	77
1995	—	50	—
1995 P	—	—	77

BULLION COINS

SILVER EAGLES

SILVER EAGLES
ONE DOLLAR—1 OUNCE

DIAMETER: 40.6mm
WEIGHT: 31.101 Grams
COMPOSITION: .9993 Silver,
.0007 Copper
DESIGNER: Adolph A. Weinman (Obverse)
John Mercanti (Reverse)
EDGE: Reeded
PURE SILVER CONTENT: 1.000 Tr. Oz.

DATE	MINTAGE	MS-65	Prf-65
1986	5,393,005	10	—
1986 S	1,446,778	—	19
1987	11,442,335	7.95	—
1987 S	904,732	—	19
1988	5,004,646	7.95	—
1988 S	557,370	—	57
1989	5,203,327	7.70	—
1989 S	617,694	—	18
1990	5,840,210	7.70	—
1990 S	695,510	—	20
1991	7,191,066	7.70	—
1991 S	—	—	21
1992	5,540,068	7.60	—
1992 S	498,552	—	19
1993	—	7.60	—
1993 S	—	—	52
1994	5,540,068	7.85	—
1994 S	498,552	—	36
1995	—	7.35	—
1995 S	—	—	23

EDMUND'S 1996 U.S. COIN PRICES

BULLION VALUES OF UNITED STATES COINS

SILVER COINS

Price Per Troy Ounce	$3.50	$4.00	$4.50	$5.00	$6.00	$7.00	$8.00	$9.00	$10.00
Wartime Nickels									
1942-45 (.350 Fine)	.20	.23	.25	.28	.34	.39	.45	.51	.56
Dimes (.900 Fine)									
1964 and Earlier	.25	.29	.33	.36	.43	.51	.58	.65	.72
Quarters (.900)									
1964 and Earlier	.63	.72	.81	.90	1.09	1.27	1.45	1.63	1.81
Half Dollars (.900 Fine)									
1964 and Earlier	1.27	1.45	1.63	1.81	2.17	2.53	2.89	3.26	3.62
Silver Dollars (.900 Fine)									
1935 and Earlier	2.71	3.09	3.48	3.87	4.64	5.41	6.19	6.96	7.73
Half Dollars (.400 Fine)									
1965-1970	.52	.59	.67	.74	.89	1.04	1.18	1.33	1.48
Ike Dollars (.400 Fine)									
(S-Mint)	1.11	1.27	1.42	1.58	1.90	2.21	2.53	2.85	3.16

GOLD COINS

Price Per Troy Ounce	$325.	$350.	$375.	$400.	$425.	$450.	$475.	$500.	$525.
Gold Dollars (.900 Fine)	15.72	16.93	18.14	19.35	20.56	21.77	22.98	24.19	25.39
Quarter Eagles ($2.50)									
(.900 Fine)	39.31	42.33	45.25	48.38	51.40	54.42	57.45	60.47	63.50
Three Dollars (.900 Fine)	47.16	50.79	54.42	58.05	61.68	65.30	68.93	72.56	76.19
Half Eagles ($5.00) (.900)	78.61	84.65	90.70	96.75	102.79	108.84	114.89	120.94	126.98
Eagles ($10.00) (.900)	157.22	169.31	181.41	193.50	205.59	217.69	229.78	241.88	253.97
Double Eagles($20) (.900)	314.44	338.63	362.81	387.00	411.19	435.38	459.56	483.75	507.94

EXPLANATION OF BULLION VALUE CHARTS

Many newcomers to numismatics have the erroneous opinion that the prices of gold and silver are closely related to their bullion value. This assumption is quite far from the truth. Bullion value determines only the base value of coins. This value applies to the most common dates of the series, and usually only to coins that are not in choice condition. No U.S. silver coins minted before 1892 are affected significantly by this base value because they all have numismatic value in excess of their bullion value even in the lowest collectible grades.

For those who are interested in using the bullion value charts, the following information should be noted: Dealers will generally pay considerably less for silver coins than their full melt value (listed above). At the time that this book is being written, dealers were paying as much as 40% below melt value for silver.

The prices dealers are paying for bullion related (common date) United States gold coins are quite different. U.S. gold coins have already sold for a premium over actual melt value. This premium has changed considerably in the present volatile market, so we recommend that anyone wishing to sell common date gold coins should get several offers from dealers before selling to the highest bidder.

EDMUND'S 1996 U.S. COIN PRICES

UNITED STATES MINTS AND MINT MARKS

The United States Mint at Philadelphia is the "parent" mint of the United States. Regular issue U.S. coinage was commenced at Philadelphia in 1793. From that time to date, all dies for U.S. coinage have been made at Philadelphia. It has been customary for coins of the Philadelphia mint to not carry a mint mark. The exceptions to this practice are the nickels of 1942-1945 and the Susan B. Anthony type dollar.

From time to time, branch mints have been established to increase coinage production to keep up with increasing commercial needs for coins. To distinguish coins struck at these branch mints, a letter (or letters) was punched into the dies sent from Philadelphia to the branch mints. The mint marks of these mints are as follows:

MINTMARK	MINT	DATES OF OPERATION
P	Philadelphia, Pennsylvania	1793 to date
O	New Orleans, Louisiana	1838-1861 and 1879-1909
D	Dahlonega, Georgia	1838-1861 (gold coins only)
C	Charlotte, North Carolina	1838-1861 (gold coins only)
S	San Francisco, California	1854-1955 & 1968 to date
CC	Carson City, Nevada	1870-1893
D	Denver, Colorado	1906 to date
W	West Point, New York	1984

Mint Mark Locations

DENOMINATION	TYPE	SIDE OF COIN	LOCATION OF MINT MARK
Cent	Indian Head	Reverse	Below Wreath
Cent	Lincoln	Obverse	Below Date
Three Cents (Silver)	—	Reverse	At Right of C
Five Cent Nickel	Liberty Head	Reverse	At Left of Cents Below Dot
Five Cent Nickel	Buffalo	Reverse	Below Five Cents
Five Cent Nickel	Jefferson 1938-64	Reverse	At Right of Building
Five Cent Nickel	Jefferson (Wartime)	Reverse	Large Mintmark Above Building
Five Cent Nickel	Jefferson 1968-Date	Obverse	Below Date
Half Dime	Liberty Seated	Reverse	Above or Below Bow of Wreath
Dime	Liberty Seated	Reverse	Above or Below Bow of Wreath
Dime	Barber	Reverse	Below Wreath
Dime	Mercury	Reverse	At Right of ONE
Dime	Roosevelt 1946-64	Reverse	At Left of Torch
Dime	Roosevelt 1968-Date	Obverse	Above Date
Twenty Cents	—	Reverse	Below Eagle
Quarter Dollar	Liberty Seated	Reverse	Below Eagle

EDMUND'S 1996 U.S. COIN PRICES

UNITED STATES MINTS AND MINT MARKS

DENOMINATION	TYPE	SIDE OF COIN	LOCATION OF MINT MARK
Quarter Dollar	Barber	Reverse	Below Eagle
Quarter Dollar	Standing Liberty	Obverse	At Left of Date
Quarter Dollar	Washington 1938-64	Reverse	Below Wreath
Quarter Dollar	Washington 1968-Date	Obverse	At Right of Ribbon
Half Dollar	Cap bust, Reed edge	Obverse	Above Date
Half Dollar	Liberty Seated	Reverse	Below Eagle
Half Dollar	Barber	Reverse	Below Eagle
Half Dollar	Liberty Walk 1916-17	Obverse	Below Motto
Half Dollar	Liberty Walk 1917-47	Reverse	Below Leaves at Left
Half Dollar	Franklin	Reverse	Above Yoke of Bell
Half Dollar	Kennedy 1964	Reverse	At Left of Branch
Half Dollar	Kennedy 1968-Date	Obverse	Above Date
Silver Dollar	Liberty Seated	Reverse	Below Eagle
Trade Dollar	—	Reverse	Below Eagle
Silver Dollar	Morgan	Reverse	Below Wreath
Silver Dollar	Peace	Reverse	Below ONE at Left of Wingtip
Dollar	Eisenhower	Obverse	Above Date
Dollar	S.B. Anthony	Obverse	At Left of Head
Gold Dollar	All Types	Reverse	Below Wreath
Quarter Eagle	Classic Head	Obverse	Above Date
Quarter Eagle	Coronet	Reverse	Below Eagle
Quarter Eagle	Indian Head	Reverse	At Left of Fasces
Three Dollars	—	Reverse	Below Wreath
Half Eagle	Classic Head	Obverse	Above Date
Half Eagle	Coronet 1939	Obverse	Above Date
Half Eagle	Coronet 1840-1908	Reverse	Below Eagle
Half Eagle	Indian Head	Reverse	At Left of Fasces
Eagle	Coronet	Reverse	Below Eagle
Eagle	Indian Head	Reverse	At Left of Fasces
Double Eagle	Coronet	Reverse	Below Eagle
Double Eagle	Saint-Gaudens	Obverse	Above Date

RECOMMENDED READING

A fairly extensive listing of recommended books and periodicals concerning United States coins is being included because the editor believes that it is very important to read as much information as possible before spending large sums of money for coins. While Edmund's United States Coin Prices is intended to give you accurate price listings for all United States regular issue and commemorative coins, there is a wealth of detailed specific information in the publications on the following pages.

Periodicals

COIN WORLD (Weekly) Post Office Box 150, Sidney, OH 45365
COINS MAGAZINE (Monthly) Iola, WI 54945
COINAGE MAGAZINE (Monthly) 17337 Ventura Blvd., Encino, CA 91316
NUMISMATIC NEWS (Weekly) Iola, WI 54945

General Reference

Yeoman, R.S., *A GUIDE BOOK OF UNITED STATES COINS*, 36th edition,
 Racine, WI 1983
Taxay, Don, *THE U.S. MINT AND COINAGE*, New York 1966, Reprinted 1969
Bressett, Ken and Kosoff, A., *OFFICIAL ANA GRADING STANDARDS FOR
 UNITED STATES COINS*, Racine, WI 1977
Bowers, Q. David, *THE HISTORY OF UNITED STATES COINAGE, AS ILLUSTRATED
 BY THE GARRETT COLLECTION*, Los Angeles, CA 1979
  IBID., *ADVENTURES WITH RARE COINS*, Los Angeles, CA 1979
  IBID., *COINS AND COLLECTORS*, New York, NY 1971
Stack, Norman, *UNITED STATES TYPE COINS*, New York, NY 1977

Specialized Reference

NOTE: The following books are recommended to the collector who wishes to specialize in a particular series of United States coins. At the end of this listing, we have included a few books covering Colonial coins, Pattern coins and mint errors. These coins are somewhat related to the collecting of U.S. regular issue coins, but are not within the scope of this book.

Gilbert, Ebenezer, *UNITED STATES HALF CENTS*, New York 1916, Hewitt Reprint, Chicago, IL
Sheldon, Wm. H., *PENNY WHIMSY (1793-1814)*, Lawrence, MA 1976
Newcomb, H.R., *UNITED STATES COPPER CENTS 1816-1857*, New York 1944
Valentine, D.W., *THE UNITED STATES HALF DIMES*, New York 1931
Kosoff, A., *UNITED STATES DIMES FROM 1796*, New York 1945
Ahwash, Kamal M., *ENCYCLOPEDIA OF UNITED STATES LIBERTY SEATED DIMES 1837-1891*,
 Kamal Press 1977

RECOMMENDED READING

Browning, A.W., *THE EARLY QUARTER DOLLARS OF THE UNITED STATES 1796-1838*,
   New York 1925
Haseltine, J.W., *TYPE TABLE OF UNITED STATES DOLLARS, HALF DOLLARS AND
   QUARTER DOLLARS*, Philadelphia, PA 1881, Reprinted 1968
Cline, J.H., *STANDING LIBERTY QUARTERS*, 1976
Kelman, Keith N., *STANDING LIBERTY QUARTERS*, 1976
Beistle, M.L., *REGISTER OF UNITED STATES HALF DOLLARS VARIETIES AND SUBVARIETIES*,
   Shippensburg, PA 1929
Overton, Al C., *EARLY HALF DOLLAR DIE VARIETIES 1794-1836*, Colorado Springs, CO 1967,
   Revised 1970
Bolender, M.H., , Freeport, IL 1950
Newman, Eric P. and Bressett, Kenneth E., *THE FANTASTIC 1804 DOLLAR*,
   Racine, WI 1962
Willem, John M., *THE UNITED STATES TRADE DOLLAR*, Racine, WI 1965
Van Allen, Leroy C. and Mallis, A. George, *COMPREHENSIVE CATALOGUE AND ENCYCLOPEDIA
   OF U.S. MORGAN AND PEACE SILVER DOLLARS*, New York 1976
Akers, David W., *UNITED STATES GOLD COINS, AN ANALYSIS OF AUCTION RECORDS*
   VOLUME I GOLD DOLLARS, 1849-1889, Englewood, OH 1975
   VOLUME II QUARTER EAGLES, 1796-1929, Englewood, OH 1975
   *VOLUME III THREE DOLLAR GOLD PIECES 1854-1889 AND FOUR DOLLAR
      GOLD PIECES 1879-1880*, Englewood, OH 1976
   VOLUME IV HALF EAGLES 1795-1929, Englewood, OH 1979
   VOLUME V EAGLES 1795-1933, Englewood, OH 1980
   VOLUME VI DOUBLE EAGLES 1849-1933, Englewood, OH 1982
Slabaugh, Arlie R., *UNITED STATES COMMEMORATIVE COINAGE*, Racine, WI 1975
Taxay, Don, *AN ILLUSTRATED HISTORY OF U.S. COMMEMORATIVE COINAGE*, New York 1967
Breen, Walter, *WALTER BREEN'S ENCYCLOPEDIA OF UNITED STATES AND COLONIAL
   PROOF COINS 1722-1977*, Albertson, NY 1977
Judd, J. Hewitt, MD., *UNITED STATES PATTERN, EXPERIMENTAL AND TRIAL PIECES*,
   Sixth edition, Racine, WI 1977
Herbert, Alan, *THE OFFICIAL PRICE GUIDE TO MINT ERRORS AND VARIETIES*,
   Orlando, FL 1978
Durst, Sanford J., *COMPREHENSIVE GUIDE TO AMERICAN COLONIAL COINAGE*, New York 1976
Crosby, S.S., *THE EARLY COINS OF AMERICA*, Boston, MA 1875
   (Reprints, 1945, 1965, 1975)
Kessler, Alan, *THE FUGIO CENTS*, Newtonville, MA 1976

Notes

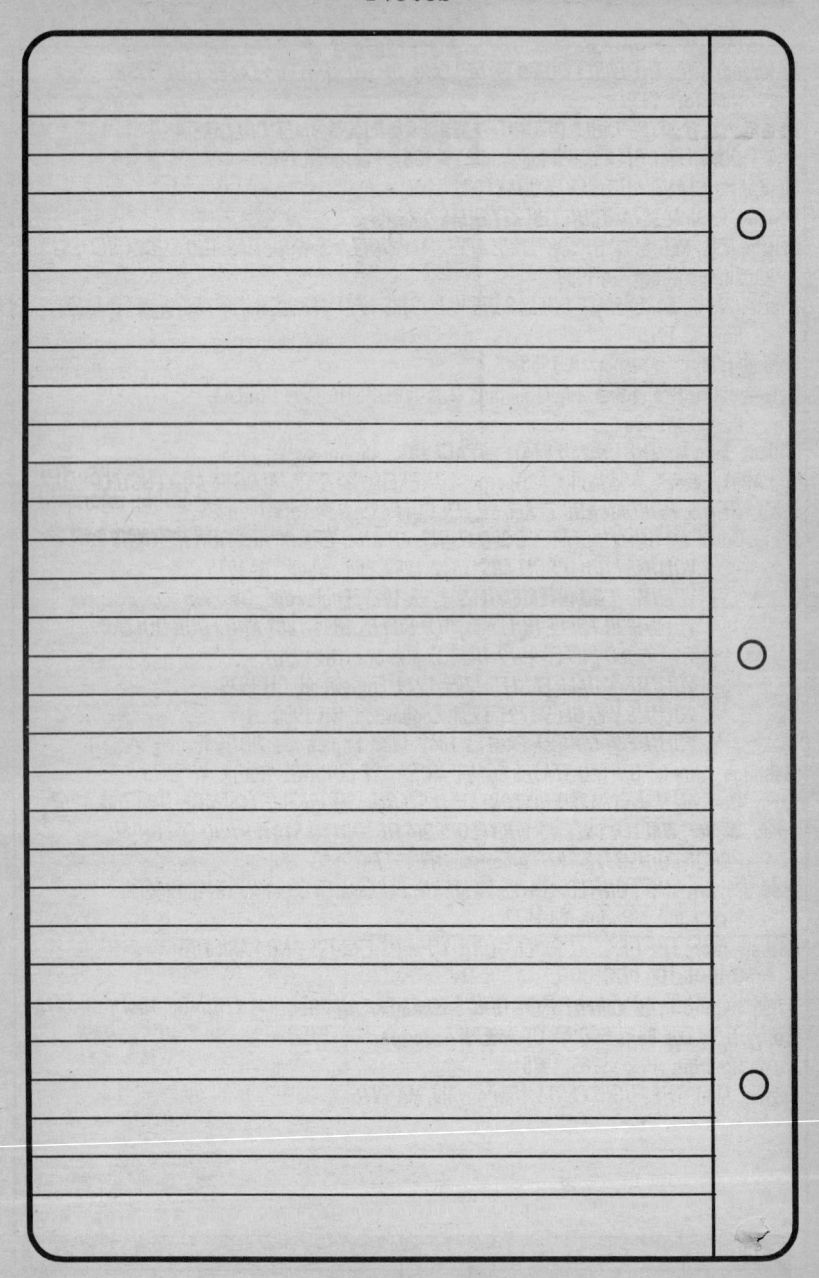

Edmund's **Perfect Partners**

USED CARS: PRICES & RATINGS

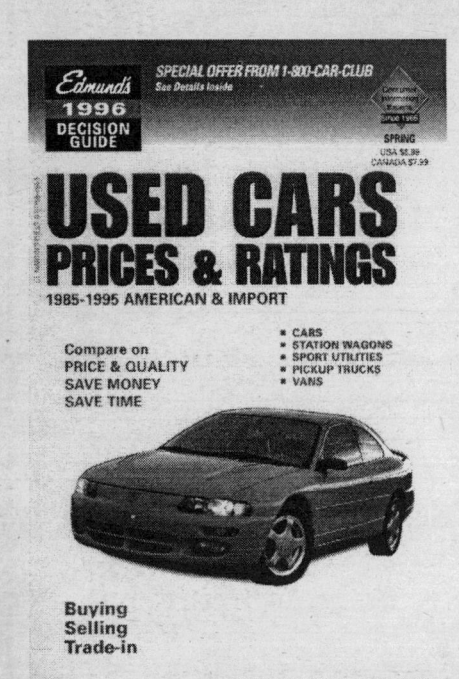

For 30 years, Edmund's has guided smart consumers through the complex used car marketplace. By providing you with the latest wholesale and retail pricing, you are able to determine fair market value before negotiations begin.

Whether buying, selling, or trading, Edmund's *Used Cars: Prices & Ratings* gives all the information you need to get your very best deal.

√ Prices All American and Imported Used Cars, Pickup Trucks, Vans, and Sport Utilities

√ Shows Summary Ratings Graphs for Most Used Vehicles

√ Listings Cover Models Over Last 11 Years

√ Price any Vehicle Quickly and Accurately

√ Adjust Value for Optional Equipment and Mileage

$6.99 CANADA $7.99

Also look for Edmund's other automotive books - *New Cars: Prices & Reviews* and *New Trucks: Prices & Reviews*.
Visit us on the Internet at
http://edmund.com

For information on all Edmund's Automotive Books, call 914-962-6297

Edmund's SUBSCRIPTIONS / ORDER FORM
U.S. COIN PRICES

As a collector and/or investor in U.S. coins, I am interested in receiving the next **two** issues of **Edmund's U.S. Coin Prices** for just **$13.80**.

Name _____

Address _____

City, State, Zip _____

PAYMENT: __ MC __ VISA __ Check or Money Order-Amount $ _____

Rates subject to change without notice

Make check or money order payable to:
Edmund Publications Corporation P.O.Box 338, Shrub Oaks, NY 10588
For more information or to order by phone, call **(914) 962-6297**

Credit Card #: _____ Exp. Date: _____

Cardholder Name: _____ Signature: _____

EDMUND PUBLICATIONS
P.O.Box 338, Shrub Oaks, NY 10588